THE GREATEST BOOK IN THE WORLD
AND OTHER PAPERS

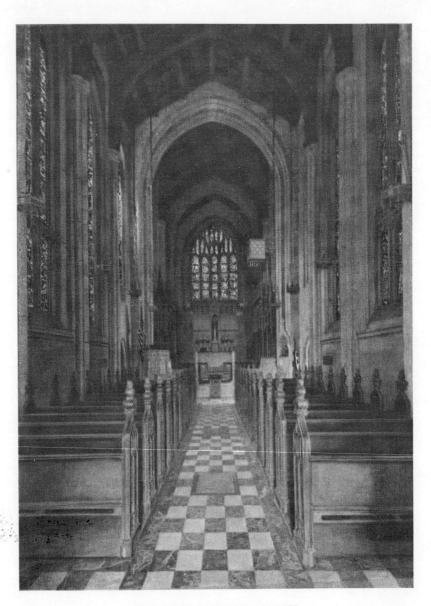

WASHINGTON MEMORIAL CHAPEL
VALLEY FORGE, PENNSYLVANIA

THE GREATEST BOOK
IN THE WORLD

AND OTHER PAPERS

BY

A. EDWARD NEWTON, 1864-1940.

AUTHOR OF

THE AMENITIES OF BOOK–COLLECTING

WITH ILLUSTRATIONS

KENNIKAT PRESS/PORT WASHINGTON, N. Y.

THE GREATEST BOOK IN THE WORLD

Copyright 1925 by A. Edward Newton
Reissued in 1969 by Kennikat Press
Library of Congress Catalog Card No: 78-86572
SBN 8046-0579-3

Manufactured by Taylor Publishing Company   Dallas, Texas

ESSAY AND GENERAL LITERATURE INDEX REPRINT SERIES

PREFACE TO THIRD EDITION

To the critics of the first edition of *The Greatest Book*, etc.:

"I would rather be attacked than unnoticed," said my friend Dr. J. So say I.

It don't make much difference whether Fred Leslie or E. J. Lonnen sang "Killaloe." Both singers and the song are dead. So am not I.

I maintain that Florence St. John was always called Sinjin and no doubt Mr. Pope called his friend St. John, Sinjin too. He certainly did so in the lines

"Awake! my St. John, leave all meaner things
To low ambition and the pride of Kings."

The correct pronunciation of English proper names is a life's study.

I am sorry that I made a slip in the spelling of Le Fevre's name.

If I was wrong in saying that my Uncle Toby was sunning himself on a bench when the Widow Wadman courted him, it is because I have a picture of the old gentleman, so sitting, looking for the mote in the widow's eye. Some of my critics are looking for motes in mine.

I don't think that I positively asserted that "Rasselas" was written in Gough Square. I am familiar with the arguments for and against this theory.

My prize blunder remains, as yet undiscovered. But it will come to the surface.

And now I am off for a fine ramble with John Burns through Limehouse and Poplar.

A. E. N.

London, *September 23, 1925.*

EPISTLE DEDICATORY
TO
HENRY HANBY HAY
The Founder of The Club

SIR,

You cannot fail to remember that forty years ago you were the leader of a small group of young men in Philadelphia who decided to form a club. It was to devote its energies to the study of English literature, particularly to the lesser lights thereof, and it was to have no name, no officers, no dues, no rules; in a word, no organization of any kind.

In due time you communicated your plan to Henry H. Bonnell and Felix E. Schelling, who approved it; and the matter was then discussed with John R. Moses, who subsequently became a clergyman, and Lawrence B. Ridgely, now the Dean of a Divinity School in China. Ridgely was promptly advised that in proportion to its number there would probably be more heathen in the Club than there were in China, but he insisted upon working in the larger field. These men, together with John Thomson, were the charter members. Subsequently other men, including the writer, were included in the little circle.

You will remember that at an early meeting it was agreed that subsequent members were to be admitted only upon the approval of all present, after probation, the length of which was not clearly defined, and that subsequently it was discovered that, if it was difficult to secure admission to the Club, it was impossible to get out of it, no one having authority to accept a resignation. Meetings of the Club were to be held every fortnight during the winter months at the houses of the different members, and four papers were to be read. One was upon the author who had been selected as the subject of the evening; another was upon his times; the third was upon his works; and the last was to be an imitation of his style. After the papers came light refreshments of crackers and cheese and beer.

For some years the Club pursued the uneven tenor of its way. We were serious men in our early days: we thought and worked hard. Gradually changes were introduced; men balked at the paper called the imitation: it was difficult to write and not too easy to listen to. You will remember that when it became my turn to write an imitation of Ebenezer Elliott, the corn-law rhymer, I, having no gift for rhyming, induced you to write my imitation for me; and that it was, nevertheless, so bad that I barely escaped with my life; and that, until now, I have kept your secret.

It was, too, upon your motion that the papers were reduced to one, and the meetings to one a month; and when, finally, the reading of formal papers almost ceased and the men were expected to know their subjects so thoroughly as to be able to talk their papers against interruption, ribald or serious, you made no objection, although we had to stand an enormous amount of heckling.

Eventually, when the light suppers developed into excellent dinners, where you sat was the head of the table; and when, after twenty years, some of us had made our way in the world along paths that were not too easy, you permitted no man, however respected outside the Club, to speak *ex cathedra* in it, except yourself.

Sir, it is a pity that we did not keep a complete list of our members. First and last we must have had over a hundred, though our meetings were usually attended by not more than eight or ten. Do you remember how welcome we made everyone, provided he had a real contribution to make? Have you forgotten that certain rich man who once entertained the Club at dinner, and how one of our members, sadly under the influence of his excellent wine, nominated him for membership, and declared him duly elected, and how we, nevertheless, declined to permit him to attend our meetings, our excuse being that no merely rich man should ever be one of us?

Sir, the Club you founded was a good one; there never was a better; the papers, with certain brilliant exceptions, were excellent; but best of all was the talk, wise or witty as the case may be, which followed or punctuated the remarks of the speaker of the evening. Do you remember how, in rubbing our wits against one another, we sometimes made the sparks fly, but more frequently produced only the effect of something burning? Of course you do; I ask these questions merely to get them into the record.

Sir, you will admit that, between us or among us, we came to have a pretty good knowledge of that glorious and continuing thing we call English literature. The complete list of the authors we discussed would be enormous; it would begin with Lord Acton and end with the poet Young.

In brief, Sir, to be a member of the Club was to receive a liberal education; at all events, it was the only one the writer ever received. And you know, Sir, that as we approached our fortieth milestone the Club languished;

one can hardly keep one's enthusiasms forever. The responsibilities of business pressed hard upon some of us; you left the city; some of us were caught up in the suburban movement; several of our most distinguished members died. Since the passing of Francis B. Gummere, of honored memory, we have never had a meeting. But we shall have one more dinner, at which a copy of this volume shall be presented to you.

Sir, I am becoming tedious; that you would never have permitted. In closing, let me say that, while my debt to you and to the Club can be acknowledged, it can never be paid.

I am, Sir,

Yours very affectionately,

A. Edward Newton

"Oak Knoll"
Berwyn, Pennsylvania
March 1, 1925

MARKS AND REMARKS

Mr. Frank B. Bemis of Boston is the owner of the "elopement letter" from which I have taken my title: "Skinner Street News."

For several illustrations of rare Bibles I am indebted to Mr. T. Edward Ross of Philadelphia.

The Color Plate of the Washington Memorial Chapel at Valley Forge was photo-engraved by R. B. Fleming of London, from a photograph made and colored by Henry Troth of Philadelphia.

The other color plates and the half-tones were made by the Rembrandt Engraving Company of Philadelphia.

"Sir," said Dr. Johnson, "People seldom read a book which is given to them . . . The way to spread a work is to sell it at a low price."

"A man will even write books to get money to buy books."
— Henry Ward Beecher

The End of all Scribblement is to amuse.— Byron

The blunders in this book — and already I know of one nice one — are exclusively my own.

A. E. N.

TABLE OF CONTENTS

TABLE OF CONTENTS

LIST OF ILLUSTRATIONS

THE GREATEST BOOK IN THE WORLD
AND OTHER PAPERS

"THE GREATEST BOOK IN THE WORLD"
AND
OTHER PAPERS

I

"THE GREATEST BOOK IN THE WORLD"

MOST emphatic statements will be challenged by someone, but that the Bible is the greatest book in the world will, I think, be admitted. To be sure, a person seeking an argument might say, "What Bible do you mean?" to which I, being anxious to avoid a discussion, would reply, "Any of them," for there are many; but I have in mind chiefly two, the two that the English-speaking world knows best: the Latin Bible, usually called the Vulgate, and the Authorized or King James Version, published in London in the year 1611.

For many centuries — just how many any scholar will tell you; I do not know — the writings of learned men upon stone, clay, papyrus, parchment, and finally upon paper, had resulted in the creation of a caste: men who could read, men who sitting silently before a written or painted manuscript could follow in their minds the thoughts of other men. This, I submit, is the greatest achievement of the human mind; it is a sort of "radio" into that space which we call time. No "aërial" was required; there was no sound; yet a man sitting silently behind the written page could, with a little skill, learn all the best that has been thought or done in the world. Needless to say, these manuscripts, the product of a staff of writers and illuminators who worked upon them, — for years, it may be, upon a single book, — were of very great value, and it was not unusual for them to carry upon the first page, by way of warning, a notice which might be thus translated: "He who steals this book or conceals it, it having been stolen; or deletes this inscription, is excommunicate." Not much, but enough.

With the growth of learning there arose an ever-increasing demand for books; but the method of producing them by means of a quill and brush made them so costly that they were the exclusive posses-sion of princes, either of the Church or of the State. Museums and libraries of the Old and, to a lesser extent, of the New World, now possess many superb examples of these books, and when we peer at the priceless treasures of the past, carefully screened with glass, in museums, we exclaim: "How wonder-ful!" And yet, wonderful as they are, they are as nothing compared with the printed page.

The story of the printed book, reduced to its simplest terms, may be briefly stated. Scholars are generally agreed that the art of printing, as we know it, had its birth in Germany. In the earliest examples

of printing, not only illustrations but text were cut
in relief on solid blocks of wood, but it was not until
the invention of movable metal types, capable of
innumerable combinations of letters forming words,
that printing may be said to have come into existence. The honor of this great discovery has been,
by general consent, awarded to Johannes Gutenberg.
Of his life we know relatively little, but we know
that about 1450 he was negotiating with one Fust,
a goldsmith, for a loan to carry on his invention, and
that a few years later there was a falling-out between
the two men, as is not unusual between inventors,
over the division of the resulting profits or losses;
meantime the great Bible was completed.

It is possible, before the work of printing so important a book was undertaken, that several smaller
ventures were made, but no book has yet been discovered in which are employed the types used in
this Bible, and we are sure that the Bible was the
first important effort of the great inventor. As an
example of printing it has never been surpassed. Of
all the arts, printing at its birth more nearly reached
perfection than any other. It has indeed been said
that it is the only art in which no progress has been
made: that the first example of printing is the best.
And to Gutenberg is given the credit for the great
discovery of this "art preservative of the arts."
The time, 1450–1455, the place, Mainz or, as we
would call it, Mayence.

It is a great book, the Vulgate, a wonderful book:

Incipit plogº in apocalipsim.

Ohannes apostolus et euangelista
a cristo electus atꝫ dilectus · in tanto
amore dilectionis vberior habitus ē
ut in cena supra pectus eius recumbe-
ret et ad crucem astanti soli matrem
propriam commendasset : ut quem
nubere volentem ad amplexum virgi-
nitatis asciuerat : ipsi ad custodiendā
virginem tradidisset . Hic itaqꝫ cum
propter verbum dei ꞓ testimonium ihe-
su cristi in pathmos insulam sortire-
tur exilium·illic ab eodē apocalipsis
pre ostensa describit:ut sicut in princi-
pio canonis id ē libri geneseos incor-
ruptibile pricipiū ꝑnotat̄: ita etiā in-
corrupnbilis finis ꝑ virginē in apoca-
lipsi redderet̄ dicentis . Ego sū alpha
et o:iniciū et finis. Hic est iohannes· ꝗ
sciens superuenisse sibi diem egressioniſ
de corpore conuocatis ĩ epheso discipu-
lis descendit inde fossum sepulture sue
locum:orationeqꝫ ꝯpleta reddidit spi-

PORTION OF ONE COLUMN OF THE GUTENBERG BIBLE
almost exact size of original

the production of a monk, who, fifteen hundred years ago, exchanging the luxury and learning of Rome for the barren seclusion of a cell at Bethlehem in Palestine, carried through, practically unaided, a translation and revision of the Hebrew Scriptures and, with the help of Greek and Latin manuscripts of the New Testament, produced a book which for more than a thousand years reigned supreme and unchallenged throughout western Europe. The monk, whom the world calls Saint Jerome, served it well; the most learned man of his age, his work has been called "the pride and pillar of the Latin Church," and a great Anglican scholar says, "It is to Saint Jerome that Europe stands forever indebted for the preservation of her spiritual and intellectual inheritance from the blind deluge of Northern barbarism." What a tribute! And it is repeated by Dr. Penniman, the Provost of the University of Pennsylvania, who points out in his *Book about the English Bible* that it was upon the Vulgate that the whole literature and art of Western Europe depended from the time that Christianity became the prevailing religion down to the time of the Reformation; citing, as an example, that Michelangelo derived from that famous text his authority for placing horns on the head of his famous statue of Moses, the lawgiver.

A word as to the book itself. It gives no information as to the time when it was printed, or the place, or the printer. It has no title-page or colophon, its six hundred and forty-one pages are unnumbered,

and there are no catchwords to help us in collation.
It is printed in Latin, in large Gothic characters in
double columns, forty-two lines to a column. In the
first issue of this noble book the first few pages were
printed forty lines to a column. After printing a few
leaves, the printers decided to get more lines to a
page and also to increase the size of the edition,
which necessitated reprinting the pages that had first
passed through the press; these pages have forty-
two lines. Hence this Bible is frequently referred to
as the "forty-two line Bible," and it is also sometimes called the Mazarin Bible, for the reason that,
while it was believed to exist, no copy was known
until it was discovered in the library of the great
French Cardinal. The printing was done both upon
vellum and upon paper; which was first used, cannot
now be determined, but it is generally believed that
the paper copies are the earliest.

The printing was done in imitation of writing,
which by some it was at first believed to be, in a brilliant black ink of a quality which has defied the
centuries. The headlines, the accents, — that is to
say, the red marks which stress the capital letters, —
and the illuminated initials, where they occur, are in
every case supplied by hand, and in varying degrees
of beauty and excellence. In a copy in the Bibliothèque Nationale at Paris there is a manuscript
note in which the rubricator, that is, the one who
did the hand illumination, says that he finished his
work on the twenty-fourth of August 1456, adding

thereafter, as was not unusual, the word "Alleluia."
Less than thirty examples on paper and on vellum
are known to exist, many of them in imperfect condition, and all copies vary slightly. With a very
few exceptions they are all in public libraries.

What is the money value of a Gutenberg Bible?
It is a hard question to answer. When Mr. Henry
E. Huntington, certainly the greatest book-collector
of modern times, purchased through the late George
D. Smith a vellum copy for fifty thousand dollars,
he paid the highest that up to that time had ever
been given for a book. This was on Monday evening, April 24, 1911, and I well remember the round
of applause which followed the fall of the auctioneer's hammer when this figure, breaking all records,
was reached. But we live in days when records of
all kinds are easily broken and, should such an item
again come on the market, it might easily fetch
several times this sum. Indeed, if we can imagine
in the far-off future a Gutenberg Bible coming up
for sale, some wise rich man or richly endowed
museum might gladly pay a million dollars for it.

Of its emotional value it is not for me to speak.
For centuries no word of it was challenged; it was
regarded as a divine thing.

The first Gutenberg Bible to come to this country
was the copy now in the New York Public Library,
dispatched in 1847 from London by Henry Stevens
to James Lenox, who had instructed his agent to
buy the book, — which was coming up at auction

at Sotheby's, — without fixing any limit. The result
was that the book was purchased for him at the then
"mad price" of five hundred pounds, which for a
time so incensed Mr. Lenox that he was tempted to
repudiate the transaction; but, as the narrator of
the story says, he finally took the book home and
lived to cherish it as a bargain and the chief ornament of his library.

By a coincidence I have copies of the correspondence
that passed between Henry Stevens and another client, George Brinley of Hartford, Connecticut, relative to the second Gutenberg Bible to come to this
country, twenty-five years later. How Mr. Brinley,
"being as prompt as the Bank of England," took the
prize away from two lords who wanted the book but
had no ready money, need not now concern us; the
point at which I wish to arrive is this: After an
exchange of letters and cablegrams Mr. Stevens
secured the book, and dispatched it, insured against
all "risques," to its owner with this note of comment: "Pray, Sir, ponder for a moment and appreciate the rarity and importance of this precious
consignment from the Old World to the New. Not
only is it the first Bible, but it is the first book ever
printed. It was read in Europe half a century before
America was discovered. Please suggest to your
deputy that he uncover his head while in the presence of this great book. Let no custom house
official or other man, in or out of authority, see it
without first reverently raising his hat. It is not

possible for many men ever to touch or even look upon a page of a Gutenberg Bible."

Upon a Gutenberg Bible! quite so; but is it necessary? It were indeed a calamity if only those few possessors of entire Gutenberg Bibles, or those fortunate collectors who a few years ago secured from Gabriel Wells, in New York, a specimen leaf, could read, mark, learn, and inwardly digest its teachings, but no other book in the world is so generally accessible as some edition or other of the Bible.

It will be understood, of course, that for a thousand years before the discovery of printing the Bible or some portion of it was circulated in manuscript, and in several languages: in Hebrew, in Greek, and in Latin; and in many texts, dependent upon the learning or the lack of it or upon the prejudice of the transcriber, who may have been the translator also. For centuries there was — indeed, there could have been — no such thing as a national Bible, but there was what may be described as an international Bible: the Bible of an international Church, the Church of Rome, of which the Bishop of Rome, who subsequently became the Pope, was the head — the Vulgate, in Latin, the language of all the scholars of Christendom.

Of Cædmon and his Saxon songs, of Bede, commonly called the Venerable, I, knowing little, shall not speak; and scholars are not yet in entire agreement as to how far John Wycliffe was personally responsible for the translating of the Latin Bible into English. The so-called Wycliffe Bible, which dates from the end of the fourteenth century, existed only in manuscript until 1850, when it was printed in four quarto volumes.

Indeed, it is not until we come to the work of William Tyndale, who has been called the father of the English Bible, that we leave a nebulous bibliographical world, a world of conjecture. And now that we have come at last to a printed English Bible, we have also come to a time when politics and religion joined hands with murderous result. We hear much in these days of reform within the party, but in actual fact reform, whether it be political or religious, always is forced from without. Reforms from within have been well compared to efforts to raise one's self by the boot-straps: they excite our attention, but are ineffective; for this reason they are always recommended by those interested in maintaining the status quo. Never was the Church so ungodly as in the days when great and luxury-loving ecclesiastics, "corrupt and contented," forgetful of the teaching of Christ, fought like demons with one another for temporal power. As with the passage of time they lost control of the State, it was seized by another class, equally corrupt, men skilled in the law; and their decisions, however preposterous, when gravely handed down by bewigged old gentlemen, had the power of life or death upon those who heard them. It is a great game, and it seems never to be played out.

A legal decree forbade any person to translate the Bible without permission. William Tyndale found it impossible to secure this authorization. The Bishop of London, to whom he applied, would have none of him, and it may be to him that Tyndale made his famous declaration: "If God spare my life, ere many years I will cause a boy that driveth a plough to know more of the Scripture than thou dost." He was as good as his word, but of the many thousands of copies of Tyndale's New Testament which must have been printed only three mutilated fragments of the two earliest editions are now in existence: all the others have been destroyed.

We are entering upon that interesting period known as the Reformation. Bishops, however they may have differed with one another in doctrine, agreed that the purification — of others — was best accomplished, not by following the teaching of the Bible, but by fire; and to solemn or joyous burnings of religious and godly men was added the destruction, so far as was possible, of their works. Said Tyndale, "In burning my New Testament they did none other than I looked for; if they burn me also, it is God's will"; nevertheless, to escape he fled to Antwerp. Here he was seized, thrown into prison, and finally put to death. On account of his pious and exemplary life he was spared the agony of being burnt, his sentence being merely that he should be strangled and his body burnt at the stake. This was done in the name of religion.

It has been estimated that by the time of his death not less than fifty thousand copies of his New Testament had been printed, the laws which had been passed forbidding its printing and possession being ineffective chiefly on account of the tiny dimensions of the book, five or six inches by four.

Shortly after the death of Tyndale it was decreed that it was no longer a crime to translate or print or read the Bible, and Miles Coverdale, a Yorkshireman, subsequently the Bishop of Exeter, became responsible for the famous Bible that bears his name. It is a relatively small book, about twelve inches by eight, and was printed, possibly in Antwerp but more probably in Zurich, in 1535. It bears a somewhat cringing dedication to the founder of the Church of England, King Henry VIII, "defendour of the fayth and under God the chefe and supreme heade of the Church of Englande," and upon the title-page is a very suitable quotation from the Second Epistle of Saint Paul to the Thessalonians: "Praie for us, that the worde of God maie have free passage and be glorified."

Scholars are generally agreed that Coverdale had access to five Latin and several German Bibles, including Luther's, and that his influence upon the translations which followed his own has been great and enduring. We are told that he had an instinct for whatever was sympathetic and beautiful; such expressions as "tender mercy," and "loving kindness," and many similar expressions which have be-

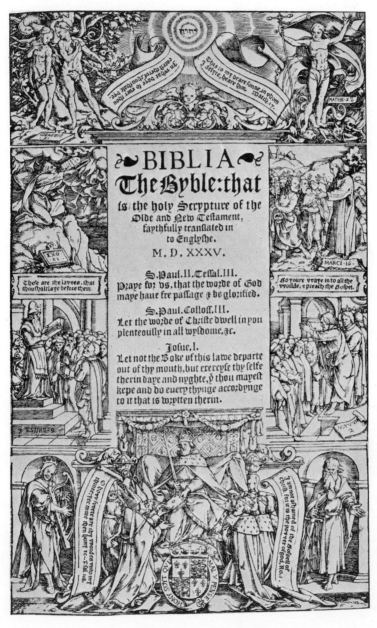

TITLE-PAGE OF THE COVERDALE BIBLE (1535)
the first complete Bible in English

come a part of our language we owe to him. It was his hope that his own work would soon be displaced by a better text, and it was, in fact, only two years later that the Matthew Bible appeared.

This version was popular during the reign of Edward Sixth, but its vogue was brief, perhaps for the reason that its actual translator, John Rogers, — who merely adopted the name of Thomas Matthew, there being in reality no such person, — was the first martyr to perish in the succeeding reign of Queen, alias "Bloody," Mary. Rogers was, shortly after her accession, condemned to be burnt to death, and this sentence was carried out in Smithfield within a few paces of the chief entrance to St. Bartholomew's Hospital, as a stone set into the wall records.

But we are anticipating. Henry Eighth was still upon his throne, busying himself, between getting married, with the affairs, spiritual as well as temporal, of his subjects. It seems to have been represented to him by Thomas Cromwell, his Chancellor, that he would do well to authorize a new edition of the Bible and, this being in accordance with Archbishop Cranmer's views, Coverdale was appealed to, to revise his text, taking into consideration the Matthew text. The result was the "Great Bible," sometimes improperly called "Cranmer's Bible," published in 1539, the authorized version of the time. It is a noble book: the type is black letter, well composed, the ink is brilliant and the paper superb. As no printer in England had the equipment necessary for the production of so sumptuous a volume as was contemplated, Henry secured a special license from Francis First, King of France, permitting his printer, Regnault, to supervise the undertaking. But even with royal permission in hand, difficulties were encountered: the type was set and some of the sheets were printed when the officers of the Inquisition swooped down upon the undertaking and great confusion ensued. Grafton, the printer, and Coverdale, the editor and translator who had come from London to be at hand while the work was "in press," as we would say, were at their "wittes endes." Originally an edition of two thousand was contemplated; how many copies were printed or destroyed was never known; some were publicly burnt, some were sold to a haberdasher for use as wrapping-paper, and some were secured by the English Ambassador, Bishop Bonner, and smuggled across the Channel. Finally the presses and types were conveyed to a place of safety and the work was completed.

These difficulties were, no doubt, exceptional, and they cause one to look upon the old book with reverence: indeed one should always look upon an old book in that way. What learning and skill entered into its production! With what hopes, or perchance misgivings, its author or its editor entrusted his manuscript to the printer! We who live in an age which seems to have adopted for its slogan, "Do it electrically," that is to say, rapidly, may well pause for a moment and think upon the places and the

TITLE-PAGE OF MATTHEW BIBLE (1537)

peoples who, three or four hundred years ago, produced those books which all the world to-day so greatly admires. Paris was indeed a town, but it was only a town in 1539; and that huge agglomeration which to-day is London was then merely half a dozen villages, connected together by rough roads, impassable in winter, dusty in summer, and always dangerous. What facilities had the printers of those days? From our point of view, none. Yet they designed and cast beautiful types which are still a delight to the eye, and set them with taste, and printed from them on rude presses in jet black ink upon paper which yet remains as sound as when it first came from the mill. Verily those old printers were artists and craftsmen, not mechanics imbued with but one idea — that of an eight-hour day. Such thoughts as these always break in upon me when I look upon a fine old book.

The "Great Bible" is a large folio, and a fine copy is to-day an extreme rarity. It bears the imprint of Richard Grafton and Edward Whitchurch. The title-page or frontispiece is an elaborate engraving, said to be from a drawing by Hans Holbein, crowded with Biblical and political allusions. At the top of the picture King Henry, seated on his throne, is giving Bibles to the clergy on his right by the hands of his Archbishop, Cranmer, while the people on his left are receiving theirs from his High Chamberlain, Thomas Cromwell. Meantime a host of figures, great and small, are shouting, "Vivat Rex" and

"God Save the Kynge," in a most engaging manner. But alas, a few months after having been created Earl of Essex, Cromwell had the misfortune to offend the King in the matter of one of his wives, and Henry caused him to be beheaded in the Tower.

Our Cromwell, Thomas, is sometimes confused with the greater Cromwell, Oliver, who beheaded King Charles First, a hundred-and-odd years later. The story will be remembered of the youth who, in an examination paper, upon being told to write briefly what he knew of Thomas Cromwell, said: "Thomas Cromwell was a great English statesman who cut off the head of his King, and as he lay upon his death-bed, he exclaimed, 'Had I but served my God as I have served my King, He would not now have left me naked to my enemies.'"

There were seven issues of the Great Bible, in the last three of which the coat of arms of Cromwell was erased from the title-page, leaving a round blank space about the size of a shilling. This Bible is sometimes improperly called Cranmer's Bible, but "the promoter of the enterprise was Cromwell, the editor was Coverdale, the printer was Regnault, the famous French typographist, with what assistance could be rendered him by his English associates, Grafton and Whitchurch." The error grew out of the fact that Cranmer composed an elaborate preface as an introduction to the edition of 1540 and subsequent issues. It may not be amiss to remind the reader that Cranmer too, in due

TITLE-PAGE OF THE GREAT BIBLE OF HENRY VIII (1539)
This plate is supposed to have been engraved from a drawing by Hans Holbein

course, died a victim of the Reformation — at the stake.

But for the moment Archbishop and Chancellor were in high favor, and a royal order decreed that every clergyman in England should provide "one book of the whole Bible of the largest volume in Englysshe, and have the same sett up in summe convenient place within the churche that he was cure of, whereat his parishioners might commodiously resort to rede yt." But this rule was not strictly obeyed, Henry having wives and other matters to attend to. For eighteen years after publication little or nothing was done in the matter of perfecting the text, and Edward Sixth, when he came to the throne, gave his name to the Book of Common Prayer, with which virtually he had nothing to do.

The Prayer Book of Edward Sixth, published in 1549, usually referred to as the "Book of Common Prayer," is not so great, not so universal a book as the Bible, but for sheer beauty of phrasing is far superior. Every page, every sentence, every word has been the subject of critical study. It is not the work of a sect, of a denomination, or indeed of an age. For more than fifteen hundred years the master minds of Christendom have been at work upon it and have made it what it is — sublime: an anthology of all that is most beautiful in Christian literature. This being the case, it is curious that collectors do not appraise the Prayer Book at anything like its true value. Next to the Bible it is the most significant book in the language; yet a man who may not hesitate to give a thousand, five, or even ten thousand dollars for some nasty Restoration drama of no merit whatever, the very name of which can hardly be mentioned in polite society, will think twice before he parts with a few hundred dollars for a book which contains the finest prose and the finest poetry in our language — or indeed in any language. Let me not be misunderstood as recommending the collection of a miscellaneous lot either of Bibles or of Prayer Books; but I maintain that no library worthy of the name should be without the keystones of our literature; and by these I mean a King James Bible and an Edward Sixth Prayer Book.

Ten years after the publication of the "Great Bible," that is to say, in 1549, the first edition of the Prayer Book appeared. Subsequent issues containing minor changes, the result of religious or political bickering, appeared from time to time, until finally, after a conference, it was decided that no further changes should be permitted; whereupon a copy known as the "sealed copy," the text of which was approved by a substantial majority, was deposited in the Tower of London as a standard to which future reference might be made. Not again until 1717 is the book-collector's attention challenged by a Prayer Book. In that year John Sturt, a London engraver, famous for the exquisite minuteness of his work, — he engraved the Lord's Prayer on a silver half-penny and the Creed upon a silver penny, —

TITLE-PAGE OF THE BOOK OF COMMON PRAYER (1549)

executed one hundred and eighty-eight silver plates from which was printed the full and complete text of the version of the Prayer Book in use in his day. It is a marvelous production: each page is adorned with borders and vignettes, and while the text is very fine, the whole of it can be read with the naked eye, except the frontispiece, which is composed of a portrait of George I, on which are inscribed the Creed, the Lord's Prayer, the Ten Commandments, Prayers for the Royal Family, and the Twenty-first Psalm! There are over five hundred ornamental initial letters, and indeed the whole production is nothing short of marvelous. I have long had a fine copy of the small paper edition, but a few weeks ago, in the Brick Row Bookshop in New York, a clergyman, overhearing a conversation on the subject of Bibles and Prayer Books, put me in the way of obtaining what I believe must be the finest copy of the book in existence. It is printed on large paper, the pages being ruled by hand with thin red, green, and gold lines; is in a fine contemporary binding; and is made additionally valuable by the bookplate of that most discriminating collector and old friend of mine, Samuel Putnam Avery. It will be observed that the Sturt Prayer Book antedates Pine's *Horace*, the other famous engraved book, by almost twenty years.

My enthusiasm for Bibles and for Prayer Books does not extend to hymnals. There are, of course, some grand old hymns, words and music, but it is difficult to write hymns and sense at the same time.

Even as a small boy I rebelled at the gruesomeness of William Cowper's "There is a fountain filled with blood," sung to the most lugubrious of tunes. I am reminded of the rejoinder I once heard a man make to another who said that he had just written a fine hymn: "I have always regarded the writing of hymns as the lowest form of intellectual effort." The remark was applauded. Let us join in singing Dr. Isaac Watts, his hymn: —

> Blest is the man whose bowels move
> And melt with pity for the poor;
> His soul in sympathizing love
> Feels what his fellow saints endure.
>
> His heart contrives for their relief
> More good than his own hands can do;
> He, in a time of gen'ral grief,
> Finds that the Lord has bowels too.

There was very little study of the Bible during the reign of Edward's violently partisan sister, "Bloody Mary," but with the accession of Queen Elizabeth the reading of the Bible of the "largest volume" was encouraged. Soon another Bible arrived from the Continent to challenge its supremacy. This was the Geneva or "Breeches Bible," so called because in it the seventh verse of the third chapter of Genesis reads, "made themselves breeches" instead of "aprons"; no fewer than sixty editions of it were published during the reign of Elizabeth alone.

In these days when questions of doctrine, that is

THE BIBLE

AND

HOLY SCRIPTVRES

CONTEYNED IN

THE OLDE AND NEWE

Testament.

TRANSLATED ACCOR-
ding to the Ebrue and Greke, and conferred With
the best translations in diuers langages.

WITH MOSTE PROFITABLE ANNOTA-
tions vpon all the hard places, and other things of great
importance as may appeare in the Epistle to the Reader.

FEARE YE NOT, STAND STIL, AND BEHOLDE
the saluacion of the Lord, which he wil shewe to you this day. Exod. 14, 13.

THE RED SEA

THE LORD SHAL FIGHT FOR YOU: THERFORE
holde you your peace, Exod. 14. reuis. 14.

AT GENEVA.

PRINTED BY ROVLAND HALL.

M.D.LX.

TITLE-PAGE OF THE GENEVA — OR BREECHES — BIBLE (1560)
The lines on this title-page were ruled in red ink with a pen

to say, what is taught, and dogma, which has been defined as arrogant expression of opinion, have paled before the blazing sun of science, it seems almost unbelievable that four hundred years ago, in what called itself a civilized and Christian country, men were persecuted and put to death for holding beliefs that arose, not so much from the Bible itself as from the expounders of it. Miles Coverdale, then Bishop of Exeter, a pious and exemplary old man of seventy, to whom we owe so much, was deprived of his bishopric and obliged to flee for his life before the bloody rage of Queen Mary. He deserves to be remembered for his saying, in a time when violence of opinions was counted for righteousness, that he was "always willing and ready to do his best as well in one translation as in another." His name is associated with three versions of the Bible: the edition of 1535, which bears his name, the Great Bible of 1539, and the Geneva Bible of 1560.

When he returned from his exile abroad, he was not reinstated in his see of Exeter, but was made rector of the Church of St. Magnus the Martyr. However, he soon gave up this living, and at his death he was buried in the Church of St. Bartholomew by the Exchange, in London. When that church was demolished, his remains were by pious hands transferred to his old church of St. Magnus, London Bridge. There has been recently some talk of the destruction of this church: it impedes somewhat the traffic approaching the north end of the historic bridge, but it is altogether probable that it will be saved because it is the final resting-place of the ashes of Miles Coverdale. A long and somewhat labored inscription to his memory may still be seen on a marble tablet on the east wall of the church, not far from the communion table.

Various reasons have been given for the popularity of the "Breeches Bible." It had a romantic background: it was the Bible of the Reformation, the Bible of Calvin and Knox and their followers, and it was of convenient size; it was portable and inexpensive. Above all, it was the first Bible that was cut up into verses which could readily be committed to memory. For all these reasons it came to be beloved by the common people as no other Bible had ever been.

But English ecclesiastics were jealous of its popularity and were determined to oust it if possible; their efforts resulted in the "Bishops' Bible" of 1568. Nothing was left undone to make this appealing; it was issued in magnificent style with a portrait of Queen Elizabeth and — in very bad taste — another of her supposed lover, Robert Dudley, the Earl of Leicester, and of Lord Burleigh, her minister. Its cost was about the equivalent of twenty pounds to-day, and an order of the Convocation of Bishops required that every archbishop and bishop should have at his home "a copy of the Holy Bible as lately published," and that it should be kept in the hall or dining-room, that it might "be useful to servants or

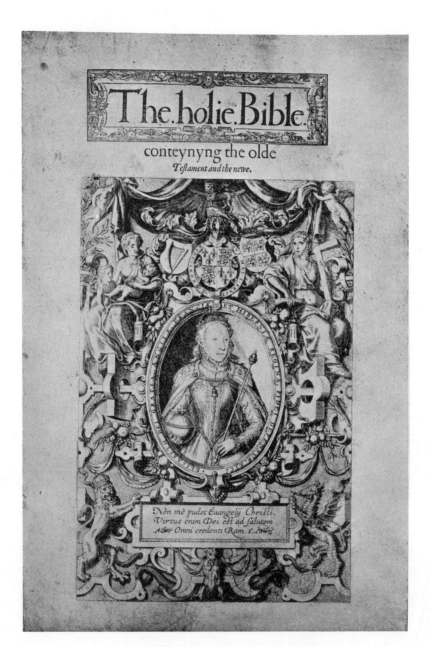

TITLE-PAGE OF THE BISHOPS' BIBLE (1568)
with portrait of Queen Elizabeth

strangers." But the best thing that could be said about the Bishops' Bible is that it served to pave the way for the King James Version.

Before coming to this, however, there remains to be mentioned another important version, the Douai Bible: the only text not based to a greater or less extent upon the translation of William Tyndale. As there were Puritan exiles at Geneva, so there were Roman Catholic exiles in the French cathedral city of Rheims, who subsequently moved to Douai upon the establishment there of a university. The Douai version is generally regarded as an effort on the part of Catholics to win back the Church of England to the Roman communion. The New Testament was published first at Rheims in 1582. It was accompanied by many notes of a controversial character and was later followed by the entire Bible, a translation from the Vulgate in 1609; this has remained since its publication the accepted Bible for English Catholics.

There is also a "Treacle" Bible, in which the text "Is there no balm in Gilead?" becomes "Is there no treacle?"; and a "Vinegar" Bible, because of the misprint which speaks of the parable of "the vinegar" for the parable of "the vineyard." This, published by one John Baskett, on account of its many blunders is usually called the "Basketfull of Errors." But the supreme blunder was made in an edition published in 1631, in which the word "not" was omitted from the Seventh Commandment, so that it reads, "Thou shalt commit adultery." This edition was instantly suppressed, and the printer fined for the slip, — if slip it was, — in the sum of three hundred pounds. Henry Stevens of Vermont, as he always called himself, says Mr. James Lenox paid him fifty guineas for a copy then believed to be unique, which is now in the New York Public Library; but "unique" books, when well advertised, have a way of reproducing themselves. Subsequently another copy, imperfect but later perfected, turned up and was secured by Mr. Panizzi for the British Museum; and several other copies have since come to light; there is certainly one in the John Rylands Library of Manchester, that great treasure-house of Bibles, for its always obliging librarian, Dr. Henry Guppy, showed it to me when I was last there.

But it is high time, and a little more than time, that we approach the "Authorized" Version, the King James Bible, the "Great He" Bible of 1611. It has a curious and interesting history.

Immediately upon the death of Queen Elizabeth, in 1603, King James came to the English throne, having reigned for some time in Scotland as James Sixth. His progress from Edinburgh to London, to be crowned, was retarded, or at least interrupted, by groups of men appointed to wait upon him to learn his royal pleasure on this subject and on that; one of the groups sought immediate changes in the Prayer Book. The Puritans thought that, having been brought up among Scotch Presbyterians, a dour lot, he would be glad to introduce what they considered

as much-needed reforms in the ritual of the Church.
Roman Catholics, on the other hand, hoped that
the new King would, with increase of responsibility,
see the error of his ways and come out strongly for
the true Church, the Church as it was before the
schism. As between the Calvinists on the one side
and the Romanists on the other, James thought it
expedient to identify himself rather with the Church
of England party, but to hear the grievances of the
Puritans. Scenting a violent theological discussion,
which he loved as other kings loved vice, he called a
conference at Hampton Court soon after his accession, to discuss the Prayer Book, he himself acting
as Moderator.

As a result of this conference, a few unimportant
changes were made in the Book of Common Prayer,
but the meeting gave the King, as he said, an opportunity to "pepper the Puritans" soundly. Then,
perhaps to relieve the sting, he fell in with the suggestion of one of their leaders, John Rainolds, President of Corpus Christi College, Oxford, one of the
great scholars and linguists of the time, that the
Bible should be newly edited under the King's royal
patronage, contending that those versions which were
allowed in the reigns of Henry Eighth and Elizabeth
were corrupt and not answerable to the original.
Thus it was that a conference called for one purpose
accomplished another.

The time was singularly propitious for a new edition: the English language had attained a degree of

fixity that it had before lacked; a man speaking it knew that he was using a language which was understood by all who heard him; at the same time its phrasing had not yet become hackneyed. It is necessary only to compare the Bibles of a relatively few years before the one we are now considering, to note the amazing change that had taken place. The men who made this translation were more than scholars; they were artists, using that word in the sense in which it is used when one speaks of an orchestra, and they used their instrument — the English language — with studied skill. Not only was the right word sought, — I will not say found, — having in mind the meaning of the original text, but great regard was paid to cadence, to rhythm. Equal scholarship several generations before could not have produced a work so nervous and vigorous, and it is equally certain that succeeding generations have not done so. Considering its bulk, it is remarkable that its accuracy remained practically unchallenged for two and a half centuries.

It is usual to dismiss King James First of England as a pedant; he was a pedant, but he was more; had he not been a king he would have been a scholar, and unless I have altogether misread the history of the making of the Version bearing his name, he was largely instrumental in drawing up the rules which governed the several groups of scholars who worked upon it.

The idea of making the new edition was not the

King's; he did not formally authorize it, nor did Parliament, nor did any bishop or bench of bishops. Moreover, so far as is known, the King did not contribute a penny toward the undertaking: he was a Scotsman, it will be remembered. Indeed, and for very similar reasons, the new version might be likened to the so-called "Dawes Report."* Everyone knows that this report is backed, in effect, by the United States Government, yet no whippoorwill in the Senate has a right to challenge it, for no one in that body authorized it, nor was a dollar appropriated toward the expenses of the men who made it.

Shortly after the adjournment of the Hampton Court Conference the King called upon all the greatest scholars in England — with the exception of one man who was known to be quarrelsome — and instructed them to proceed forthwith upon the new translation. For the better understanding of their duties, each man was provided with a set of rules which were intended to guide him in his task. There were originally fifty-four men, but for some reason their number dwindled, and the names of only forty-seven have come down to us. The revisers were divided into six groups: two groups to work at Oxford, two at Cambridge, and two at Westminster. As soon as one group had finished a portion of its allotted task, a transcript of the work was sent to each of the other five groups for criticism. In this

*Note: This report was, in fact, written by Mr. Owen D. Young of New York City.

way the knowledge of all was placed at the disposal of each, coöperation was secured, and an evenness of tone maintained throughout.

A preface of considerable length, if of admirable temper, set forth what the translators did or sought to do. They "never thought to make a new translation, nor yet to make of a bad one a good one, but to make a good one better, or out of many good ones, one principal good one." Nor did they "disdain to consult all previous translators and commentators" in whatever language, nor hesitate "to bring back to the anvil that which they had hammered"; they "feared no reproach for slowness nor coveted praise for expedition," and they pointed out that "nothing is begun and perfected at the same time," and that second thoughts are best. In this admirable spirit, after something less than four years' work the Authorized Version was issued to the public.

"And now," to quote Old Fuller, "after long expectation, the greate desire came forth, the new Translation of the Bible by a select and competent number of Divines, appointed for that purpose, not being too many, lest one should trouble another; and yet many, lest many things might haply escape them."

At first, as is usual when a very great book is given to the world, nothing happened. No attempt was made to force the book upon an unwilling public; the public were, in fact, satisfied with the Bible of Calvin, the "Breeches" Bible. Not at once, then, but gradually the new version displaced all others

and, by reason of its simplicity and beauty, wound
its way into the hearts and heads of the people who
would have been quick to resent it, had it been
"required" reading. James First was not very popular; he might have "queered" the version that bears
his name had he attempted to force it upon them.
Whereas previously one version had been read in
church and another at home, now all parties and
classes turned of their own accord to the same version and adopted it. No longer was the Bible looked
upon as an arsenal from which the several parties
could secure ammunition to hurl at one another;
every word had been a battleground, but was so no
longer. Thus it was that the King James Version
quieted and tended to soothe the whole nation.

It might be well to pause for a moment and think
what the Bible meant to a seventeenth-century
reader. In the first place, it was regarded as a privilege to look therein, a privilege which had from time
to time been denied the common people. In Henry
Eighth's reign a statute permitted the reading of the
Bible only by the nobility and gentry; any artificer,
apprentice, journeyman, servant, or laborer, or any
woman not of noble or gentle birth who dared to
read the Scriptures incurred liability of a month's
imprisonment for each offense. Could any means
have been employed more likely to secure a world of
readers? Then the Book was regarded from end to
end as the Word of God. Every word was sacred:
"In the beginning was the word, and the word was

with God, and the word was God." There it was as
plain as print: could anything be clearer or more conclusive? Only an evil man would challenge it.

Let us imagine that we are in the year 1611. The
Virgin Queen was no more, but her spacious days
were hardly over. England was a nest of singing
birds. Shakespeare was alive; he had, indeed, made
his exit from the stage and was living in retirement
in Stratford; but Bacon was at work: he had published
his *Advancement of Learning* and was busy upon the
Novum Organum. His disciples say that he had much
to do with the Bible, and he may have done so, for
he was the greatest scholar then living in England.
They make much of the fact, for fact it is, that in
the forty-sixth Psalm the forty-sixth word from the
beginning is "Shake" and the forty-sixth from the
end is "speare," and they say Bacon put it there;
it is a coincidence of course, for practically this
same arrangement occurs in the Bible of 1539,
published some years before Bacon was born. Ben
Jonson was at the height of his fame. Dekker and
Marston, — the latter a cleric as well as a dramatist, — Webster and Massinger, Beaumont and
Fletcher, all were at work making their contribution
to that glorious thing we call English literature.
The whole world was in a ferment: the Renaissance
was in full flower; imperialism was in the air; England
had found herself; the seas were swept by her ships;
Drake had circumnavigated the globe; Robert
Thorne, a Bristol seaman, only voiced what was

in all men's minds when he said, "There is no land uninhabitable, no sea innavigable to an Englishman." It was in this spirit that Captain John Smith sailed west to the land that was to be Virginia.

The line between priestcraft and statecraft, not yet sufficiently drawn, was, at the beginning of the seventeenth century, as imaginary as the equator, as indistinguishable as the line that separated the pirate from the privateer, for the great explorers were but little more. The one thing needful to weld together the empire — for England was an empire long before Disraeli made the announcement — was a common language, simple and direct enough to be understood by all, yet of range sufficient for the scholar. This "The Book," the Bible, the Authorized Version, supplied. No book has ever had, no book can ever have, the influence of the English Bible. It did for prose what the First Folio of Shakespeare did for verse. It is an older, a nobler, and a greater book. Poetry is for our exalted moods; prose does the work of the world. The Bible gave character not only to our tongue but to the people who used it. No man ever hears of a French or a Spanish or an Italian Bible; a Luther Bible, indeed, there is, but it is the Bible of a sect, repudiated by a large part of the German nation, and outside of that nation its existence is practically unknown. The English Bible is the Bible of the world.

And for the privilege of reading it men have given their lives; they were willing to fight for it, for the reason that its possession was synonymous with liberty. Men and women read their Bibles in full confidence of the inspiration of its every word. Their well-thumbed Testaments, Old and New, opened almost automatically to passages of unequaled simplicity and beauty. What comfort, what solace, was to be found in its pages! In those far-off days all men were "fundamentalists"; that is to say, they believed enormously and were content. The physical world was their oyster which any man with a sword could open, but the oyster has told somewhat of its secret, and now it is our souls that we explore. In the words of Walt Whitman:

> Sail forth! steer for the deep waters only,
> Reckless, O soul, exploring, I with thee and thou with me,
> For we are bound where mariner has not dared to go,
> And we will risk the ship, ourselves, and all.

The creation of the world, as described so vividly in the first chapters of Genesis, can no longer stand in the blaze of light which science has focused upon it; but the clergy, — many of them, — unwilling to jettison beliefs no longer tenable, have made unwise attempts to cling to texts that had done their work. Instead of saying frankly, the Bible is literature, not to be taken literally; science is one thing, religion, which is or should be a guide to right living, is another — they joined issue with the scientists and insisted that its every word was inspired, the word of God. This resulted in their complete discomfiture,

and there arose a group of ribald jesters like the late
Robert G. Ingersoll, with his lecture on the "Mistakes of Moses," a cheap and flippant attempt to
destroy the faith of the unthinking. How different
is the attitude of that great scientist, Thomas Hux-
ley, who says of the King James Bible: —

Consider this great historical fact, that for three centuries this book has been woven into all that is noblest
and best in English history; consider that it has become
the national epic of Great Britain, and that it is as familiar
to noble and simple from John o' Groat's to Land's End
as Tasso and Dante once were to the Italians; consider
that it is written in the noblest and purest English, and
that it abounds in exquisite beauties of literary form, and
finally, consider that it forbids the veriest hind, who never
left his native village, to be ignorant of the existence of
other countries and other civilizations, and of a great past
stretching back to the furthest limits of the oldest nations
of the world.

Not enough of us appreciate — or sufficiently —
the nobility of our English language, the language of
literature if not of science. The impossible Germans
have told us so much of the merits of their tongue
that we have grown forgetful that it was in the language of the King James Bible that Shakespeare
unlocked his heart.

It is our fate to live in a time of transition, a time
when many of the statements of the Bible have been
disproved. Science has destroyed our belief in the
God of our fathers, and the teachings of Jesus are
not yet come into full bearing. It is useless for us to

blink the fact that the Bible is no longer read as it was a few generations ago, and as on account of its wisdom and beauty and essential truth it deserves to be. I am told that a generation is growing up in entire ignorance of this great Book; I believe it and regret it. One of the wisest sayings of any man was that of the archskeptic Voltaire: "If there were no God we should have to invent one." That is what we have been doing since the beginning of time, creating God in our own image.

I am not concerned with your belief — that is not a book-collector's business; for myself I find that not all parts of the Bible have the same value; some are trivial, some historic, some sublime. There is indeed something to be said for the Roman Catholic point of view that not all the Bible requires reading; but the omission of certain parts leads to tampering with others; I want deletions from the Bible, not additions. In this I am in accord with Thomas Jefferson who, you will remember, arranged for his own personal use a book usually called the Jefferson Bible, but which he called the "Life and Morals of Jesus of Nazareth," in which the teachings of Jesus, extracted in his own words from the Evangelists, in four texts, Greek, Latin, French, and English, were arranged in parallel columns. Writing of this book — it is now in the Smithsonian Institute at Washington; I saw it there only a few months ago — he said, "A more beautiful or precious morsel of ethics I have never seen: it is a document in proof that I am a real Christian, that is to say, a disciple of Jesus."

There are too few of them: it is the notes, glosses, and explanations of men like ourselves that bring the Church into disrepute. Christianity, which flows from the Bible, not alone supplies a creed adapted for society as it existed eighteen hundred years ago or for society as it exists to-day, but supplies us with an ideal toward which the world is tending. It has never yet been tried on a large scale, least of all by those who think that Christianity means their particular brand of belief. Christianity is far greater than any church: Christianity produced the Sermon on the Mount; the Church produced the Athanasian Creed, which is, roughly speaking, to this effect: "I believe in the incomprehensible, and the more incomprehensible the more I believe in it." Disraeli said this was the most splendid ecclesiastical lyric ever produced by the genius of man. I regard it as a horror. And I wish that trials for "heresy" might cease — those tragic farces at which kindly old men of excellent character are goaded and made miserable by *criminal lawyers* — what a happy phrase that is! — at the instance of other old men. To be sure, we no longer burn them or behead them, as we used to do; we merely "unfrock" them and break their hearts. It is something, but it is not enough; the world moves slowly.

"Are you a fundamentalist or a modernist?" a lady asked me not long ago, in a bookshop where I was looking at a Bible. The question was staggering and, seeking counsel, I was advised not to answer, on the ground that to do so might tend to degrade and incriminate me. I seem to remember a text to the effect that the letter killeth but the spirit giveth life. Fortunately, I am so happily tempered as to believe that the poet can save where the priest may fail. But the priest and the lawyer move me as little as a soothsayer come from ancient Rome.

One's meditations sometimes take one far afield; once again let us imagine we are in the year 1611, and that the Authorized Version has just been published. Let us examine the volume. It is a large book, and to quote Old Fuller again, "most beautifully printed"; the manuscript was probably lost in the great fire. The printer, Robert Barker, had had no little experience in Bibles, for we see his imprint on several earlier editions. His son Matthew, in a lawsuit after the father's death, stated that his father had paid three thousand five hundred pounds for the exclusive right to print, and claimed that by reason of this payment the right descended to him. Be this how it may, no one seems to know who got the money; the translators certainly did not, and although Barker was "king's printer" and enjoyed several monopolies, in his old age he became involved in financial difficulties and was committed to the King's Bench Prison, where he remained until his death.

A first issue of the first edition of the Bible is excessively rare; an immaculate untouched copy of the

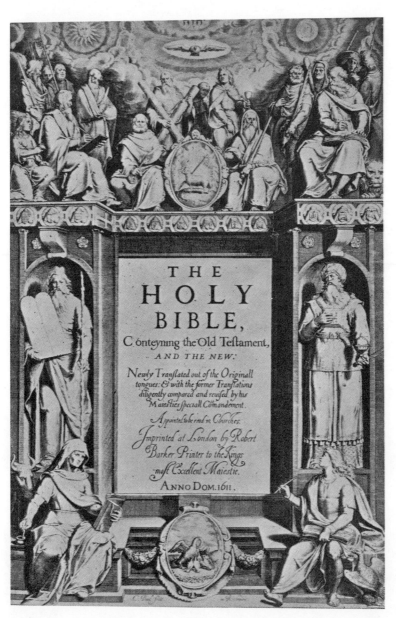

ENGRAVED TITLE-PAGE OF THE GREATEST BOOK
IN THE WORLD — "GREAT HE" BIBLE (1611)

first issue is practically unobtainable. A letter before
me from Mr. E. H. Dring (Quaritch), who has been
searching for one for years, in reply to a letter from
me states that he does not remember ever to have
seen such a copy and despairs of getting one. This
led me to secure the best copy which has come upon
the market for some years, and with which I shall be
content. It has been carefully collated by Francis
Fry, a rich old Quaker gentleman of Bristol, England,
who devoted the leisure of a long life to the study of
the bibliography of the Bible, and a most fascinating
study it is. My Bible is described by him in a manuscript note inserted therein, as being a clean, sound,
fine copy in the old binding. He goes on to say, "I
have examined every leaf and certify this as a standard copy of the First Issue with the rare edition of the
Genealogies, with the title-page and a good map."

There are several "points" which should be looked
for in buying a King James Bible. In the first place,
there were two title-pages, both bearing the date
1611. One is engraved on copper; the other is a woodcut border with a panel of text printed from type in
the centre; the engraved title is preferred. It is also
necessary to have a repetition of three lines of the
text at Exodus xiv. 10. And making sure that you
have the "genealogies," which are not more interesting than genealogies are wont to be, look especially
that you get the map of the land of Canaan, "Begun
by Mr. John More and continued and finished by
John Speede." The map is a fine and fascinating

specimen of the cartography of the time. It is dotted
with numbers which refer to a table in the margin
showing where many famous Biblical events took
place: for example, it is possible to see the exact spot
where David slew the giant and, most wonderful of
all, the ship from which Jonah was expelled so uncere-
moniously and the very whale which swallowed him.
Indeed, the "Ægiptian" Sea is full of these strange
animals. These corroborative details did not indeed
belong to the Bible, but Speede, having a "pull" with
the King, secured from him an order that they should
be inserted at an additional cost of two shillings for
large, eighteen pence for medium, and a shilling for
small Bibles.

The great point, however, remains to be mentioned.
There are two issues of the first edition, known
respectively as the "Great He" and the "Great She"
Bible, from a difference in the printing of the last
clause in the fifteenth verse of the third chapter of
the Book of Ruth. In the earliest impression it
reads, "He measured five measures of barley . . . and
HE went into the citie"; in the subsequent issues
the last line becomes "SHE went into the citie." A
comparison of the spacing of the words in the two
issues clearly shows that the missing "S" in the "He"
Bible is not occasioned by the accidental dropping of
the letter. It is the "He" Bible that is sought by
museums, libraries, and collectors alike.

"Never was so important a literary enterprise
carried out with so little record thereof." It was not

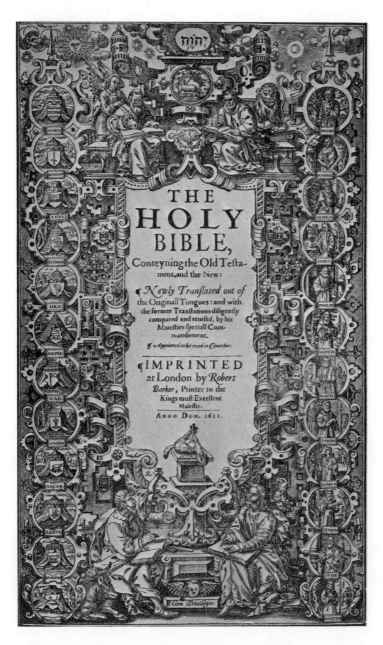

TITLE-PAGE OF THE "SHE" BIBLE (1611)
The same border is also used in certain of the "He" Bibles

entered at Stationers' Hall, as was usual, so that no
one knows in what month it appeared. Presumably,
two printing-houses were engaged upon the work,
for the different errors of the press can be accounted
for in no other way. A large edition — some say as
many as twenty thousand copies — was printed; if
so, what has become of them? The answer is simple:
a large book, if it be much handled, almost invariably
loses the first leaf or the last leaf, or both. The first
issue of the Bible went into few great houses, but
chiefly into parish churches, where it was accessible
to all, with the result that it was thumbed, not out
of existence so much as out of condition. One can
follow in one's imagination the decline and fall of a
Bible on a reading-desk in a country church. With
the passage of years the pages become loose and
finally detached from the volume, but they are carefully kept, and as often as they fall to the floor they
are replaced. Finally they disappear; but plenty is
left — who reads a title-page, anyway? And after
the volume has continued to shed its first and last
leaves for a century or two the old Bible is discarded,
and a newer and more easily read edition substituted.

This may be as good a place as any for me to refer
to the Bibles printed in America, prefacing my
remarks by stating that the first Bible printed in
what is now the United States was the so-called
Eliot Bible, with an unpronounceable title, published
for the use of the Indians. This was printed in Cambridge, Massachusetts, in 1661. A Bible in German

was printed by Christopher Sauer at Germantown, Pennsylvania, in 1743. The mother country never permitted her colonies to print a Bible in English: every copy had to be imported from England, although a profitable business was done in smuggling Bibles printed in English from the Continent — especially from Holland — into this country.

During the Revolutionary War, Bibles, like many other things, were scarce. At the end of that war Robert Aitken, a Scotsman who had come to this country some fifteen years before and established himself in Philadelphia as a bookseller, publisher, and binder, determined it was time to print a Bible in English. The matter was laid before Congress, then sitting, and after some discussion the following resolution was adopted: —

Resolved; That the United States in Congress assembled highly approve the pious and laudable undertaking of Mr. Robert Aitken, as subservient to the interest of religion, as well as an instance of the progress of arts in this country, and being satisfied of his care and accuracy in the execution of the work, they recommend this edition of the Bible to the inhabitants of the United States, and hereby authorize him to publish this Recommendation in the manner he shall think proper.

Thereupon Mr. Aitken went to work, and in due course printed a small volume — the page measures six by three and a half inches — which bore upon its title-page the coat of arms of the State of Pennsylvania. It was suggested that every soldier upon

THE FIRST BIBLE IN ENGLISH PRINTED
IN THE UNITED STATES (1782)

laying down his musket receive a copy; Washington applauded the idea. The matter was debated and debated; meanwhile the soldiers, anxious to get home, were disbanded — and nothing was done. How up-to-date it all seems. I have before me an autograph letter of Washington in which is this paragraph: —

Your proposition respecting Mr. Aiken's (*sic*) Bible would have been particularly noticed by me, had it been suggested in season. But the late Resolution of Congress for discharging Part of the Army, taking off near two-thirds of our numbers, it is now too late to make the attempt. It would have pleased me well, if Congress had been pleased to make such an important present to the brave fellows, who have done so much for the security of their Country's Rights & Establishment.

More highly praised than any other book, the Bible has also been more criticized, and from every angle; inevitably what we call the higher criticism has worked havoc with readings which were so entirely satisfactory to our ancestors. It will be remembered that the translations from both the Old and the New Testament were made from — if not a corrupt text, certainly from a text which might be described as composite; and if one calls to mind the photographs which we used to see years ago of a dozen or twenty faces, taken one upon another on the same plate, one will get an idea how blurred are many of the passages about which theological battles have been fought. The Hebrew text of the Old Testament translates well, we are told, into English; the Greek

text of the New Testament for some reason does
not. No scholar is ever entirely satisfied with the
translation of another; one stresses sense, another
sound. There were no exact equivalents in English
for many of the words in the original text, hence
words were used which only approximated the meaning; and we have to remember that we are dealing
with the works of highly imaginative writers, poets
in fact, as well as prophets, philosophers, historians,
and evangelists. But perhaps the chief cause of error
in our Bible arose in this way: a translator or a scribe
would interline a word of explanation or a note of
assent or dissent, which a later scribe would write
into the main text; this is the simple explanation of
many contradictions which disturb the mind of the
careful reader.

Our own scholar, the late Dr. Morris Jastrow, in
his volume, *A Gentle Cynic,* — which was his playful
title for the Book of Ecclesiastes, — shows with exactness just how and where this occurred in that
famous book. But would a father, seeking to train
up his child in the way he should go, reading to his
son that glorious twelfth chapter which begins, "Remember now thy Creator in the days of thy youth,"
be helped by the knowledge that the true meaning
of that chapter is: "Eat, drink, and be merry, for
verily all is vanity and vexation of spirit"?

It is because the sayings of the Preacher are as
beautiful and as poetic as the *Rubáiyát* of Omar
that the believer and the cynic alike know them by

SUPERB EXAMPLE OF A NEEDLEWORK BINDING
an English art which flourished in the time of James First.
The original is 9 x 13 inches, both sides and back embroidered

heart and open the book as they go to an organ, for its music, rather than for their literal meaning. It was, I feel certain, in this spirit that my friend, John Henry Nash of San Francisco, our greatest printer, "set the book in type," as he says, "entirely for my amusement, with my own hands," making thereby one of the most beautiful volumes I have ever seen. Who can be interested in the fact that bread, which is mentioned in the Bible some two or three hundred times, did not exist when either Testament was written; or who needs a more correct rendering of the text, "the candle of the wicked shall be put out"; or who is distressed that there are several trivial variations in the Lord's Prayer?

Are we more convinced of the truth of the pretty fable of the creation of Adam and of Eve by being told that it took place in a "park" (!) rather than in the Garden of Eden? Or that Noah escaped destruction from a great flood on a "barge," rather than in "an ark of gopher wood," pitched "within and without with pitch"?

We are celebrating this year, 1925, the four-hundredth anniversary of the first printing of the Tyndale Bible, by publishing a flood of new versions of and articles about the Bible, with most of which I am in complete disagreement. I yield to no man in my reverence for the Bible; indeed it is because of my reverence that I do not wish it tampered with. Men, in their efforts "to make a good translation better" or in striving for exactness in a matter which is of no earthly importance, have lost all sense of beauty, which is its own excuse for being. Scientists and scholars may destroy our belief in a text which was entirely satisfactory to our ancestors, but what shall we say of a school which hopes to "popularize" the Bible by vulgarizing it? In one text Salome is described as "a young lady who danced with inimitable grace and elegance." The superb *Magnificat* in the first chapter of St. Luke becomes: "My soul with reverence adores my Creator, and all my faculties with transport join in celebrating the goodness of God, who hath in so signal a manner condescended to regard my poor and humble station."

Esau's exchanging his birthright for "a mess of pottage" gave us a phrase — like "Naboth's vineyard" — in which is condensed a long story which is a part of our literary inheritance. One shudders for the mentality of a man who prefers the reading: "Let me have a bite of that *red omelette* there." (The phrase "a mess of pottage," curiously enough, is not in the text of any Bible. It is from a chapter-heading in the Matthew Bible of 1537, and it also occurs in the Great Bible of 1539 and several subsequent issues.)

Reader! recite if you can the Twenty-third Psalm, or, if you cannot, get someone to take down your Bible and read it to you. If you are not impressed with its beauty, consult an alienist. Now listen to some of the improvements suggested by the Reverend Doctor Moffatt:

The Eternal shepherds me, I lack for nothing;
He makes me lie in meadows green,
He leads me to refreshing streams,
   and revives life in me.
He guides me by true paths,
   as He himself is true.
My road may run through a glen of gloom,
   but I fear no harm, for thou art beside me;
   thy club, thy staff, they give me courage.

"Glen of gloom"! What wise man was it who re-marked, "Beware of the pitfalls of alliteration"? Verily, the Doctor is beside himself: much learning hath made him mad.

It was inevitable, too, in these days of woman's rights, that we should have a woman's Bible. The idea appears to have been born in the mind of Elizabeth Cady Stanton. In a stout pamphlet, published in New York in 1897, — I have a copy before me of the third edition, — the lady, having appointed a tentative committee of twenty-three women — and lo! the Reverend Phœbe Hanaford's name led all the rest — instructed each member of it to purchase a Bible and go through it from Genesis to Revelation, marking all the passages in which women were mentioned; these passages were then to be cut out and pasted in a blank book, and correct readings and comments thereon written underneath.

This may cause a smile, but there is, indeed, something to be said for it, if not in this country at least in England, where the law, ecclesiastical and civil, has from time out of mind discriminated shamefully

bunge vs to God, and was kplled, as per-
teininge to the flelhe; but was quickened in
the spirite.

☞ In which spirite, he also wente and prea-
D ched vnto the spirites that were in prison,
which were in tyme passed disobedient, when
the longe sufferinge of God abode exceainge
pacientlp in ȳ dapes of Noe, whyle the arcke
was a preparing wherin fewe (that is to saie
viii. soules) were saued bp water, which signi-
fpeth. c. baptisme that nowe saueth vs, not ȳ
puttinge awape of the splth of the flelhe, but
in that a good conscience consenteth to God,
bp the resurreccion of Jesus Christe, whyche
is on the right hande of God, †and is gone
into heauen, aungelles, power, and mighte,
subdued vnto him.

The notes.

a. He dwelleth wpth his wyfe accordinge to
knowledge, that taketh her as a necessarye
healper, and not as a bonde seruaunte or a
bonde slaue. And pf she be not obedient and
healpfull vnto hpni, endeuoureth to beate the
feare of God into her heade, that therbp she
mape be compelled to learne her duitie and
do it. But chiefly he muste be ware that he
halte not in anye parte of his dutie to her
ward. ffor his euill exemple, shall destrope
more then al the instruccios he can geue, shall
edifie.

b. Erasmus in his annotacions, noteth out of
Sainct Jerome, that this honoure is not the
bowynge wpth the knees, nother the decking
wpth gold and preciouse stones, neither pet
the settinge of the in the vpper seates & high-

Gene.ri.b
Mat.rriij.d
Luc.rvij.f

To dwell w
a wyfe accor-
dinge to
knowledge.

To geue ho-
nour to the
wyfe.

spnne, th
as much
not after
of God.
spent the
wil of the
lustes, or
in abomii
☞ And i
that pe ru
excesse of
of pou, w
that is red
this purp
.a. vnto th
ypke othei
before G
ges is at
† Be pe
mape be
ges haue
couereth t
berous ol
ginge. At
minister t
nisters of
anpe mar
spake the
stre, let h
God min
thinges n
Christ, ł

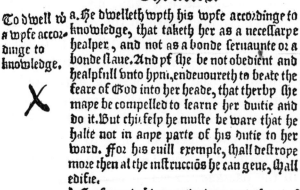

A PORTION OF A PAGE OF AN EARLY BIBLE

*showing how a "note" might easily be incorporated
into the body of the text, as has, indeed,
frequently been done*

against women. Women had, in fact, for centuries, had no rights which a man was bound to respect. Upon marriage she became his: his property, his chattel; and her property became his too. The promise of the wife to obey was no empty form, and the Church service closed with the admonitive words of Saint Paul addressed to the wife — the "weaker vessel" — in which she was told that her duty was plainly set forth in Holy Writ. She was to hold herself in subjection to her husband, and in all things to reverence and obey him, for the husband was the head of the wife, "in like manner" as Christ was the head of the Church. It all sounds a bit thick to-day; it is admittedly difficult for a woman to reverence a man who, coming home drunk, beats her up: the law in England still permits a husband "to beat his wife with a stick no thicker than his thumb," and while this privilege is not often exercised, the man still has it.

There is, too, a note in the "Bug" Bible, — so called on account of the familiar line in the Psalms, "Thou shalt not be afraid for the terror by night," being translated into "So that thou shalt not nede to be afrayed for any bugges by night," — a note, not at the bottom of the page, not in the margin, but set right in the text in the same type as the Scripture itself. It reads: "If she be not obedient and healpfull" unto her husband, let him endeavour "to beate the fear of God into her heade." Persons using this strong language — I have heard it in the streets

— can hardly know that they have for their authority a note published in a Bible that appeared so long ago as 1549.

I have already referred to the ease with which contradictory and inexplicable passages have crept into texts written by ignorant or careless scribes, passages which have proved stumbling-blocks throughout the ages. Why should we, then, be surprised that the advanced woman of to-day objects to the old idea of a masculine Trinity, and would substitute therefor a Godhead composed of a Father, a Mother, and a Son, basing her contention upon the twenty-seventh verse of the first chapter of Genesis: "So God created man" — that is to say, mankind — "in his own image, in the image of God created he him; male and female created he them," simultaneously, rather than upon the version which almost immediately follows, in which God caused a deep sleep to fall upon Adam, during which, from one of his ribs he made a woman and gave her to the man.

But the one for whose sanity I most tremble is that of a professor of a Western university who feels that we have all too long depended upon what he calls English-made translations, and declaring that the zest for improvement, which is so characteristic of the American, demands a translation into American-English, he promises to supply it! Prepared now for anything, we are not surprised when he goes further and plumes himself upon the receipt of a letter from a Negro living in New York, congratulating him upon the idea, adding that he has received no higher compliment. I can well believe it.

I am reminded of a cartoon which appeared in *Punch* some years ago, at an instant of calm in a strenuous life, when Theodore Roosevelt issued his famous edict vigorously demanding simplified spelling. The President, as he then was, is shown with his shirt sleeves rolled up, swinging an enormous axe against the trunk of a splendid English oak, the English language, upon which he was vainly endeavoring to make an impression. Old Father Time, passing by with his scythe at rest upon his shoulder, pauses for a moment and remarks to himself, contemplatively, "Ah, well, boys will be boys."

Of greater moment, it seems to me, is the criticism sometimes made that the Bible is the worst-printed book in the world, in that the eye is not permitted to assist the mind in recognizing at a glance the difference between passages in prose and in what may well be called poetry. I speak, of course, of the usual editions.

It will be remembered that in the early texts there were neither "chapters" nor "verses"; these purely arbitrary divisions have been made for the sake of clarity, and no doubt more could advantageously be done. An example of what might be printed as poetry is that wonderful passage about the wise man who built his house upon a rock —

> And the rain descended,
> And the floods came,
> And the winds blew,
> And beat upon that house,
> And it fell not;
> For it was founded upon a rock.

Or that glorious passage from the first epistle of Saint Paul to the Corinthians, too long to quote, which is and should always be read as poetry, which forms a part of the beautiful burial-service of the Church of England, and which ends with

> Death is swallowed up in victory.
> O death, where is thy sting?
> O grave, where is thy victory?

What we most need is not new versions or new printings but a better understanding of the significance of the version we have. But I am forgetting that I am a book-collector and not a preacher.

I return for a moment to the "Great He" and the "Great She" Bibles: they are the parents of a large family and have taken very literally the text, "Be fruitful and multiply, and replenish the earth and subdue it." The Bible exceeds in circulation, if circulation may be judged from publication, the next ten most popular books put together. Complete Bibles have been published in one hundred and thirty-five languages, and the New Testament in over one hundred additional. The British and Foreign Bible Society, organized in 1804, alone has printed hundreds of millions of Bibles. The American Bible Society, founded in Philadelphia a few years later, has since its inception printed and distributed more than twenty-five million Bibles, and over a hundred million New Testaments. Counting the output of the great presses of the Universities of Oxford and Cambridge and the presses in this country as well, it is reckoned that the annual output of complete Bibles and parts thereof is in the neighborhood of three million copies. On the other hand, in proportion to its circulation, it is very little read. This is to be regretted, because from every angle it is the Greatest Book in the World: so great that if a man can be found in a civilized country who has never heard of the Bible, it nevertheless influences his life, and influences it for good.

You will fancy that I have forgotten the words of Koheleth, "Let us hear the conclusion of the whole matter," and you may, if it pleases you, think of me as one who has just discovered the beauties of the Bible. Very well; let me say to you as the young curate did to his astonished congregation: "If the King James Version was good enough for Saint Paul, it is good enough for me."

II

LONDON is a marvelous place. One can turn a sharp
corner or pass under an arch, and in an instant find
one's self in the country. Fine old trees are growing
on well-kept lawns, the birds are twittering, the noise
of the city is distant and forgotten; in an instant one
has passed from the turmoil of the twentieth century
into the calm of the eighteenth.

Another thing: London is a city of ghosts; the
people one sees are not important, they are merely
shadows; the actualities are the people one can see
only with the help of a little imagination; it does not
require much, the settings are so perfect. Climb
Ludgate Hill, for example, and as you approach St.
Paul's swing round to your left, make a turn or two
and get lost, and you will stumble upon the Dean's
Garden. It's a lovely spot. There, right in the heart
of London, only a stone's throw from the great
cathedral of which it is a part, is a quiet Old World
garden, and facing it is a row of red-brick houses
beautifully tempered with age. In the largest of
these houses lives the dean of the cathedral in just
such rural luxury as a prince of the Church should,
who is the head of an immense and costly ecclesiastical establishment, the foundations of which go deep

down into history. But Dean Inge, the Gloomy
Dean, as he is called, is not, as might be thought, a
"rural dean"; I am quite sure, for I asked him the
question one evening when I sat next to him at a
dinner; but in answer to my rather flippant question
he merely looked sadly down his nose, seemingly
heavily packed with a cold, and replied, "No." I
was tempted to inquire whether a rural dean is the
same thing as a common or garden dean, but jesting
with a great dignitary of the Church of England is
apt to prove a serious business, and I lost the best
opportunity I ever had of discovering what a rural
dean is; I only know that they grow them in London;
probably in out-of-the-way places. Speaking of
Church dignitaries, I never make much progress with
them — I never did. There is a legend in my family
that at the age of four I was sent into a parlor to be
blessed of a bishop, for I had ecclesiastical bringing-
up. After the blessing I turned and, regarding the
bishop doubtfully, remarked, "I never liked bishops,"
and then added, as an afterthought, "nor pliecemens."
So early did I resent any form of authority; and this
characteristic has lengthened and strengthened and
thickened with years.

But Dean Inge is only one of the inhabitants of
his house and garden: Dean Milman is just as real
to me, although he died years ago. In life he wrote
plays, and good ones too, rather to the scandal of
the clergy; and finally, when he settled down, he
devoted himself to the study of history rather than

to the duties of deaning — whatever they may be.
I wish for his greatness' sake that I could summon
the ghost of Dean Swift in this garden, but he put
his money on the wrong horse, politically, and only
became Dean of St. Patrick's, Dublin, a very different matter. There was, of course, Dean Donne, but
that was several centuries ago.

The story goes that a letter was once addressed
to "Mr. Smith, No. 1, London," and that it was
delivered at Apsley House, at Hyde Park Corner,
the town residence of the Duke of Wellington, that
being, in the opinion of the post office, the beginning
of things — the Number One of London. Now, were
I commissioned to deliver a letter so addressed, I
think I would look round for a residence in a corner
of the circle — or more properly the oval — surrounding the great cathedral, and if I finally gave
up looking for a corner in a circle, I think I would
ask to be directed to the Dean's, that certainly being
Number One at this end of the town. And having
delivered my letter and being told, as I should be,
that there was "no answer," I would walk westward,
loiteringly, looking for other equally charming back-
waters; for one of the intoxicating joys of London is
the unexpectedness of one's finds, and if I failed to
stumble upon another Dean's Garden, I might come
upon another fine old house, also in its garden, the
house of the Master of the Temple. Who the present
Master is, I do not know, but if the old Master were
alive, Ainger, I would certainly go in and have a chat

with him; for I had a pleasant correspondence years
ago with him about Charles Lamb. Before E. V.
Lucas came along with his learning, Canon Ainger
was the accepted authority upon everything relating
to the greatest of English essayists. And threading
my way back to the Strand, I would certainly pause
for a moment on the other side of the Temple Church,
at the grave of Oliver Goldsmith. He died in debt
and was buried here, rather in a hurry one night, in
order that his body might not be seized by his creditors; and the grave was not marked for some time,
for the same reason. Poor Goldy! I hope John Filby,
your tailor, from whom you had the bloom-colored
suit, was not among them.

Every little court and alley in this part of London
has its colony of ghosts, and wandering among them
I would certainly, sooner or later, stumble upon
Gough Square. It is not too easy to find. I usually
enter it by Wine Office Court, in which is located
the Cheshire Cheese, that famous eating-place which
only became firmly identified with Dr. Johnson after
his death, because I like to pass and frequently enter
the one quaint old tavern which remains exactly as
most London taverns were a century or two ago, and
because tradition says that Goldsmith lived in this
court when he wrote *The Vicar of Wakefield.*

Reaching the top of this narrow channel and turning sharply to the left, one faces the famous house,
Number 17, the house in which Dr. Johnson lived for
ten years from 1748 to 1759, during which he compiled

the greater part of the Dictionary and wrote innumerable "Ramblers" and "The Vanity of Human Wishes"; from which he dispatched his smashing letter to Lord Chesterfield, and to which he returned "unshaken as the monument" after the failure of his play, *Irene*. It is the house, too, in which his wife died and in which, in all likelihood, he wrote *Rasselas*. It is not an amusing fiction, but I quite agree with the judgment of Christopher North, that "it is a noble performance in design and in execution," and that "never were the expenses of a mother's funeral more gloriously defrayed by a son than the funeral of Samuel Johnson's mother by the price of *Rasselas*, written for the pious purpose of laying her head decently and honourably in the dust."

Get someone with a good voice to read aloud the opening paragraph: read it if possible out of the first

THE

HISTORY

OF

RASSELAS,

PRINCE OF ABISSINIA.

AN ASIATIC TALE.

THE TWO VOLUMES COMPLETE IN ONE.

VOLUME THE FIRST.

The Labour or Exercife of the Body, freeth Men from Pains of the Mind ; and 'tis this that conftitutes the Happinefs of the Poor: For if a Man don't find Eafe or Content in *himfelf*, and his *Rational Employments*, and *Connettions*, 'tis in vain to feek it *Elfewhere.——Duke De La Roche Foucault.*

AMERICA:

PRINTED FOR EVERY PURCHASER.

MDCCLXVIII.

American edition, and having done so, pass the book on to me. It is excessively rare. Professor Tinker, of Yale, who recently discovered the volume, has been lording it over me in a manner more suggestive of a Captain of Industry than a mere college professor. The fact is that it is a hitherto unknown "item." Johnson called his "fable" *The Prince of Abissinia*. An obscure printer in Philadelphia called it "Rasselas" and *Rasselas* it has, since that time, remained. Johnsonians will remember that Bishop White of Pennsylvania sent Dr. Johnson a copy of it, and the Sage remarked that, while the impression was not magnificent, it was flattering to the author.

I would like to think that the Doctor's Elegy, — the Latin poem with a Greek title, — which he wrote on the completion of the revision of the fourth edition of his Dictionary, was written in Gough Square, but it is dated 12th December 1772, at which time he had deserted the Square for Johnson's Court. The manuscript of the poem, as well as an excellent translation of it, is one of my treasures. It is a portrait of the old man as he appeared to himself, as like as a painting from the brush of Reynolds. In writing the poem he seems to have had in mind the well-known lines from Pope's "Essay on Man":

> "Know then thyself, presume not God to scan.
> The proper study of mankind is man."

He commences by referring to the work and learning of the great French scholar, Scaliger, and to his

alleged epigram that the drudgery of words would be
one of the punishments of the damned.

[*Trans.*] The drudgery of words the damn'd would know,
     Doom'd to write lexicons in endless woe.

Dr. Johnson then breathes into his verse a feeling of
humility, the result of his own want of success (!)
and his fears for the future, evincing the feeling of
melancholy under which he was at that time laboring.

[*Trans.*] What then remains? Must I, in slow decline,
     To mute inglorious ease old age resign?
     Or, bold ambition kindling in my breast,
     Attempt some arduous task, or were it best,
     Brooding o'er lexicons to pass the day,
     And in that labor drudge my life away?

But we are wandering in London. Thomas Carlyle, who when he died was likened to Dr. Johnson, —
though this, to me, seems profanation, — was one of
the first to make a pious pilgrimage to the Gough
Square house, which he discovered, he says, "not
without labour and risk." This was in 1832, and ever
since that time it has been more sought and visited
than any similar shrine in London, though when its
present owner bought it, some years ago, it had fallen
on very evil days indeed. It is no small honor to
have secured and restored and for many years maintained at his own expense so delightfully haunted a
house as 17 Gough Square; that distinction belongs
to my friend Cecil Harmsworth.

In Dr. Johnson's day Gough Square was a genteel
— indeed one authority says it was a fashionable

17 GOUGH SQUARE

The famous house in which Dr. Johnson wrote the Dictionary

neighborhood; certainly it was the most dignified residence the Doctor ever had, and of all the many houses in which he lived it is the only one which is known and spared to us. He took it, it may be remembered, when the publishers had agreed to pay him fifteen hundred-and-odd pounds for compiling his Dictionary, which he thought a generous sum; and he used it as his residence and workshop. He was probably fixed in his determination to become a householder in this particular location by the convenience of being near his printer, William Strahan, who was one of the first partners in the firm of Messrs. Eyre and Spottiswoode, which eminent firm still continues to flourish in premises not far off. The house dominates the Square, which is not in itself imposing: a small paved parallelogram, not much frequented now except by members of the printing trade who work in the neighborhood.

Let us pause for a moment, and see if we are as alone in the Square as we seem to be. Is there not a shabby man walking toward the door from under a near-by arch? Yes, and it must be Robert Levett, the "humble practitioner of physic" who lived with Johnson and whose patients were recruited from among the very poor. He married a streetwalker, it will be remembered, much to Johnson's amazement, who said, "The marvels of that alliance make commonplace the occurrences in the *Arabian Nights*." And the old lady with him, who moves a little uncertainly, that would be blind Mrs. Williams, another pensioner. And that courtly gentleman who enters the Square from the northeast corner, carrying an ear trumpet into which talks excitedly a small man with never-to-be-forgotten eyes. What! you don't know who they are? That, sir, is Sir Joshua Reynolds, and with him is David Garrick; and that curious-looking man who has just entered the Square by the way we came — can that be Oliver Goldsmith? No doubt of it, for Dr. Johnson is giving a party to-night, and if we wait long enough we shall see probably Mr. Cave and Dr. Hawkesworth, and perhaps Lord Southwell and the Earl of Orrery. And after the Dictionary was published and the money spent, and the Doctor was poorer than ever, — for what was £1575 spread over eight years and paying for the hire of six amanuenses? — came, too, to this same door one evening two scoundrelly-looking men, and arrested the Doctor for debt, so that he was obliged to send a note by his black servant, Frank, to Mr. Richardson, the author of *Clarissa*, who lived hard by, saying: —

I am obliged to entreat your assistance. I am now under arrest for five pounds eighteen shillings. Mr. Strahan from whom I should have received the necessary help in this case, is not at home and I am afraid of not finding Mr. Millar. If you will be so good as to send me this sum, I will very gratefully repay you, and add it to all former obligations.

I am, Sir,
Your most obedient
and most humble servant
SAMUEL JOHNSON

Gough Square, 16 *March* [1756]

What has become of that letter? How one would like to own it! How many more times than the debt itself would the letter fetch if it were put up at auction with the Johnsonians of the world bidding? If old Samuel Richardson had no other fame, he deserves to be remembered for having come to the rescue of Dr. Johnson when he was arrested for debt. Well might the Doctor have written in that house those two famous lines in "The Vanity of Human Wishes":

> There mark what ills the scholar's life assail,
> Toil, envy, want, the patron and the jail.

The house in Gough Square is a substantial brick building of three stories, a basement, and an attic, and seems to date from the time of Queen Anne; it suggests comfort, if not luxury; indeed, I think if I were offered a house in the City to live in and could not persuade either Dean Inge or the Master of the Temple to vacate his mansion in my favor, that my next choice would be the Johnson house in Gough Square, especially if I could turn the square into a garden and transplant a few trees. At night not a sound is to be heard, for London is the quietest city in the world; occasionally a strayed reveler from the Johnson Club, who has been dining in the attic, lets out an uproarious laugh; I know, for I have often joined these parties; but more frequently I have entered the seemingly deserted Square during my midnight rambles. Then it is that the ghosts walk.

Let us enter the house. Raise the knocker and

wake the dead. Perhaps the Doctor will come to the door, poker in hand, ready to defend himself, as he did one night when his friends Topham Beauclerk and Bennet Langton, out on a frisk, knocked him up in the middle of the night, when, discovering who it was, he joined them and they rambled about until morning — and London mornings do not come with the sun, it will be remembered. But more likely we shall knock on that door about tea time and the chain will be drawn, and a lady — either an old one, Mrs. Dyble, or her daughter, Mrs. Rowell — will open the door and bid you welcome. I urge you to be on your best intellectual behavior, for these ladies are not the mere parrots that one too frequently meets in old houses and museums, but excellent Johnsonians, as several members of the Johnson Club have reason to know. Perhaps, if you are very nice to them and can pass your Johnson examination creditably, they will secure Mr. Harmsworth's permission for you to give a little tea to some of your friends in one of the rooms, and will attend to the details for you, and very charmingly too. It was Mr. Harmsworth's idea that there was to be as little as possible of the museum about this house. As he once said to me, "In a year I could fill it full to overflowing with trash; I don't want to do that. A few prints, a few pictures, a few books, a few autographs, and as few show-cases as possible." It is a good resolution; I hope his successors will stick to it.

But to return to the front door. As it closes, your

attention will be drawn to the curious chain-bolt that stretches across it: one end is secured to a staple, the other engages upon a spiral hook in such a manner that it cannot be disengaged therefrom by a wicked boy operating with a crooked stick through the fanlight. Then perhaps you will be permitted to descend the winding stairs into the kitchen with its great beams and roomy fireplaces. It stretches under the entire house, and one may "presume" a jack, a spit, or whatever gear may be required for the preparation of food on the generous scale of Dr. Johnson's hospitality.

Returning to the first floor, you will observe a small room on either side of the hall but, before entering either of them, note the winding staircase which leads above and below. The substantial balustrades are quite a feature of the house; the guide books say they are of oak, but actually they are of pine, and have been preserved, I suppose, — for they are original and in good condition, — by countless coats of paint. Think how many and what hands have rested upon them. Think how often these stairs must have creaked with the weight of the great Doctor. Perhaps before you go to the second floor you will care to enter the "powdering closet" in the north room, to have your wig powdered and made presentable — that's what that closet in the corner was used for; and gradually you will work your way to the attic. I never enter it without thinking of Le Gallienne's lines: "To see a place where something was really written, a place where the fire once came down, is a good deal — or nothing at all, as one happens to be constituted." And Carlyle was right when he said, "Had Johnson left nothing but his Dictionary, one might have traced there a great intellect, a genuine man. There is in it a kind of architectural nobleness; it stands there like a great, solid, square-built edifice, finished symmetrically, complete. You judge that a true builder did it." And the Dictionary was born in this room! After great labor! Here the definitions were coined that have given the world so much amusement: "Windward" and "leeward" and "tory" and "oats" and "pension" and "pastern" — which Johnson defined as the knee of a horse. You remember, of course, his reply to the lady who taxed him with the blunder and asked him how he came to make it: "Ignorance, madam, pure ignorance."

What a wonderful book it is! As the little boy said, "full of words, and all of 'em different."

Boswell did not know the Doctor at the time the Dictionary was published; we are therefore forced to fall back upon Sir John Hawkins's account of his life at this time.

Johnson, who before this time, together with his wife, had lived in obscurity, lodging at different houses in the courts and alleys in and about the Strand and Fleet Street, had, for the purpose of carrying on this arduous work . . . taken a handsome house in Gough Square, and fitted up a room in it with desks and other accommodations for amanuenses whom, to the number of five or six, he kept constantly under his eye. An interleaved copy of Bailey's dictionary in folio he made the repository of the several articles, and these he collected by incessant reading of the best authors in our language. His method was to score with a black-lead pencil the words by him selected, and to give them over to his assistants to insert in their places. The books he used for this purpose were what he had in his own collection, a copious but a miserably ragged one, and all such as he could borrow; which latter, if ever they came back to those who lent them, were so defaced as to be scarce worth owning, and yet some of his friends were glad to receive them and entertain them as curiosities.

"Scarce worth owning!" How amazed Sir John — "the unclubable Knight," Johnson once called him — would be if he could know that to-day any scrap of Johnson or Boswell interest is worth owning and much of it is practically priceless. Yet he only expressed the opinion of his time.

Dr. Johnson died in a house in Bolt Court, only a few yards away, on December 13, 1784; a few months later his books — his literary property we would now call it, "was sold at auction by Mr. Christy in his great room in Pall Mall," with this result:

In all six hundred and fifty lots were disposed of, not including one hundred and forty-six engraved portraits, of which fifty were framed and glazed, which sold in lots of four, or eight, or even ten together. . . . The sale was largely attended, many people desiring to buy a book which had once belonged to the great lexicographer.. . . The total obtained was two hundred and forty-seven pounds and a few odd shillings.

To-day the proceeds of such a sale would make a man rich. What was Johnson's phrase? He would be in the possession of wealth "beyond the dreams of avarice."

I have often fancied how I would furnish the Gough Square house if I were going to live in it. Let us return to the square hall on the first floor. The little room on the left-hand side, with a door going out into a garden about the size of a pocket-handkerchief, should be the drawing-room. It should be formal in character, simply but elegantly furnished in mahogany. To this end, if I were living in Dr. Johnson's time, I would go to Thomas Chippendale's, his shop in St. Martin's Lane, and tell him to take his time and to do his best; otherwise I should haunt the auction rooms where alone to-day good furniture is to be had, until I had secured the finest specimens of this famous cabinet-maker's work that were available. The fact that the chairs would probably be uncomfortable would not disturb me, for I would not encourage visitors who would spend much time in the drawing-room. On the walls would be all the fine mezzotints I could collect of Johnson and his circle, and I would have a few fine books in carefully glazed and locked cases and a few pieces of fine old silver.

The room across the hall would be my dining-room — a bright, cheerful room, as a dining-room should be. The powder closet I don't think I would use for its original purpose; I would go to Mr. Chubb and tell him I wanted a good stout lock put on that closet door, and I would keep it stocked with well-filled

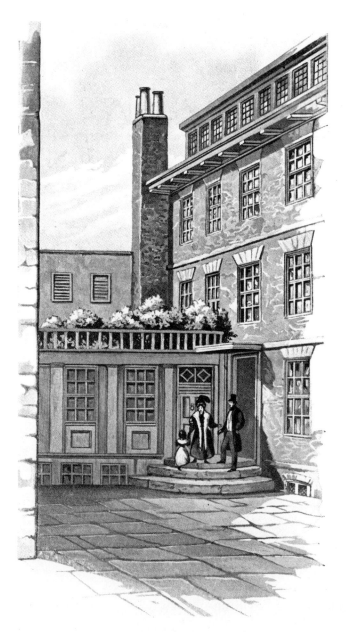

HOUSE — NOW DESTROYED — IN BOLT COURT
in which Dr. Johnson died

bottles. The furniture in this room should likewise
be mahogany, and the chairs should be stout and
comfortable, and the table, when the cloth was
drawn and the walnuts and wine placed thereon,
should shine like a mirror. On the wall over the fireplace should hang my Johnson portrait by Reynolds,
and I would endeavor to get a portrait of Boswell —
and little more. The walls of a dining-room should
not be too completely pictured; there should be
nothing to distract one's attention from the pleasures
of the table; every fish and roast should come on,
a picture, and be removed, a total ruin.

The furnishing of the rooms above gave me much
concern; I long considered taking a leaf out of the
book of Sir John Soane, whose house, now a museum
in Lincoln's Inn Fields, is not far away, but upon mature consideration I found that it would n't do. He,
it will be remembered, in order to get space for his
pictures, put several walls on hinges in order that he
might swing them out; a wall, on being drawn out,
revealed another wall within. In like manner, I
thought, by swinging the hall partitions on the second
floor back against the windows I would be able to
throw the rooms together, so that I could entertain
large parties upon occasion. But the question arose
as to what was to be done with the bookshelves; and
then I remembered that large parties are not so nice
as small ones, and I decided to leave the partitions
as they are and use one room for my collection of
first editions and the other for my reading-library.

Johnsonians will remember that the Doctor has given his ideas upon the spacing of bookshelves, and I am not sure that they can be improved upon; the modern collector, however, eschews big books as far as possible, fully agreeing with the doctrine that "a small book that can be carried to the fire and held readily in the hand is the most useful, after all."

There would be no period furniture here. Comfort only is considered; the tables are conveniently placed, the chairs are easy, the light falls over the left shoulder, the couch invites repose and the walls are covered with books — what wall-covering is as fine? Certainly not the leather of Cordova, no; nor prints, nor paintings, however costly. — No, nothing is so beautiful as the backs of substantially bound books, ranging row upon row from floor to ceiling. I have often wondered why this is. Is it the mellow leather in its rich diversity of color and its bright or tarnished gold, or is it, perhaps, because even the back of a book calls up before the inward eye some scene which the book contains? I know no greater pleasure than to light a good cigar, throw myself in an easy chair, and let my eyes range over a wall covered with books. I love to try to recall the names of all the different books in a row, or as many of them as I can. Over there is my Trollope, complete in every item. What novelist has given me greater pleasure? His characters are my old friends. And there is my Sterne, and Fielding, and Dickens, and Dumas, — and not a Russian among 'em, thank God! That entire case

is devoted to Johnson and his Boswell. And all the
books on that side of the room are essays, with Lamb
in the place of honor; that set of small, well-worn
volumes is Augustine Birrell, whose essays I adored
as a young man, — and still do, — little thinking
that I should be able to call him friend, as an old one;
and that entire wall over there is covered with books
about London, the microcosm, the world in miniature. It was a stroke of genius in Lucas to call
London "The Friendly Town." Who would think of
applying that epithet to New York, the most brutal
of cities?

You want to see my bedrooms? They are furnished
as bedrooms usually are, except that on the walls
you will observe only portraits of women; the Doctor
was a great admirer of the fair sex, and we are apt to
forget that no man of his day — and it was a great
day — could turn a compliment more neatly than he.
The place of honor, of course, goes to Mrs. Thrale
who, as he said in one of his last letters to her, had
"soothed twenty years of his life, radically wretched."
Yonder is Fanny Burney; as Fanny, I adore her, but
as Madame d'Arblay she bores me to tears. In that
group are the "Blue Stockings," Mrs. Chapone,
Mrs. Montagu, Mrs. Lenox, and the rest. Mrs.
Carter is my favorite; she translated Epictetus, and
is said to have had, in addition to Greek and Latin,
half a dozen modern languages at her fingers' ends,
"and a working knowledge of Arabic," whatever
that means. But it was not alone for her scholarship

that Johnson admired her; with the penetration and lack of cant which is his distinguishing characteristic, he one day remarked, "A man is, in general, better pleased when he has a good dinner on his table than when his wife talks Greek; my friend Mrs. Carter could make a pudding as well as translate Epictetus." I know as little of her translations as I do of her puddings, but the beauty of her face is not easily forgotten.[1] Although she was always addressed as Mrs. Carter, she lived and died an old maid.

On that wall are the actresses — and worst — of the Doctor's acquaintances: Peg Woffington, Garrick's friend, and Kitty Clive, and Frances Abington, whose morals were doubtful, if her jellies were — as the Doctor said, and he was a judge — better than Mrs. Thrale's. That is Mrs. Siddons, whose character was without flaw; and that is Kitty Fisher, who had no character at all, but whose lovely portrait by Reynolds now smiles at us from the walls of the Wallace Collection. That vacant space I am keeping for the picture, when I can find it, of that Scotch hussy who climbed on to the Doctor's knee one evening in a tavern and surprised him with a kiss. Surprised, and pleased him too, for he said, "Do it again, my dear; let us see who gets tired first."

Observe my bathroom, how conveniently placed it is. It is a concession England has reluctantly agreed to make to America. Guestrooms? No, unluckily we are in rather close quarters here, but I have taken

[1] See the portrait opposite page 160.

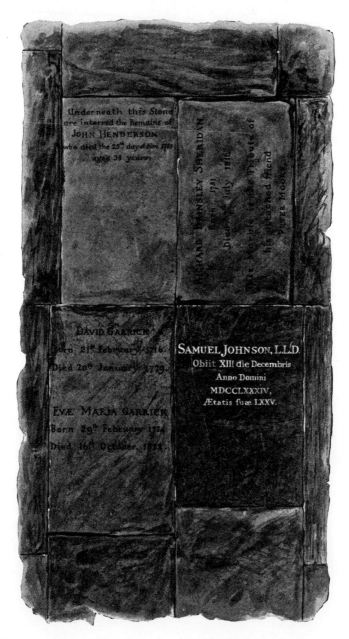

A PART OF THE FLOOR OF THE POETS' CORNER IN WESTMINSTER ABBEY

After a drawing by Gosden

rooms for you at Anderton's Hotel, near by, in Fleet
Street, and there is excellent authority for the statement that "there is no private house in which people
can enjoy themselves so well as in a capital tavern . . .
the more noise you make . . . the more trouble you
give, the welcomer you are . . . . You will find the
Master courteous, and the servants obsequious to
your call . . . Sir, a tavern chair is the throne of
human felicity." Such is the hospitality I offer you.
Your bill will be presented to Mrs. Dyble, or her
daughter Mrs. Rowell, and promptly paid; for of
course I should continue them in their present employ at a largely increased honorarium, whatever
it may be, that I might constantly have the
pleasure of talking Johnson to such excellent good
people.

Before you go, peep again into the attic: you may
see nothing in it but one old chair with three legs.
It was Dr. Johnson's, and I have left it there in case
the ghost of Old Sam himself should not wish to
stand — upon ceremony — in his own house. I am
not up in the requirements of ghosts. Hamlet's
walked a good deal in cold weather, I remember;
whereas Marley's not only could but did take a chair,
as if he were quite used to it. But this room is not
deserted, as it seems; it is in fact overcrowded; be
careful how you move about; you may disturb a
shade.

I am dreaming, of course. Am I actually in London or in the strong room of "Oak Knoll," in Daylesford, Pennsylvania? No difference. When this mortal shall have put on immortality, who shall say that he may not join the choir invisible that made the world the better — and the merrier — for their presence, the ghosts of Gough Square.

III

SHAKESPEARE AND THE "OLD VIC"

"I AM sure that much of the respect which we pay to an elderly man is due to our suspicion that he could avenge any slight by describing the late Charles Mathews in *Cool as a Cucumber*. Theatrical reminiscence is the most awful weapon in the armory of old age." I am quoting from that delightful essayist, Max Beerbohm, only now beginning to come into his own; and I am about to draw that "awful weapon," not in self-defense, but because it will give me pleasure to flourish it; I shall not, I think, do much harm, and it is barely possible some good may come of it. And now for the preliminary flourish.

It will, I think, be admitted by any Londoner whose memory carries him back to the palmy days of Irving and Terry, that the theatre in that great metropolis is now in a very parlous state. We do not greatly care for the revival of plays a quarter-century old, plays which once shocked us but which shock us no longer, and in which we remember — But never mind: Gladys Cooper is not a fair exchange for Mrs. Pat Campbell, and Cyril Maude disporting himself as "Lord Richard in the Pantry" does not make us forget but rather long for Forbes-Robertson.

Even the music-hall has gone to h——, I was going to say. The cozy, old-fashioned music-hall, smoky, and witty, and often vulgar, has given way to the gaudy theatre in which *revues*, tedious and meaningless, are given month after month; performances which would seem to be chiefly a challenge to the police. To one who remembers Lottie Collins and Marie Lloyd — to mention only two names, but memory calls up a dozen; to one to whom Dan Leno was a delight and who frequently joined Herbert Campbell in a chorus; who has breathlessly watched Cinquevalli successfully defy the laws of gravitation, and who has learned his coster songs from Albert Chevalier and Gus Ellen; the passing of the "halls" is nothing short of tragic, but it might perhaps be borne had not the theatre practically disappeared. Then suddenly something happened — and it happened at the Old Vic.

And now, and only now, is this paper fairly started.

I know a man who has written two or three books about modern London, who confessed to me that he had never been in the Old Vic; comparatively few Londoners know where it is, and many of those who do have but a hazy idea of its character. I stumbled on it quite by accident, in the delightful little cathedral city of Wells, while spending a day or two at the Swan. One evening two young ladies were ushered to our table for dinner; they were young, attractive girls, and after the usual preliminaries, the exchanging of mustard for salt, and so forth, we fell into conversation, and I soon discovered that my tablemates were college girls on a holiday. They were taking a walking-trip and were about finishing four hundred miles. Then I learned, too, that they were actresses from London; and at length it developed that they had been playing Shakespearean parts at the Old Vic.

"The 'Old Vic,'" I said to myself, wonderingly; "I seem to remember a more or less disreputable music-hall of that name on the Surrey side of the river; surely such cultivated women as my companions cannot be playing there — not even Shakespeare!" Yet it was so. Little by little the story was told of how, many years ago, an enterprising woman, a Miss Emma Cons, had secured the old place and by degrees redeemed it; then she died, and someone else had taken up and carried on the work. When we parted next morning, I was fully determined to visit that theatre at the first opportunity.

Immediately upon my arrival in London I started out to learn exactly where the Old Vic was; the newspapers had not a word to say; finally someone told me it was in Lambeth in the New Cut; then someone else said it was in the Waterloo Road. Finally, it appeared that both my informants were right, that it was in the New Cut at the corner of the Waterloo Road; and by dint of reading and inquiring, this is what I discovered.

In 1811 there was building a great stone bridge over the Thames, for a long time known as the New Bridge; it was completed soon after the glorious battle of Waterloo, which gave a name to many

things, including the new bridge and the approaches
to it. Shortly after the completion of the bridge,
a theatre was begun in the marshes of Lambeth,
about half a mile from the Surrey end, and in 1817
its cornerstone was laid, by proxy, by Prince Leopold
of Saxe-Coburg, uncle to Queen Victoria, afterward
to become famous as the King of the Belgians. No
one seems to know if or how the Prince became interested in the theatre, but in any event it was named
after him, the Royal Coburg Theatre. With due
regard for the character of the surrounding population, it was at once given over to the crudest kind of
melodrama and the most vulgar of pantomimes.

The theatre had been erected in a dangerous
slum, one of the worst in London, and for a time, in
an effort to entice visitors from the other side of the
river, it was announced that special guards were
posted on the bridge and its approaches, in order
that the audience might feel safe both before and
after the performance from the attack of thugs and
pickpockets. This announcement did not much mend
matters.

From the first the theatre had a checkered career:
it prospered occasionally, but it usually was in financial or other difficulties. In 1833, in an effort to revive
its fortunes, it was given a new name, the "Royal
Victoria," in honor of the young princess who was
then heir presumptive to the crown. But no one was
deceived thereby. Edmund Kean acted there for a
brief moment; but Grimaldi, the famous clown, was

more to the taste of its patrons.   However, nothing really succeeded.   Its location was desperate, if not positively dangerous.

With the coming of gas, and finally of electricity, and the better policing of the streets, it became relatively safe; but why travel such a distance to see performances of varying degrees of badness? For a hundred years its record was ten failures to one success.   Drinking in the theatre was allowed (and still is), and fights were frequent; the audiences were fierce, in the proper use of that term.   Missiles, overripe fruit, mellow eggs, and occasionally an empty beer-bottle, were thrown at the villain on the stage, while the heroine and the still more virtuous hero would invariably be encouraged by loud cries of approval.   "Never will I give my consent to bring a virtuous girl to a life of shame!" was a sentiment that, we may be sure, brought the audience of half-drunken men and women to their feet in a burst of delirious applause.

But it was no go.   No one seemed to want legitimate drama in the Waterloo Road at the corner of the New Cut; and the "Old Vic," as it had come to be called, became a music-hall — about as common a music-hall as there was in London.   Then it was that I made its acquaintance — but we hardly became friends.   It was, before the coming of the taxi, in an out-of-the-way part of the town, and the performances, if cheap, were bad, very bad.

But it is always darkest just before dawn.   A

woman conceived the idea of giving good drama, not trash, at popular prices; and while her success was not great, she turned the tide. When she died, her assistant, Miss Lilian Baylis, took up and carried on the work. With the coöperation of Mr. and Mrs. Matheson Lang and the help of Ben Greet, and at long last, with the assistance of Russell and Sybil Thorndike, success came to the Old Vic.

"Take me to the Old Vic," I said one evening to a taxi-driver, shortly after I reached London.

"To where, sir?" he replied.

"Don't you know the Old Vic in the Waterloo Road?" I inquired.

"I do, sir, but I wasn't sure that I heard you right."

We entered, and in a few moments we were rolling through St. James's Park and over Westminster Bridge into Lambeth. On we went, under the great railway bridge which forms the approach to Waterloo Station, through the Lower Marsh, into the Waterloo Road where, just ahead of us, was the New Cut.

It is a busy, noisy thoroughfare, "pestered" on both sides, as far as the eye can see, with open-front shops and booths and hand-barrows, lit up at night with flaming naphtha torches, where food and clothing of every kind and character are exposed for sale. Hawkers were crying their wares; the whole neighborhood was swarming with men, women, and children, doing their daily shopping; for in this part of London everyone works when he can, and the pur-

THE ROYAL COBURG THEATRE — NOW THE "OLD VIC"

in the Waterloo Road at the New Cut

chase of necessities begins when the day's work is done. We were in — not the famous East End, but the equally sordid South Side of London.

It was nearing seven as we stepped out of our taxi; and going to the ticket-office, I discovered that the play that evening was *Henry IV, Part I*, and that the curtain rose at seven-thirty sharp. "Give me two stalls; how much?" I inquired.

"Five shillings each, including war-tax," was the reply.

Pocketing the little pieces of paper, I stepped out and looked around for a place in which to eat.

"When in doubt, ask a policeman." Of all forms of authority I respect a London policeman most: upon the subjects within his range he speaks with the certainty of a college professor, and he carries himself with the bearing of a bishop. Going up to one, and touching my hat, — for I would not have a policeman outdo me in politeness, — I said, "As man to man, if you were standing with your best girl where I am and had only twenty minutes in which to get something to eat, where would you go?"

"Hi'd go, sir," he said promptly, "to the Wellington Buffet" (spoken as spelled); "you'll find it hexcellent."

And we did: bread and butter, a cut of cold ham, a Welsh rabbit, and several bottles of Bass; I ask no more and I ask no better.

When the curtain rose a few minutes later, we were in our stalls, four rows from the front, and I was just beginning to enjoy my after-dinner cigar.

Reader, when did you last see *Henry IV, Part I?* Have you ever seen it? If you have not, you perhaps think of it as one of Shakespeare's historical plays. Nonsense! the historical part is mere setting for the greatest comic character in all literature, Falstaff. But first let me describe the audience and the house.

The theatre was packed with a quiet, orderly crowd of plain people; I should say there were about as many, or as few, of what might be called common people as of people from the upper walks of life; there were perhaps as many as half a dozen men and women in evening dress.

Everything in the house was of the plainest and simplest: there was no attempt at decoration, the seats were not too comfortable, and when the curtain went up, it was at once evident that rigid economy had been the watchword on the stage also. There were no footlights; from either side of the proscenium arch two flood-lights played upon the actors, while from the centre hung a long, narrow box containing six or eight lights, which lit up the whole or any part of the stage with white or amber lights as desired.

Of scenery there was almost none. A simple backdrop sufficiently indicated the scene; heavy curtains formed the wings; stage carpentry was conspicuous by its absence. It was at once evident that the play was the thing.

In all the arts of the theatre Henry Irving began where Charles Kean left off; he utilized all the mechanical, engineering, and æsthetic devices of his time to perfection; and after him, under Beerbohm Tree at His Majesty's, stagecraft almost superseded acting; indeed, it was not until the magnificent and spectacular could no further go, that the reaction against the stage upholsterer and electrician came.

Now I could, if necessary, write a very pretty paper on lighting-effects, and I am in some degree acquainted with the merits of "remote control," electrical apparatus, "dead-front" switchboard devices, and the rest (if the truth must be told, I make and sell them); but I object to the switchboard attendant usurping the province of the actor. A dark purple sky, slowly changing to blue, to orange, to amber, until the whole scene is of dazzling whiteness, is interesting, but it does not take the place of acting; neither do gorgeous costumes and expensive scenery; indeed, these things may so distract attention that the word and suiting the action to the word — which is what acting is — is lost sight of.

The cost of mounting a magnificent spectacle is to-day almost prohibitive; for costumes alone fifty thousand dollars may be spent, and twice as much more for the scenery and incidentals. If the play is a success, it is money well invested, but if not — well, only a very rich *régisseur* can stand the strain.

Now at the Old Vic everything depends upon the actor — no, not everything: the actor depends upon his lines, and he has gone back to Shakespeare to get them.

Our great Shakespearean scholar, the late Dr.

Furness (and these remarks would, I think, equally apply to his distinguished son), was never at his ease when one began to praise Shakespeare. "Shakespeare is," he thought, "beyond praise. I don't care who wrote the plays, the important thing is we have them. Whoever it was, I am glad we know so little about him; pretty much all talk about him is twaddle, especially eulogy." Such, in brief, was his attitude. Such seems to be the idea at the Old Vic; the stage is cleared, the actors and actresses come and give their lines with what skill they may, and go, and there's an end on't.

No, not quite an end; for when the play is over, one goes home with the idea that one has seen the real Shakespeare. Generally speaking, there is not the change of a scene or the omission of a word. The plays are given just as they have come down to us; they are given rapidly — there is only one intermission of about five minutes, just time for a man to stroll to the back of the house, drink a bottle of Bass, light his pipe, and get back to his seat as the curtain goes up again. Be it remembered that Shakespeare did not write for highbrow audiences; he had no idea that his was the greatest intellect that had ever been given to mortal. He wrote for the average man of his own time, and he packed into his plays everything that he could think of that would amuse and interest him. And he was some thinker, with remarkable powers of expression. Dr. Furness would, I think, have permitted me to say that much. The audiences that first saw the plays were much such audiences as now see them at the Old Vic.

The people of Shakespeare's day wanted to be amused, just as we do; they wanted the action to go right on; a long wait just as the play was getting interesting would never have been tolerated; so it is to-day. At the Old Vic the curtain goes up at seven-thirty and stays up, usually with one brief intermission as I have said, until eleven or even twelve o'clock. *Hamlet*, which is usually cut to death on our stage, is given in two versions: the short version, which takes almost four hours, and the play in its entirety, which takes considerably longer. It is, as it ever has been, enormously popular.

When, not long ago, Robert Atkins, the producer greatly daring, considering the paucity of his equipment, gave *Antony and Cleopatra*, he achieved an enormous success. If ever a play permitted the use of all the devices that the magician-manager has at his disposal, it is this story of the love of the doting Roman general for the serpent of old Nile; but according to report, although given without scenic splendor or any of the magnificence of the modern stage, it was a great success and played to crowded houses. Why should it not have been? For the speeches in *Antony and Cleopatra* are almost blinding with color.

But the great moment in the life of the Old Vic was the night when they gave *Troilus and Cressida*. It was the eve of the tercentenary of the publication of the First Folio, and Miss Baylis sent upon the stage a half-dozen men, one after another, producers, who had been responsible in turn for all its thirty-six plays. It was a marvelous achievement to have given in ten years, four of which covered the Great War, all the thirty-six plays attributed to Shakespeare. No other theatre in the world had ever attempted this great feat. An interesting recital of the difficulties met and overcome by Miss Baylis was subsequently published: —

A volume could be written about Miss Baylis's heroic achievements at the Old Vic; the war did not stop her; air raids were ignored, as was the discouragement of acting to an almost empty theatre with an absolutely empty treasury. Every member of the staff, from Miss Baylis down, "lived on half of nothing, paid 'em punctual once a week," as Kipling has it, but Shakespeare survived.

At times actors were so scarce that practically no men, except very aged ones, were available; at these times almost all the parts were taken by the women of the company, many of whom took two or three or more parts in a single evening. In this connection the names of Sybil Thorndike and Florence Saunders will always be remembered.

Performances were given while air raids were in progress. They played *King John* one night while German bombs were dropping and a whole row of houses a few hundred yards away were destroyed. Overhead, above the theatre, were the aeroplanes: all through the noise the play went on, everyone roaring at the top of their voices, so that they could be heard. At the very moment that the lines,

> Some airy devil hovers in the sky
> And pours down mischief,

were given, a bomb dropped on Waterloo Station just

across the way, but they went on acting. The atmosphere in the house was so electrical in its patriotism when the closing lines of the play were spoken,

> This England never did, nor never shall,
> Lie at the proud foot of a conqueror,

that the management, in commemoration, had the words, said more proudly that night than ever before, painted above the proscenium arch:

> Come the three corners of the world in arms
> And we shall shock them: nought shall make us rue,
> If England to itself do rest but true.

Although they knew that they would be out of a job if she had accepted their proposition, after the performance several of the actresses said to Miss Baylis, "If you feel that you can't open to-morrow we shall quite understand."

Miss Baylis's reply should become a part of the history of the theatre: "We shall open; and if the roof is blown off the theatre, we shall give the play in the cellar." The nerving effect upon the people in the neighborhood was wonderful: dwellers in the humble streets near by began to use the theatre as an air-raid refuge! "It seems to help us so, when we just look at those words"; and no doubt it did.

That Mr. Atkins could, and he would, use those resources which sometimes eclipse the work of the dramatist, is shown by his selection to arrange the historic tableaux which were presented with such success at St. Bartholomew's Hospital on the occasion of its celebrating the eight-hundredth anniversary of its foundation. The reader will not remember, but "Bart's," as everyone affectionately speaks of St. Bartholomew's, is my hospital. In it many years ago I passed hours of agony after a serious accident and many tedious weeks of convalescence, and I always think of it with great affection. In imagination I can see the fine old quadrangle I know so well, with its gray and grimy walls, a fitting background for a gorgeous mediæval spectacle. I can fancy Arthur Bourchier (who will be remembered as Henry VIII in Tree's fine production) stepping, so to speak, out of his frame, the living image of the portrait of that monarch by Holbein, which hangs in the great hall. Henry VIII was, after Rahere, its founder, the most distinguished patron of Bart's, which indeed has been a royal hospital ever since King Henry I gave permission to establish a cloth fair outside its gates to assist in its erection and maintenance. This event subsequently became the famous St. Bartholomew Fair, long since disappeared, as most picturesque things have been done or are doing.

But we are wandering far from the Old Vic. Let us get back to *King Henry IV* and the Prince of Wales, and Hotspur, and above all to Falstaff, the glory of the English stage. The first scene, short as it is, is all too long; we await so anxiously the second: "London. An apartment of the Prince's. Enter the Prince of Wales and Falstaff" — and the fun begins, and continues almost without interruption for almost four hours. Now, mind you, I do not mean to say that this was the best performance I have ever seen, or that Wilfrid Walter was the greatest Falstaff that ever trod the boards. I do not say that; but with the contentment which comes from sandwiches and Welsh rabbits well bestowed and several bottles of the best of all beverages, Bass (prohibitionists, this is not an advertisement of an intoxicant), with the knowledge that I had a pocketful of cigars and, my physician being far away, I intended to smoke them, I settled myself for an evening of unalloyed delight, and had it.

What does Horace Walpole say of *Henry IV?* "Now I hold a perfect comedy to be the perfection of human composition, and I firmly believe that fifty *Iliads* could be created sooner than another such character as Falstaff." And this perfect comedy has not been seen on the American stage for years; indeed a generation has grown up that has hardly heard of it.

And a few nights later we saw the Second Part of the same play. Let critics decide which is the better, and let who will, read plays: I want to see them acted. It may be that a Lamb or a Coleridge could derive as much pleasure from reading the plays as from seeing them; but for myself, I can never get the fine points of a play until I have seen it on the stage. This was brought home to me in the scene where Falstaff delivers himself of his famous soliloquy: "What is honor? 't is a word. . . . Who hath it? he that died o' Wednesday," and the rest. I knew it, of course, but I did not get its full significance until, in a later scene, after the battle in which Sir Walter Blunt is killed, Falstaff, coming by chance upon the body, turns it over with his foot, and discerning who it is, remarks, "There's honor for you." The acting gave pith and point to the soliloquy, which it had lacked before.

Henry V I have never seen, nor have I read it in close sequence with *Henry IV*. I could not bear to. In it Falstaff is dead: it may be that, buried in that mountainous mass of flesh, he had a heart which broke when Prince Hal, become a king, neglected him. Anyway he is dead, and Mistress Quickly and Bardolph and Pistol, without Falstaff, are not so interesting to us as they were; Falstaff, their great sun, which warmed and vitalized them, has set. It is almost impossible to think that a man with such a gust for living as Falstaff could die, and like the Hostess of the tavern in Eastcheap, we are sure he is not in hell, and with Bardolph, we would be with him wheresome'er he is.

The scene in which the Hostess tells Bardolph of his master's death is one of the most wonderful in all literature.

Quite recently an English magazine took a census of opinion as to the most humorous and at the same time pathetic passage in English literature: several votes for passages from Sterne were cast, but the vote for the scene of the death of Falstaff was practically unanimous.

Just between twelve and one, even at the turning of the tide . . . after I saw him fumble with the sheets, and play with flowers, and smile upon his fingers' ends, I knew there was but one way . . . and a' babbled of green fields.

We hear of the death of better men undisturbed; or as Prince Hal has it, we could have better spared a better man. What is it about Falstaff, the thief, the liar, the coward, the braggart, that so fascinates us? He is as subtle as Hamlet, and much more wonderful as a creation. Do you challenge this statement? Then think of the many great tragic characters whose names at once occur to us. Good. And now of the comic. Falstaff, Mr. Pickwick, and who else? — Don Quixote, perhaps. Every actor has a feeling that he can play Hamlet, but how many essay the character of Falstaff? In recent years, Lionel Brough and Beerbohm Tree. Of the latter I recently heard a good story illustrative of the acid wit of W. S. Gilbert. Sir Beerbohm, dressed in the several feather-beds the part of Falstaff requires, hot and sweating with exertion, seeing Gilbert wandering about behind the scenes, goes up to him expecting, quite naturally, a word of praise, for Tree was great in the part. And what does the sharp-tongued gentleman say? Looking at the perspiring actor before him, he remarks icily, "Your skin is acting well this evening."

I foolishly did not keep my programmes of the Old Vic performances, but I am sure that I am right in crediting Ethel Harper with the excellent rendition of the part of Mistress Quickly, an early Mrs. Malaprop. She had the quality of pure comedy about her, the kind of humor which we were wont to associate with Mrs. John Drew. Fascinated against her will by the old rogue Falstaff, to whom she could deny neither her kisses nor her silver, deceived and abused by him, but always forgiving him, she hoped to the last that he would keep his promise to make her a Lady, his wife; and it was not until after his death that she consented to become the wife of Pistol — a sad falling-off to be sure, but anything is better than dying a maid, if indeed she ever was one.

The *Merry Wives* should be seen before and not after *Henry IV*. Whether or not the legend be true that Queen Elizabeth, having rejoiced in the character of Falstaff, gave orders that Shakespeare should write a play showing him in love, the play presents a falling-off in the characters which have so delighted us: they lack spontaneity; humor has degenerated into horseplay; one does not much delight in seeing Falstaff buried in a basket of soiled linen, and Mistress Quickly, now become a servant to Doctor Caius, is not very convincing. We have, to be sure, those excellent romps, Mistress Ford and Mistress Page; but as for sweet Anne Page, you that love her may have her; in other words, the charm of a mature woman more fetcheth me than does that of any bread-and-butter miss whatever.

I had not expected greatly to enjoy *The Taming of the Shrew;* but when I saw it at the Old Vic, I seemed to see it for the first time and see it whole. Many years ago I saw Booth in a little play arranged by Garrick, called *Catharine and Petruchio*. I remember nothing of it but Booth's leaping upon a table and snapping his whip; he used it as a foil to *The Fool's Revenge*, in which he excelled. Later, John Drew and Ada Rehan in those delicious Daly days enjoyed in it for a season their usual success. Augustin Daly was too much of an artist to omit the Prologue, or the "Induction," as Shakespeare calls it; but of late years it has not been given; and as, on account of its noisy and boisterous quality, too few people read the play, not everyone remembers that *The Taming of the Shrew* is a play within a play; without Christopher Sly, the tinker, it loses half its point.

Bear with me while I remind myself of the joy I had one evening at the Old Vic. The story is this: Christopher Sly, a tinker, drunk, being turned out of an alehouse upon a heath, falls asleep; a noble lord, on his way home from a day's hunting, comes upon him by chance, and inquires of his attendants whether he is dead or drunk. Upon being assured that he is only drunk, he has the bright idea of having him gently picked up and conveyed to his (the noble lord's) house and put to bed in his best room. When he awakens, he is to be attended as if he were a lord: servants are to hand him a silver basin filled with rose-water in which he may wash his hands and lave his face. Food and wine are to be given him; and he is to be asked what his pleasure is, what apparel he will wear. He is to be made to believe that he is a wealthy nobleman awaking from a long sleep.

The lord's retainers enter into the spirit of the jest,

and, when the drunken tinker awakes, the sport begins; there never was such fun. Sly, rousing himself from his drunken slumber, calls for a pot of ale, and is offered wine instead by one servant, while another perplexes him with the question, "What raiment will your honor wear?" "Raiment!" cries Sly, "ne'er ask me, for I have no more doublets than backs, no more stockings than legs, nor no more shoes than feet." There never was such make-believe out of a fairy tale, which in some sort this Induction is; and it continues until all the actors (except Sly) and the audience are choking with merriment. Finally Sly believes himself actually to be a lord, and when he is told that his entertainers are come to perform a merry comedy, he bids them play. "We shall ne'er be younger, let the world slip," he says, and *The Taming of the Shrew*, five acts of farce, begins.

There is no need to detain the reader with the story. The scene is laid in Italy, but the characters are English, the fun is English, the sort of slapstick fun which three hundred years ago kept — and should forever keep, if it be played rapidly — an audience in a roar. How the play ends by Petruchio taming the obstreperous Kate, until in a pretty speech she places her hand under her husband's foot, all the world knows, and the play ends — according to Shakespeare; but at the Old Vic there are a few lines more, taken from an older play, *Taming of A Shrew*, which forms a fitting epilogue, as it were, to what has gone before.

The evening is spent; the noble lord is tired and would go to bed. Sly, too, has fallen asleep; two servants enter and are told to take him up and throw him out upon the heath. When he awakens, thinking now that he is a lord, he calls for his servants to bring him wine and is jeered at. "What, am I not a lord?" he cries; and is told that he is Christopher Sly, a drunken tinker; that he may have been dreaming; that his wife at home is waiting for him. At these words, he rises, pulls himself together, and saying he knows how to tame a shrew, he staggers off. One has a feeling that he will be the master in his house for that night at least — and the curtain falls.

Now play this rapidly, play it, not as a refined comedy, which it is n't, but as the greatest farce ever written, which it is, and it will run for months.

We all remember the story of the man who sent the manuscript of a novel to a popular magazine: when it was returned to him, as manuscripts usually are, it was with the notation that it could, perhaps, be used if it were shorter. "You take up too much time with preliminaries," the editor said. "Cut out the landscape and sky effects and get down to a recital of the facts. In its shortened form perhaps we can use it." When the manuscript was again submitted, it began this way: "'Oh, hell!' said the duchess, who up to this time had taken no part in the conversation." *Richard III* begins in much the same way. Whether originally it was longer than it now is, we do not know; but certainly not an instant is lost at starting.

The curtain goes up on a deserted street in London; a moment later the Duke of Gloster, afterward Richard III, lounges around a corner and begins: —

> "Now is the winter of our discontent
> Made glorious summer by this sun of York."

Only a man determinèd to be a villain would begin his life upon the stage with so murderous a pun, and he rants and indulges in every kind of claptrap until, at the end of the fifth act, no one responding to his despairing cry, "A horse! a horse! my kingdom for a horse!" he is killed, and Richmond makes the announcement, "The bloody dog is dead."

I don't think I am mistaken in saying that *Richard III* is the finest melodrama ever written. When a man sets out to make a melodrama nowadays, such performances as they used to give at the Adelphi, but which are now given at Drury Lane, by the use of elaborate scenery and mechanism, he secures effects which bewilder the audience and keep it in suspense; but Shakespeare had to work another way. He got his effects by the play and interplay of his characters. So Richard woos and wins his bride at a funeral, admitting that the lady's beauty had caused him to kill her husband. It is a misuse of words to call this scene theatrical; it is simply verbal horseplay. Richard says so himself, after it is over, in the soliloquy:—

> Was ever woman in this humor woo'd?
> Was ever woman in this humor won?

To this double question there can be but one answer—

No; but what difference does it make? The audience is having such a wonderful time that it does not stop to analyze the situation, and the play goes right on, one extravagant scene after another; people die like flies and nobody cares, until at last, having used every trick in his box, Shakespeare brings the play to an end, and we go home satisfied.

It is now the fashion to berate Colley Cibber for altering this play almost beyond recognition; but I don't think he really did it much harm. It is good old Cibber, and not Shakespeare, who splits our ears with "Richard's himself again," and —

"My lord, the Duke of Buckingham is here."

"What! Buckingham here? Off with his head. So much for Buckingham."

These speeches are perfectly in key with the rest of the play, otherwise they would not have survived for a hundred and fifty years. They did n't offend Garrick; it was the play in which he made his first appearance and he always delighted in it; nor Dr. Johnson, who knew his Shakespeare, and enjoyed Garrick's performance quite as much as if Shakespeare had been the author of every line. In those days an acting version of a play was one thing; a version "for the closet," as it was called, was another. At the corner of the Waterloo Road and the New Cut no Cibber is permitted, and the play crowds the house.

Finally, as the preacher says, rousing his congregation from its slumbers, what lesson can we draw from the performances at the Old Vic? Is it not that Shakespeare can be performed as written, without transpositions to make it suitable for the stage? That cuts should be simply eliminations of prosy passages, of which there are plenty, which interrupt the progress of the play and which fatigue audiences and actors alike? That elaborate scenery and expensive costumes are not essential if the acting is good; and that we have accustomed ourselves to taking Shakespeare too slowly, too seriously, too reverently?

Let us forget the author in his work; Shakespeare wrote to amuse; even his tragedies, *Macbeth* and *Lear* and the rest, did not depress his audiences as they do us. They got a lot of fun out of murders and poisonings and ghosts; we do not, and have come to believe that seeing Shakespeare is a serious business. Often we go from a sense of duty, in much the same way as we go to church; and we get about the same amount of pleasure out of it. One can imagine too many domestic conversations something like this: —

WIFE. Charley, don't forget that Nelly Watson is going to be with us next week, and that she will expect us to take her to the theatre.

HUSBAND. I'm not likely to forget it. What shall we take her to? I'm told that there is an excellent show at the Broadway.

WIFE. What's the name of it?

HUSBAND. I've forgotten the name, but Connie Constance is in it.

WIFE: I know: *Men's Playthings*. They say her gowns are magnificent, they were all made in Paris; I should like to see them, but you know Nelly Watson is sort of highbrow. What would you say to our going to see *Twelfth Night?*

HUSBAND. O Lord!

WIFE. I know, but after all we're going to please her, not ourselves.

HUSBAND. Very well, have it your way. I'll get the tickets.

WIFE. And what would you say to our asking Fred Hamilton? He's a nice fellow, and rather fond of Nelly.

HUSBAND. He won't stand for *Twelfth Night*. I know Fred.

WIFE. Oh, yes, he will; we must give a little party, and you will have to dress.

HUSBAND. That's another bore.

WIFE. I know, but it's Shakespeare, my dear.

There is a hasty dinner; there is no time for the usual cigar; everyone starts out in a bad humor. And in this frame of mind our friends go to see one of the loveliest comedies ever written.

How much longer, I wonder, will the fiction be kept up that smoking is objectionable to ladies? In Queen Victoria's day a man was obliged to go to his own bedroom and smoke out of the window; or perhaps, sitting on the floor in front of an open fireplace, blow the smoke up a chimney, fearful all the time that he would be detected. And there was the idea that tobacco smoke ruined the plush lambrequins and other hangings characteristic of the period. Now that the lambrequins have gone, let us enjoy ourselves: to-day women smoke as much as men do, some of them smoke more. A cigar or a cigarette would add to the delight of a good play, and would be a solace if the play were bad. In England smoking is permitted only in certain theatres, not of the best class; but in all of them, between the acts, young ladies are permitted to cry their wares: "Teas and ices; ice and teases," rather to the annoyance of those who are obliged to assist in their delivery to the consumer.

I have n't the least doubt that flaws could be picked with the performances at the Old Vic. It is easy to find fault. Grant that not all the actors are up to their parts, that not all of them can read blank verse correctly. Reading blank verse is not easy, and it may become a lost art unless, as now seems probable, a Shakespearean revival is seriously undertaken. At the moment we are doing better than the English. A few months ago in New York five Shakespearean performances were running at the same time. It was not too soon; it is of the utmost importance to keep a place upon our stage for actors of the old school; we must preserve the unwritten tradition of the stage: the "business," as it is called, which is handed down from one generation to another; its loss would be a calamity.

But to return to London. The Old Vic is one of the intellectual assets of the town: it is badly in need of funds: the appointments of the stage are poor, and conveniences for the actors are — well, practically, there are n't any. The management made its wants known and the hat was passed, but these are hard times in London. Then the London County Council came around and insisted upon expensive structural changes. Miss Baylis was in despair: what was to be done? Then out of a clear sky, anonymously, came a substantial gift of thirty thousand pounds. Could it be possible? Who was the donor? Was it stage money? No, current paper of the realm, "legal tender for any amount," was paid in, and gradually it became known that George Dance, the well-known dramatic author and theatrical manager, had saved the Old Vic. All honor to him! King George and I are in complete accord, for I read in the newspapers only a few days ago that a knighthood was to be conferred upon him.

Who shall say that it was not deserved? Certainly not the patrons of the Old Vic.

While the managers have been telling us that "Shakespeare spells ruin" and the intellectuals have been talking about the necessity of establishing a national playhouse, the people, not a mile from the spot on which three hundred years ago stood Shakespeare's "Globe," have loyally been supporting such a theatre — a theatre to which it is admittedly an honor to belong and in which it is a joy to spend an evening. And remember, dear reader, that all this is to be had for a shilling, for the greater part of the house; the gallery is sixpence, I believe. If the "talkies" are not to be put out of business by the "movies," which heaven forfend, we must have a theatre to which a man can take a girl without having to put a mortgage on his already heavily encumbered automobile.

IV

FATHER. My son, throw an armful of wood on that fire; then bring up a chair and let's have a good talk. There's nothing so good for a man as the give and take of conversation. I hate a man who wants to do all the talking himself. I was trained to be a good listener; your mother saw to that.

SON. Have you — ?

FATHER. I have, my son — There is tobacco in the jar over there; in those boxes are cigars; and if you must smoke cigarettes, that silver box is full of them — or was, unless your sister has smoked them all. It is positively dreadful the way girls smoke nowadays.

SON. But, father —

FATHER. I am as free from prejudices as my friend Dr. Johnson, who once remarked, "I am a man of the world and take in some degree the color of the world as it moves along"; but —

SON. Father! you are not —

FATHER. No, my son—I am not going to talk about Dr. Johnson, or Boswell either, although it was the most remarkable partnership the world has ever seen, except one which was even more wonderful — that of Gilbert and Sullivan. You have heard me speak of them?

SON. Often, father. You —

FATHER. I remember when I was a boy away from home at school, — it's forty, going on fifty years ago, — all the boys coming back to school after the Christmas holidays were singing songs that I never heard before. I remember one of them informing me that he was the "monarch of the sea." "What's that?" I asked. "*Pinafore*," he replied. Then another boy, who confided to me that *he* was called "Little Buttercup," when I asked him why, also replied, "That's from *Pinafore*." While I was pondering the matter, another announced in a loud treble that he was the "Captain of the Pinafore"; and the problem was not simplified when someone replied, "And a right good captain, too."

I hated to appear ignorant, but I had to know. "What's the Pinafore?" I inquired. Whereupon they turned from me in disgust and someone said, "He's from New Jersey and don't know nothin'; why, the *Pinafore* is an opera; I saw it four times; it's the most beautiful opera that ever was written — I heard my father tell my mother so." It appeared that I was the only boy that had not heard *Pinafore*, and I was much ashamed. My time came to hear it, at Easter, and like my companions, I heard it not once or twice but many times.

SON. How many times?

FATHER. I have n't the least idea; all told, twenty, perhaps. You can't imagine how this dainty little operetta swept over the land. There was no operatic copyright in those days, or the laws were defective, or something; anyhow, no royalties were paid, and opera companies were formed by the score. *Pinafore* was played in every city in the country, until finally one's conversation got so cluttered up with bits of it that if a man chanced to say to another, "I never smoke more than four cigars after dinner," he met with the rejoinder, "What, never?" and replied, "Well, hardly ever"; then they both laughed as if they were great wits and much pleased with themselves.

SON. Was *Pinafore* the first — ?

FATHER. No, Gilbert had written a number of successful plays, some of which are not quite forgotten; and Sullivan was famous as an organist and a composer of sacred music when he was asked to write the music for an operatic extravaganza, the book of which had been supplied by Gilbert; I have forgotten its name, it makes no difference. It was not a very great success, but it survived the critics, and when it was in due time followed by *Pinafore*, the world went mad. It was in the spring of 1878 that *H. M. S. Pinafore* was first produced in England; and it must have been in the following winter that it struck this country with the force of a cyclone.

SON. What does "H. M. S." mean?

FATHER. "Her Majesty's Ship" Pinafore. There never was anything like it. No church choir so mean as not to provide a tenor who for a moment sank his differences with the soprano so far as to sing to her, —

"Farewell, my own!
Light of my life, farewell!"

And every plump maiden in the land with a teaspoonful of voice felt that nature had especially endowed her for the part of Buttercup, and was perpetually offering "scissors and watches and knives" to all and sundry. Men felt an urge for a dramatic and musical career, which was hard to resist when the sailors struck up the robust chorus: —

"We sail the ocean blue,
    And our saucy ship's a beauty;
We're sober men, and true,
    And attentive to our duty."

And when the sisters and the cousins and the aunts came dancing on, everybody was glad to be on board, as a little flirting seemed to be in prospect.

SON. But there had been comic operas before?

FATHER. Lots of them, but they were different. Not since Gay fitted the words of *The Beggar's Opera* to any music he could find, had there been such a success.

SON. How about the French and the Viennese operas?

FATHER. Well, you see, originally the words of those operettas were risqué rather than clever; and when they were translated into English, they were merely stupid. Now Gilbert was a poet, and he had an advantage over most poets in that he had ideas and was a most painstaking workman; he made him-

SIR WILLIAM GILBERT

self a master of the technicalities of his craft: rhyme, rhythm, and alliteration.

Son. And Sullivan?

Father. Sullivan was the son of an Irishman who was a professional musician. At twelve years of age he knew something of all the instruments in his father's band; at thirty he was an accomplished composer. When he wanted to secure a certain effect, he knew just how to go about it. Gilbert's words and Sullivan's orchestration fit together so perfectly that, to one who has heard the operas, the words suggest the music, and the music the words. Sullivan's mother had Italian blood in her.

Son. That accounts for much.

Father. It does, my son: that's the stock that produced one of the most talented musicians that England has ever had.

Son. You rank them high.

Father. With the immortals — both of them. They were so great that they have not yet fully come into their own. The world is slow to realize that a great comic poet is quite as rare a phenomenon as a great tragic one — and much more useful.

Son. How useful?

Father. Why, my boy, the lives of most of us are so hideously commonplace that anything that makes us forget how stupid we are, anything that lifts us up and makes us merry, is useful. Gilbert may be remembered when A. Tennyson and R. Browning are forgotten. Too many people believe that the only stuff that survives is that which gives us furiously to think, as someone has said. Falstaff is a greater creation than Hamlet. And a poet who has his verses set to music is doubly blest: they are assured of a long life. Who was it who said, "If I can write the songs of a nation, I care not who writes its laws"?

SON. I don't know.

FATHER. Neither do I. We were talking of *Pinafore.*

SON. Do you think a New York audience would stand for it to-day?

FATHER. Stand for it! Why, my boy, about ten years ago — maybe it's fifteen, time passes so quickly — they gave a production of *Pinafore* at the Hippodrome, which for bulk and magnificence surpassed anything ever done in London. I'm not quite sure that a good deal of Gilbert's wit was n't lost in the immensity of the building; but the stage pictures and the choruses were superb. The ship which was the glory of the Queen's Navee looked like a real battleship. It was anchored in real water, and Buttercup was rowed to it in a real rowboat. When Sir Joseph Porter came on board, in all his magnificence, my bosom so heaved with pride that it was all I could do not to "join up with the Navy and see the world," as the advertisements tell us to do.

SON. Sir Joseph Porter, he's the great character, is n't he?

FATHER. Well, I should n't say that; he has two capital songs to sing. Let me sing one of 'em for you.

SON. If it's all the same to you — just tell me about it.

FATHER. All right, listen: —

> "When I was a lad, I served a term
> As office boy to an attorney's firm.
> I cleaned the windows and I swept the floor,
> And I polished up the handle of the big front door.
> I polished up that handle so carefullee
> That now I am the Ruler of the Queen's Navee!"

SON. Why, it's Josephus Daniels to the life!

FATHER. Sure it is. We get lots of our ideas about government from comic operas, and then take ourselves as seriously as Sitting Bull. The English, on the other hand, don't hesitate to poke fun at themselves. For centuries Englishmen have been taught to believe that upon the invincibility of their navy Britain's greatness depends; yet when Sir Joseph Porter, a mere martinet, tells us, in a comic song of many verses, how and by what means he has risen to the control of this great weapon, they positively laugh their heads off. But if anyone in Philadelphia ventures to observe that our streets are unspeakably filthy, our mayor stops having his photograph taken, and begins talking about what Dr. Johnson said was the last refuge of a scoundrel. It's a case of the shoe pinching, I suppose.

SON. I suppose Buttercup —

FATHER. I have a theory about Buttercup. I don't think she was originally intended by Gilbert to be attractive. He designed her, I think, to be a fat, disgusting old bumboat woman, a sort of operatic Sairey Gamp, who "practised baby-farming" when she "was young and charming," many years before the story begins. I know that Gilbert refers to her as "the rosiest, the roundest, and the reddest beauty in all Spithead"; but Gilbert had a pretty taste for paradox, and did n't always say what he meant or mean what he said. I think the original Buttercup, the girl who created the part, as the saying is, preferred to be young and charming in the present rather than in the past, and got away with it: anyhow, Buttercup has always been a peachy-looking person, the sort of person who at a church fair makes you remember the price when the article is forgotten.

SON. You know the opera by heart?

FATHER. I know the Pinafore from stem to stern, and am on speaking terms with almost every member of her crew. *The Pirates of Penzance*, the next success, I don't know so well; I have n't heard it for years, but it is from it that we get the music that we sing to our national anthem: —

> "Hail, hail, the gang's all here,
> What the hell do we care!"

It must be magnificent to hear it sung by our statesmen in Washington ("all available male voices without orchestra") just after passing some particularly iniquitous piece of legislation, such as the recent tariff bill.

SON. Why iniquitous?

FATHER. Silly would be a better word. Europe owes us ten billions or so. Say it slowly, and it makes your head swim. It is payable in gold: we have the gold. Europe says, "Take merchandise." "No," we reply, in effect, "we want gold," knowing perfectly well that it is impossible for Europe to send it, and that it would be unwise for us to take it if we could get it.

SON. Don't the Secretary of the Treasury know this? I thought you were strong for Mr. Mellon.

FATHER. I am, my son, but the Secretary of the Treasury is up against an untrained mob playing politics.

SON. England seems to have plenty of money —

FATHER. Yes, and she knows how to use it. The war gave us a chance which, while we were telling the world how great we were, we let slip: all the time England was sawing wood and saying nothing. Anyone who had said two years ago that she could put her dollar exchange where it now is, and keep it there, would have been told that he was crazy.

SON. They are a wonderful people.

FATHER. They are, my son. While we were talking about making the world safe for democracy, they were making it safe for themselves.

SON. How about *Patience?*

FATHER. *Patience* is lovely! I adore it. A few years ago, going in town on the train, I picked up my copy of the New York *Sun* and read something to this effect: "Any of our readers capable of appreciating the witty rhymes of the late W. S. Gilbert will do well not to lose the opportunity of hearing De Wolf Hopper in *Patience*. His reading of the well-known verses, 'Am I alone and unobserved?' is so inimitable, that we venture to say that never before has this recitative been given with such exquisite humor."

SON. You felt personally addressed, I suppose?

FATHER. I did, my son; I went right on: I only stopped in Philadelphia long enough to send word home, "Called to New York on important business," and buy a railway ticket. When the curtain went up, I was prepared for unalloyed delight; and when the Colonel, in his gorgeous uniform, left the stage, and Bunthorne, in great dejection at being outshone, first making sure that he was alone, began his famous lines, I knew that I was having it.

> "Am I alone,
> And unobserved? I am!
> Then let me own
> I'm an æsthetic sham!
> This air severe
> Is but a mere
> Veneer.
> This cynic smile
> Is but a wile
> Of guile!
> This costume chaste
> Is but good taste
> Misplaced!
>
> Let me confess!
> A languid love for lilies does *not* blight me!

> Lank limbs and haggard cheeks do *not* delight me!
> I do *not* care for dirty greens
> By any means.
> I do *not* long for all one sees
> That's Japanese.
> I am *not* fond of uttering platitudes
> In stained-glass attitudes.
> In short, my mediævalism's affectation,
> Born of a morbid love of admiration!"

SON. It's too deep for me; what's it all about?

FATHER. Long before you were born, the whole English-speaking world, led by Oscar Wilde, became æsthetic.

SON. Became what?

FATHER. Æsthetic: that is to say, it had a yearning for an inward and spiritual grace, of which the outward and visible sign was the lily and the sunflower. A single peacock's feather in a blue vase suggested that one's mind was in harmony with one's surroundings. The craze lent itself admirably to Gilbert's peculiar humor. Listen to one of the best songs that Gilbert ever wrote or Sullivan ever set to music:

> If you're anxious for to shine, in the high æsthetic line, as a man of culture rare,
> You must get up all the germs of the transcendental terms, and plant them everywhere.
> You must lie among the daisies, and discourse in novel phrases, of your complicated state of mind;
> The meaning doesn't matter, if it's only idle chatter of a transcendental kind.
> And every one will say,
> As you walk your mystic way,

If this young man expresses himself in terms too deep for *me*,
Why, what a very singularly deep young man this deep young
     man must be!

I wish you would let me sing it.

SON. Calm yourself, my dear father; be content
with reciting it.

FATHER. Listen to this bit: —

> Oh, to be wafted away
>   From this black Aceldama of sorrow,
> Where the dust of an earthly to-day
>   Is the earth of a dusty to-morrow!

SON. Which means what?

FATHER. That's exactly the question that Patience,
the milkmaid, asked, and was told that it was poetry,
that it came from the heart — "Heart Foam," he
called it.

SON. Just chaff, in other words.

FATHER. Exactly; mere fooling. A good deal of
poetry is like that. Next to me sat a lady, a widow I
should say, of mature years, with a young man evidently her son. "This carries me back to the early
eighties," I heard her whisper to him as the curtain
fell on the first act; and as I was beating my hands
to a pulp in applause, I heard the young man say to
his mother, witheringly, "And you enjoy this sort of
thing! I call it punk." I could not restrain myself:
turning to the lady, I said, "Pay no attention to your
son, madam; he does n't know any better; I have one
just like him at home: address your remarks to me.

Was there ever such a rhymer as Gilbert or such music as Sullivan's?

> The dash of a d'Orsay, divested of quackery —
> Narrative powers of Dickens and Thackeray —
> Victor Emmanuel — peak-haunting Peveril —
> Thomas Aquinas, and Doctor Sacheverell.

"Isn't it wonderful! I don't know who invented the patter song, but no one but Gilbert knew how to use it; and the cleverer Gilbert's words are, the more delightful is Sullivan's music." We had a fine time catching one another up on our favorite lines from this opera and from that; and by the time the curtain went up on the second act, it would n't have made any difference to either of us if that unresponsive son had gone home.

Son. We've got the music of those operas some-

Oh Captain Shaw!
Type of true love kept under!
Could thy brigade
With cold cascade
Quench my great love, I wonder!
"Iolanthe" Act 2
W. S. Gilbert
31st May, 1906

where, but the words are published in book form, I suppose?

FATHER (*pointing*). Do you see those three pea-green volumes over there on the second shelf from the top?

SON (*going over to a bookcase*). These?

FATHER. Yes, that is the only presentation copy of Gilbert I have ever seen. Evidently, he gave very few books away. Those volumes were given to Captain Shaw, Chief of the London Fire Brigade. In the first volume is an inscription in Gilbert's hand from *Iolanthe:* —

> O Captain Shaw!
> Type of true love kept under!
> Could thy brigade
> With cold cascade
> Quench my great love, I wonder?

Captain Shaw, I am told, was in the audience on the first night of *Iolanthe,* and was greatly embarrassed at this reference to himself. And there is an inscription in each of the other volumes.

SON. Very nice.

FATHER. You may be sure it is. The fact is that you have never, well, "hardly ever," heard a really good operetta. It is so much easier to be stupid than witty; and as for music, why there's enough good music in *The Mikado* to make a dozen Broadway successes. Take any recent operetta and you'll find two tunes, or three at most, and not very good ones, interwoven into the piece over and over again. The men who are writing to-day have neither imagination nor training; Sullivan, if his reputation as a composer of light operas had n't overshadowed his other accomplishments, would nevertheless have been a very respectable figure in the musical world.

SON. Which was the greater? Gilbert or —

FATHER. You might as well ask which is the more important, food or drink? Gilbert wrote the book and turned it over to Sullivan, who wrote the music. He fitted the music to the words so perfectly that, clever as they are, without the melodies we associate with them they seem rather forced and unconvincing. Try the music on the piano; the result is the same: lovely, but lacking something. Put 'em together; it's a sort of wedding. "Whom God hath joined let no man put asunder." The fact is that, when after years of coöperation there was a falling out between the two men, neither accomplished anything.

SON. Did they quarrel?

FATHER. Yes, and over nothing: a strip of carpet, I believe. There was a third man in the great partnership, D'Oyly Carte, almost an equal genius. He bought a bit of carpet, which Gilbert thought was an unnecessary expense; Sullivan sided with Carte, and the fat was in the fire. Carte was the producer, a stage manager raised to the nth power. No detail was so insignificant as not to receive his attention. He was a tremendous worker — every act, every scene, as finally given, was the result of the most careful study. The world hardly realizes how much of our stagecraft is due to D'Oyly Carte. No stage had ever been lit with electric light until he first used

it, in 1881, in *Patience*, at the Savoy Theatre. It was
a great experiment, and "if it works," Carte said in
his announcement, "it will enable us to secure effects
hitherto impossible." I wish he could see upper
Broadway to-night.

SON. It's a gay white way all right. I never heard
of — what's his name, D'Oyly Carte?

FATHER. He was the greatest theatrical manager
of his day who was not an actor. I don't suppose
there ever was such an actor-manager as Irving. The
only survivor of the famous group is Rupert D'Oyly
Carte; he it is who now produces the operas in England, and he is every whit as particular as his father.
He was very nice to me the last time I was in London,
and gave me photographs of all three of the great
men.

SON. They must have had lots of fun together.

FATHER. Yes, and they worked like the very devil.
All three men were autocrats as well as geniuses.
"You are not in the picture," D'Oyly Carte would
shout at a rehearsal to someone who sought to obtrude
himself somewhat. "My music, if you please,"
Sullivan would suggest to some tenor singing off key.
And woe betide the poor wretch who dared to inject
a little wit of his own: "his doom was extremely
hard"; for Gilbert was "techy" to the last degree.
"Do you think you can improve upon my humor?"
and there was never an answer.

SON. I suppose *The Mikado* —

FATHER. You are quite right. In England *The*

RICHARD D'OYLY CARTE

Gondoliers has always been extremely popular; but *The Mikado* is, in the world's judgment, the high-water mark of their achievement. You see, its humor is not so subtle as Gilbert's humor sometimes is — as it is in *Patience*, for example. The music of *The Mikado* is marvelous, the stage pictures were novel and beautiful, and nothing could be more witty than Gilbert's verses. Of course they can't be translated, but they try to nevertheless.

SON. Have you — ?

FATHER. Yes, once: in Germany. All my life I have been told how superbly they gave opera there. "It makes no difference where you go or what you see, it will be magnificent; such orchestras, such ensembles!" Well, some years ago I found myself in Dresden. We had arrived late, and after securing a room at the Bellevue, I inquired of a man in superb uniform if he could get me two good seats for the opera. He said it would be difficult, but he would try. I told him to try hard, and I helped him to. After a dinner, quickly eaten, I got my tickets and hurried off to the Opera House, arriving just in time. Making my way over the ample feet of people who declined to move an inch, I was amazed to hear three raps of a baton, and the orchestra began the overture of *The Mikado*, of all things in the world — *The Mikado* with the humor left out. It was a conscientious German performance: the orchestra of eighty or a hundred pieces played for dear life; not a flyspeck but they played it. The stage was vast. "Die kleine Fräulein

Yum Yum" was a young giantess usually cast for Brunhild parts. The piece, usually so exquisite and dainty and full of fun, was oversung and underacted.

I felt as unhappy as I did when I once heard *Die Walküre* in Rome.

SON. London has spoiled you for —

FATHER. London has spoiled me for many things; but I have heard good performances of Gilbert and Sullivan out of London. I heard the first performance of *The Mikado* given in Philadelphia, and I remember the pretty girl I took with me.

SON. She's a grandmother now, I presume.

FATHER. She is; but do not refer to it. I am a grandfather. It is not so appalling to be a grandfather as to be married to a grandmother. We were speaking of *The Mikado*. I had end seats on the right-hand side of the front row of the balcony; they were the most expensive seats I had ever bought up to that time; and I remember that I took my girl home in a coupé. Most people used street-cars in those days, drawn by horses, the floors of which, in winter, were covered with what had once been nice clean straw, strewn knee-deep, but which soon became matted down and wet and filthy; and when the streets got blocked with snow, the cars were constantly getting off the tracks; then we were all invited to get out and push. It seems only yesterday.

SON. Who was the girl?

FATHER. Never mind, my son. You don't see such girls nowadays; they don't make 'em any longer.

All through the performance I thought of taking that girl home in the coupé. You never saw Mrs. John Drew in a play called *Engaged* — also by Gilbert, by the way? No, of course you did n't — she was John Drew's mother. Well, there is a scene in that play which came to my mind. A man and a girl get into a cab and drive off from a country inn, leaving the host to remark meditatively, as the vehicle disappears down the road, "He's got his arm around her waist, if I know anything of human nature — in a cab."

SON. No wonder you like *The Mikado.*

FATHER. The first time I heard it in England was in Weston-super-Mare. We had landed at Plymouth, and went at once to Exeter, where we put up at that charming Old World hotel, the Clarence. Driving to the hotel, I saw posters announcing a revival of Gilbert and Sullivan; and before I asked for my room, I inquired if the company was still there. "No, last night was the last night," I was told. Where had the company gone? The divinity that worked the beer-pump did n't know, but would inquire. Either to Bournemouth or to Weston-super-Mare, I was later informed, which is like saying, either to Newport or to Coney Island. After dinner, I walked around to the little provincial theatre, and there learned, to my disgust, that the company had gone to Weston-super-Mare for a week. "Very well," I said to myself, "we will go to Weston."

SON. You don't speak of Weston with enthusiasm.

FATHER. A middle-class English watering-place is pretty dreadful, and it is n't on the sea; it's on the Bristol Channel; and when the tide is out, it is n't even on that. On our arrival, we got a room at the best hotel on the esplanade. "Where is the Mare?" your mother inquired, as she looked out upon an illimitable expanse of mud, upon which young Britons were disporting themselves, seemingly by millions. You never saw so many or such sturdy youngsters. And far off in the distance was a streak of water — the Bristol Channel. "If the opera is very good, we can stand it for three days," I said to myself; and the opera was. *The Gondoliers* packed the house to the doors.

I had last seen it thirty-odd years before, with my friend Francis Wilson, the inimitable, as the Duke of Plaza-Toro, who

> In enterprise of martial kind,
> When there was any fighting,
> He led his regiment from behind—
> He found it less exciting.
> But when away his regiment ran,
> His place was at the fore, O —
>   That celebrated,
>   Cultivated,
>   Underrated
>   Nobleman,
> The Duke of Plaza-Toro —

and much more besides. How it carried me back! It had never been a success in America; even I, enthusiast as I am, had never cared much for it; but it is enormously popular in England, where it ranks with *The Mikado* and *The Yeoman of the Guard*, which we heard the next day.

SON. Did n't you hear that in New York a few seasons ago?

FATHER. No, that was *Ruddigore*. We went over to New York two or three times purposely to hear it. It was a very ambitious revival and very successful.

SON. Tell me about *The Mikado*.

FATHER. Don't rush me, my boy; I don't often get a chance like this. We were speaking of *The Yeoman of the Guard*. I had n't seen it for years, and had forgotten how lovely it is. The curtain goes up, revealing that little square plot of ground, Tower Green, on which so much of England's best blood has been shed. In the background is the gloomy old Tower of London. The scene is laid in the time of Henry the Eighth; and when the Beefeaters and the rest of the chorus crowd the stage, it makes about as pretty an historical picture as I have ever seen. There is humor in *The Yeoman* — pathos, too. You have had examples of Gilbert at play with words; hear him in serious mood:

> Is life a boon?
>   If so, it must befall
>   That Death, whene'er he call,
> Must call too soon.
>   Though fourscore years he give,
>   Yet one would pray to live
> Another moon!
>   What kind of plaint have I,
>   Who perish in July?
>   I might have had to die,
> Perchance, in June!

Son. Obviously a song for the tenor —

Father. Yes, but you should hear the duet between Jack Point, the clown, and Elsie Maynard, his sweetheart. They are two wandering minstrels singing in the public streets, as they still do in London. Jack Point is a clown out of Shakespeare.

Son. I never thought much —

Father. I feared so; but you would think a lot of Jack Point if you could hear him sing, "I have a song to sing, O!" It's positively delicious. Then the Governor of the Tower comes along, and Jack asks him if he is not in need of a jester. "What qualifications have you?" says the Governor. Jack replies, "Marry, sir, I have a very pretty wit. I can rhyme you extempore; I can convulse you with quip and conundrum." "How came you to leave your last employ?" says the Governor. "Why, sir," says Jack, "it was in this wise. My Lord was the Archbishop of Canterbury, and it was considered that one of my jokes was unsuited to His Grace's family circle. In truth, I ventured to ask a poor riddle, sir — wherein lay the difference between His Grace and poor Jack Point? His Grace was pleased to give it up, sir. And thereupon I told him that whereas His Grace was paid ten thousand pounds a year for being good, poor Jack Point was good — for nothing. 'T was but a harmless jest, but it offended His Grace, who whipped me and set me in the stocks for a scurril rogue, and so we parted."

SON. How can you remember all that?

FATHER. That's nothing. I have a memory for the unimportant; but I can't be sure of my own telephone number. There's some more; you see Gilbert could write clever prose as well as clever verse. It takes nerve for an author to say, "Now I'm going to be witty," and get away with it. To return: "I don't think much of that," says the Governor; "is that the best you can do?" "It is much admired, sir. But I will try again," says Jack. "Say that I sat me down hurriedly on something sharp?" says the Governor. "Sir, I should say that you had sat down on the spur of the moment," says Jack. "Suppose I caught you kissing the kitchen wench under my very nose?" says the Governor. "Under her very nose, good sir — not under yours! That is where I would kiss her. Do you take me, sir?" says Jack.

But for all this fooling, the play ends in gloom; for Elsie marries the handsome tenor, which is a habit pretty girls have on the stage, and Jack Point dies of a broken heart.

SON. Which is unusual in a comic opera.

FATHER. That brings up a very nice point. As originally written, Jack Point merely swoons away at Elsie Maynard's feet, after kissing the edge of her garment; that is how it was played by Grossmith, who created the rôle. Well, years ago, Henry Lytton, the last of the great Savoyards, was playing the part in Bath. He, on his own, *died* on the stage. The stage-manager was furious, and he telegraphed to Gilbert in London: "Lytton impossible as Jack Point. What shall I do?" Instantly Gilbert took train for Bath and, unknown to the company, witnessed the performance. After the last act he went behind the curtain, said that he had greatly enjoyed the performance, shook hands cordially with Lytton, and without another word returned to London. It was evident to all, although not a word had been said, that the great man was not displeased with the innovation, and so the part has been played that way ever since.

SON. Don't present-day actors "gag" their parts?

FATHER. Not much or often. The other day I read a story of Charles Workman, who was singing the song, "Said I to myself said I," in *Iolanthe*, when a fire broke out and filled the theatre with smoke. "Don't stop; go on, for Heaven's sake, go on!" shouted the manager. "Give it 'em strong!" In a moment he had grasped the situation, and "gagged" the song this way: —

> "I'll assure all my friends who are ready to choke
> That the fire they fear is nothing but smoke;
> It's only a sort of Gilbertian joke,
> Said I to myself, said I."

He said afterward it was the first and only time that he had ever dared to play tricks with Gilbert and Sullivan.

SON. Pretty work! What is your favorite?

FATHER. The last one I have heard; but the world

says *Mikado*. It is comic and it is an opera — with talk; Gilbert at his very best, likewise Sullivan. It was the last opera we heard at Weston. Glory! how compact it is with fun and with music! It is a *tour-de-force*, both in words and music: Sullivan contrived to give a pseudo-Japanese character to a lot of his choruses; and the fact that some of the best of his duets and quartettes might have been sung in church did not interfere with their effectiveness when given by men and maidens in Japanese costume.

SON. Do the English —

FATHER. Certainly they do. Everyone knows his Gilbert and Sullivan as well as, or better than, I do.

SON. That's going some.

FATHER. One day last summer John Burns and I had a day's bookhunting together. We started from his house on Clapham Common shortly after breakfast one morning, and as we were tramping through Battersea Park a man passed us whistling *The Mikado*. "Do you know that song?" I inquired. "Know it!" Burns replied, "of course I do, every word of it. I have played in it," he continued. "What part?" I inquired. "The Mikado," he replied. Of course, with his deep bass voice, I might have known it. Instantly he began,

> "A more humane Mikado never
>   Did in Japan exist;
>   To nobody second,
>   I'm certainly reckoned
>   A true philanthropist.

It is my very humane endeavour
To make, to some extent,
  Each evil liver
  A running river
Of harmless merriment."

I waited impatiently for him to get through, when I struck up "A wandering minstrel"; then both of us began, "Taken from a county jail," and no one hearing us would have supposed that we were a pair of elderly book-collectors out for a day's sport.

SON. Gilbert's wit is pretty caustic —

FATHER. At times, yes. He created for our amusement a topsy-turvy world, but a world no more grotesque than that created in all seriousness by our political marionettes at Washington. The law against flirting, for example, —

Our great Mikado, virtuous man,
When he to rule our land began,
  Resolved to try
  A plan whereby
Young men might best be steadied.
So he decreed, in words succinct,
That all who flirted, leered, or winked
(Unless connubially linked),
  Should forthwith be beheaded, —

is no more ridiculous than our law against the sale of intoxicants.

SON. Speaking of intoxicants, I met Bill Nye at the Club to-day and he told me to ask you if you wanted to buy any perfectly good Scotch; that he knew —

FATHER. If we are going to discuss buying whiskey, come over here where the Chief of Police won't hear us.

SON. Don't bother about the Chief of Police: he has been fixed by the prohibition officer.

FATHER. Now, there you are! That illustrates just what I have been saying: our so-called prohibition is quite as absurd as anything created by Gilbert in his whimsical moments. Infractions of the law against flirting in his comic kingdom on the stage were punished by decapitation; whereas we very gravely reward our lawbreakers with fortunes beyond the dreams of avarice. A prohibition officer allows it to become known that out of a salary of three thousand a year he expects to save a million. He can give points to Pooh-Bah, and beat him at his own game. One feels that Pooh-Bah is fooling with stage money; but our officials are playing with the real thing.

SON. I should worry.

FATHER. Indeed, you should, my son, more than I, because it's your world rather than mine that the politicians are making such a mess of under the guise of reform. Do you remember what kind of stage they had in England when they reopened the theatres that had been closed under Cromwell?

SON. No.

FATHER. It was the worst ever.

SON. You were talking about —

FATHER. After *The Mikado* anything would have been an anticlimax; so early the next morning we got a fast train up to London.

SON. Where you felt happy?

FATHER. Yes. "My Old Lady London" was in tears when we arrived; but I got my arm around her very considerable waist and gave her a hug, and she brightened up; and what is more, stayed that way.

SON. So you think Gilbert and Sullivan have come to stay?

FATHER. Forever, I should say: as literature and as music. Centuries hence some gifted professor of English, like Charley Osgood of Princeton, will be lecturing on the stage in the time of Victoria, and in his despair will temporarily adjourn his class while a piano is got in upon which to demonstrate the words of Gilbert with the music of Sullivan. Hazlitt attributed the great success of a revival in his time of *The Beggar's Opera* (a revival of which, in our own time, recently had its thousandth performance in London) to the uniting of sense with sound. To these two things these men united another: namely, wit; and wit without nastiness is one of the rarest things in the world. Never before, not since, and maybe never again, will two such great artists work together in such perfect harmony for the amusement of the world. One of the marvels of Gilbert and Sullivan is that, throughout all the years of their alliance, there was never a word spoken that could not have been spoken in church, or a costume worn that would not pass almost unnoticed in the streets to-day; that is to say, girls now reveal quite as much

SIR ARTHUR SULLIVAN

of themselves on the streets as they used to do on the stage. I don't see any reason in morals why they should n't display themselves for nothing on the streets quite as much as they do for money on the stage; but in my time it was n't done. I wonder what D'Oyly Carte would say to the indecency of the *Frolics* and *Follies* and *Scandals* of to-day?

SON. Did you ever see either of —

FATHER. I once saw Sullivan go through the motions of conducting the orchestra for a part of *The Mikado*. I was in the gallery of a very large theatre when the interesting event took place; and the back of his head, from where I sat, looked in no way remarkable. Actually he looked like a successful stockbroker. The distinguished-looking member of the trio was D'Oyly Carte. Gilbert I never saw.

SON. He must have had a host of friends.

FATHER. I think not. Sullivan was much more popular. Gilbert was always saying something that rankled. A good story was told me only the other day by Austin Gray. Gilbert's next-door neighbor in the country was a Sir Thomas Day, of Day and Martin's Jams and Pickles.[1] Having acquired a title and got into society, Sir Thomas had become very aristocratic, and strongly disliked any reference being made to the way in which he had made his money. One day Gilbert's dogs got into his coverts and killed a

---

[1] Reader, be good enough not to write me that Day and Martin are manufacturers of blacking; that I mean Crosse and Blackwell; I know that; but I am trying to disguise a real name, so that when this book is reprinted in London I shall not be sued for slander.

few partridges. Sir Thomas wrote haughtily to Gilbert, ordering him to keep his dogs in better order. Gilbert wrote back politely — "Dear Sir Thomas, I have just received your letter about the loss of your partridges, and I am taking steps to keep my dogs from trespassing on your preserves in the future. Yours sincerely, W. S. Gilbert. P. S. You will pardon the use of the word 'preserves,' won't you?"

SON. Clever!

FATHER. I'll say it was. But Gilbert could wield a very nasty pen when he wanted to. When *Ruddigore* was being played, a certain high dignitary of the Church wrote a letter to the *Times* deploring "the unpleasant title," as he called it. Whereupon Gilbert wrote, "Should I refer to his lordship's complexion as being ruddy, his lordship would probably be pleased; but should I, as I do not intend to, refer to his lordship's 'bloody cheek,' he would most certainly be offended — as I am."

SON. Some letter! Tell me another one.

FATHER. Oh — there is no end to 'em! Gilbert one evening having strayed by mistake into a hall in London where a number of clergymen were holding a convention, was recognized by one of the clerics, who said to him, "Ah, Mr. Gilbert, you must feel a little strange here!" "I do," was the reply, "I feel like a lion in a den of Daniels."

SON. Not so good.

FATHER. No; every time the clock strikes it don't strike twelve. There is another story, of Gilbert's remark to Lady Tree on the night when her husband was playing Hamlet for the first time. After the curtain fell, Lady Tree went up to him and, expressing her pleasure at seeing him, asked him his opinion of the performance. "I would not have missed it for anything," was the reply; "it was funny without being vulgar."

SON. That was a nasty one.

FATHER. So Lady Tree thought.

SON. Are they always playing Gilbert and Sullivan?

FATHER. Somewhere, yes. The last time we were in England we went to Liverpool for one solid week of Gilbert and Sullivan. It was in midwinter and as cold as blazes: I suppose there are worse places than Liverpool in which to spend a week in winter, but I don't happen to know them. Luckily, we were at a good hotel, the Adelphi, the best in England, I should say. It was built by one of the great railway companies to attract American trade; then just as it was finished the war came, and the traffic was diverted to the Channel ports. The performances were superb; they gave a different opera each night and at the two matinees, and we had seats, secured in London, for them all. But the theatre! the floor was of cement; there was no cellar and no heat; I thought my feet would freeze and fall off. When we got back to the hotel we had an internal application of Scotch, rubbed our feet and legs well with Sloan's Liniment, and went to our beds and stayed there until next day at noon! Those beds! Each bed was as large as a billiard table; to roll about in one was like wallowing in a cloud. If you ever want a rest cure, go to the Adelphi in Liverpool.

SON. I'd like to have been with you.

FATHER. Your time will come. In that vast Empire upon which the sun never sets, "from morning till night," as Somerset Maugham wittily says, performances are constantly going on. At the present moment, there are two excellent companies playing in England; and I hear there is to be a revival in New York; the time is ripe for it. D'Oyly Carte, the son of his father, does not permit the slightest deviation from tradition. As the operas were given by their creators a generation ago, so are they given to-day, and so will they be given a generation hence.

SON. When did Gilbert die?

FATHER. Gilbert died as recently as 1911; Sullivan, with the turn of the century. His death was the occasion of a public funeral, and he was buried in the crypt of St. Paul's Cathedral.

SON. Are there any monuments to them?

FATHER. Yes. In the Embankment Gardens, not far from the scene of his great triumphs, there is a beautiful memorial to the man who set the whole world a-singing. It consists of a granite shaft surmounted with a bust of the composer; a bronze figure representing Grief clings to the pedestal, against which lies a broken lyre and a lute. It is one of the few successful allegorical pieces in modern London, and hardly requires the inscription, SIR ARTHUR SULLIVAN, to make it known to the passer-by. And a few hundred yards east, near the unspeakably ugly Charing Cross railway bridge, is a huge plinth of granite forming a part of the Thames Embankment. Against this has been placed a bronze portrait in profile of W. S. GILBERT, PLAYWRIGHT AND POET. Under the portrait are the words, "His foe was folly and his weapon wit." It is badly placed; it should have been nearer to the memorial of Sullivan. That it serves to relieve the monotony of an otherwise dead granite wall is nothing to the point. But after all, what difference does it make how far apart their memorials are placed? Gilbert and Sullivan, an immortal partnership, will live eternally together in the heads and hearts of those who love merriment and melody.

SON (*yawning*). I think I'll call it a day.

FATHER. Good-night, my boy. I've been very much interested in listening to you. You've grown to be an excellent talker; you take after your mother — boys are very apt to.

V

"CHANGE CARS AT PAOLI"

BUT why? the reader will ask; and where is Paoli? I address myself to those who may be coming to Philadelphia or New York over the Pennsylvania Railroad, which, before the Government laid its icy hands upon it, advertised itself as the "Standard Railroad of America." Of course, not everyone comes to Philadelphia; many persons going from Chicago to New York are so ill-advised as to take the New York Central; and some, who want to come the worst way, take the B. & O., as the old music-hall joke has it. Or, if you are living in — Boston, say, you may take the same intellectual interest in Philadelphia that we take in — Norfolk, for example, and won't come at all. Nevertheless, Philadelphia is a great city, and I am going to ask, if you approach it from the west, that you leave the train at Paoli, and continue your way by motor along what was for more than a century the Lancaster Turnpike, now the Lincoln Highway, spanning, or destined to span, the continent.

The complaint which is frequently brought against us, as a nation, is that we are not interesting. "It is a wonderful country, but it is not interesting" — so Matthew Arnold said when he was here; and he continued: "The very names of your towns and streets are lacking in distinction and suggest nothing; Washington is a beautiful, some day it will be a magnificent city; but fancy living at 17th and K Streets!"

I heard Matthew Arnold lecture on Emerson when he was in Philadelphia; but the only impression I retain of the lecturer is that he spoke with a pronounced English accent, and that he wore ill-fitting clothes; consequently, I was very much amused the other evening when I came across the following anecdote. On his return to England, Matthew Arnold called on Mrs. Procter, the wife of "Barry Cornwall." The lady was old, but not too old to be witty. He expected to be asked his opinion of America; instead, she asked what was America's opinion of him. "Well," Arnold replied, "they said that my clothes did n't fit and that I was very conceited." To which the lady made response: "Matthew, I think they were mistaken about the clothes."

We, who live along the "main line" of the Pennsylvania Railroad, know that Matthew Arnold's charge will not lie against us. Two hundred and more years ago, when the early English and Welsh settlers came here, they brought their Old World names with them. And in addition to names like Merion, Radnor, and Bryn Mawr, we have some beautiful ones indigenous to the country around us — Indian names, and names which carry us back to Revolutionary and pre-Revolutionary times. The railroad runs along a ridge of hills, almost parallel with the great highway, which is, in effect, a high street, dotted with taverns and road houses, which administered hospitality to man and beast — what time it was not illegal for a man to slake his thirst.

It is said that there were as many as sixty of these life-saving stations, or one to a mile, between Philadelphia and Lancaster, — for this was a busy road in the good old days when George III was King, — and they were of all grades, high and low. Authorities differ as to the best, but they all seem to be agreed that the worst was the Blue Ball, near what is now Daylesford station. And among the Balls of various colors, the Bulls and Lions and Spread Eagles and Sorrel Horses, there was an inn with a foreign name much favored by the aristocracy — the Paoli.

"How curious!" you may say. But listen. We are back in 1769. At that time, Pasquale Paoli's name was one to conjure with: freedom was in the air; wherever men congregated, liberty was being discussed; and Paoli, then at the height of his fame, was known as the Liberator of Corsica, the unfortunate and not very important little island in the Mediterranean, midway between France and Italy. So, when we out here at a crossroads in the country were busying ourselves about securing a license for the sale of intoxicants in the new road-house, as yet without a name, what more natural than that the name of Paoli, synonymous with Liberty, should be given to the tavern? The old house, and the more famous one which replaced it almost a century later, are now gone; but Paoli, the settlement which sprung up around the old landmark, is now a thriving town, the terminus of strictly suburban railroad traffic. Many express trains from the West stop at Paoli, and I think all will, if the conductor be properly approached; but as to this, I must not be quoted; for the officials of the railroad are neighbors of mine, and I want to live at peace with them.

Starting due east, almost before you have had time to get up to speed, you will pass the Tredyffrin Country Club; men, and women too, will be playing golf; I shall not be among them, for, although I once was president of this club, when it was discovered that I did not know the difference between a foursome and a brassie, and that the nineteenth hole was the only one I could put a ball into, I was given the choice between resignation and expulsion.

But, as I was saying: as you pass the clubhouse, turn sharply to the right, cross the first road you come to, and a few yards farther on turn again to the right, and go down a tree-bordered avenue. In a few seconds, in a swiftly moving automobile, you will come upon one of the finest old colonial houses you have ever seen. It is the birthplace of Anthony Wayne, "Mad Anthony," as he came affectionately to be called after the recapture of Stony Point from the British; subsequently Major-General and Commander-in-Chief of the United States Army. His career as one of Washington's most trusted officers is clearly written into the history of the Revolutionary War; and, if you had time, it would be a pleasant thing to swerve somewhat out of your course and visit his final resting-place, a few miles away, in the church-yard of Old St. David's at Radnor. But you must hasten on; for you are on your way to Valley Forge, where you will see much that will interest and delight you. So content yourself with strolling around the fine old Wayne mansion, and reading the tablet let into the south wall; then enter your motor and return to the highway. In a few moments you will be spinning by the concrete piers at the entrance of a drive that leads to the home of the writer of this paper.

If you observe, as you may, that these concrete piers are somewhat out of plumb, be advised, dear reader, that this fact has been called to the attention of the owner many times; the explanation is that they were erected, in his absence, by several colored brothers who had been defying successfully the provisions of Mr. Volstead, his Act.[1] Had he been sure of the hour of your passing, he would have been at home to bid you welcome; perhaps he would have met you at the station and even have acted as your cicerone for it is a great delight to him to show visitors the strip of country which lies between Paoli and Philadelphia. Indeed, it is only when approaching Valley Forge, the spot upon which was recited the winter-

---

[1] My friend Hawley McLanahan, the gifted architect, upon observing that these posts were out of plumb, was much too considerate to call my attention to the fact, but asked me if I remembered the story of the Irish mason building a wall. Someone came along and said, "That wall is out of plumb." "You're a liar," said the mason, and getting a line on it, exclaimed joyfully, "Sure, it's better than plumb!"

long soliloquy of the great Washington, that he feels
his heart beat with patriotism; elsewhere he is somewhat too inclined to question the workings of democracy; but never here; for, as someone has said, no
spot on earth is so sacred in the history of the struggle
for human liberty as Valley Forge. But you still
have several miles of good riding before you.

As you approach the Devon garage, with a picturesque log-cabin alongside it, take a sharp turn to the
left, and after climbing a short hill you will descend
into the Great Valley. The road is picturesque and, at
the moment, — thanks to the policy of our enlightened
Governor Sproul, — is in excellent repair. As you go,
you will pass the Great Valley Baptist Church, which
has been standing for well on to two centuries in a
large, well-cared-for, and well-populated churchyard.

At this point I usually tell a story. Years ago, I
had a distant relative, a poor and intensely proud old
lady whose home was in Virginia. She was once
walking in Richmond with a little girl who called her
cousin, when, as they passed a small frame structure,
the child remarked, "Cousin Nannie, what kind of
church is that?" The old lady, looking down at the
child, replied, "That is not a church, that is a chapel."
And they passed on. Presently the child remarked,
"Cousin Nannie, what's the difference between a
church and a chapel?" After a moment came the
reply: "A chapel is where Baptists worship." A few
moments later, the child put a final question: "Cousin
Nannie, is it a crime to be a Baptist?" "No, my

dear," was the answer; "it is not a crime, but it is a great social misfortune." The finest Christian gentleman I ever met I have brought up on this story. He is a Baptist, but I believe that he has in him the makings of an Episcopalian.

After a run of a few miles over an undulating road, with trim, well-kept farms on either side, there will come into your view a fine equestrian statue of Anthony Wayne; and a moment later, a large, well-proportioned arch, a memorial to Washington and his officers; and if you are properly attuned to the occasion you will begin to murmur to yourself: —

> "Breathes there the man with soul so dead
> Who never to himself hath said,
> This is my own, my native land!"

for you will be in Valley Forge Park.

And now, if you will, forget the motor car in which you have been luxuriously gliding over smooth asphalt or macadam roads; forget the friendly farms which dot the landscape, and imagine this hilly country bleak and cold as it was during the awful winter of 1777–78. The attack upon the British at Germantown, on the outskirts of Philadelphia, had ended in failure; General Sir William Howe had settled down to spend a pleasant winter in Philadelphia; and Washington sought a place where, by taking advantage of the protection afforded by a river, a stream, and a range of hills, he might remain unmolested until his army of starved and half-naked men might, with the coming of spring, once more take the field.

The history of this country — of all countries, perhaps — is the history of individuals overcoming the obstacles put in their path by groups, either willfully, or acting in the belief that they are helpers in a cause. One whose service to America has never been sufficiently appreciated, Tom Paine, the English radical, was here too, endeavoring with his pen to enhearten the fast declining spirits of the colonists. In ringing phrases, "These are the times which try men's souls," and the like, he ably seconded the efforts of Washington, dividing his time between the headquarters of the army at Valley Forge and York, Pennsylvania, where a body of men calling itself the Congress was sitting. The six months from December 18, 1777 to June 19, 1778 were undoubtedly the darkest in American history. During that time it is estimated that several thousand men perished on these Valley Forge hills; and while the soldiers were dying of neglect, Congress talked, thus setting an example which has been followed right down to the present time.

Again, if you will, forget the awful misery and suffering suggested by this gloomy picture, and in imagination come with me a short distance, less than twenty miles as the crow flies, to the city of Philadelphia, and witness a very different scene. Despite the Declaration of Independence, signed in the State House only eighteen months before, Philadelphia was largely Tory. Many of the Quakers were for non-resistance. Society was frankly pro-British: that is to say, many a pretty girl, whose brother or lover was, or should have been, fighting for his country, was flirting industriously with the British officers, while the tradespeople generally preferred the golden guineas of the British quartermaster to the constantly depreciating currency which Congress was issuing as fast as printing presses could turn it out.

In those days, war was the chosen profession of the European gentlemen; but it was not of a quality which we have recently come to understand. It was a game played by men gloriously uniformed in scarlet and gold, during those months of the year when the weather made life in the open possible, if not pleasant. With the coming-on of winter, the campaign closed; the army went into winter quarters; the men gave themselves up to vice, drinking, and cards, while the officers beguiled the time with cards, drinking, and vice.

It was about the middle of October that Howe moved his forces into Philadelphia, and, after throwing up some few entrenchments to protect his army from possible but unlikely surprise, — for he was kept fully informed of the condition of the army under Washington, — he with his brother officers settled down to enjoy a pleasant winter in what was then the gayest city on the continent. Severity in dealing with the colonists having been tried without result, a policy of reconciliation had been begun, and little or no damage was done. Clubs were formed, concerts and dances planned, money and the essentials of life were plentiful. "We have all that is necessary and much that is superfluous," wrote home a British officer, under date of January 18, 1778.

But Howe was tiring of chasing elusive Americans from place to place; he complained that he did not have the confidence of his superiors at home; and finally he wrote and begged that he might have His Majesty's permission to resign. When this was accorded him, he turned over his command to Sir Henry Clinton and, after a fête of great magnificence, known to all Philadelphians as the Meschianza, given him by his brother officers, he returned to England. Those of our ancestors who took part in this historic pageant — and mine were among them — were glad to avail themselves of the skill of the ill-fated Major André, who planned events, painted scenery, devised costumes, and worked so indefatigably that the affair was so successful that it was said no general of modern times had ever been so honored. At the end, a set piece of fireworks was exploded, and a legend, "Thy laurels are immortal," was revealed against a background of night; but it has been observed that, when General Howe arrived in London, these laurels were already faded.

A century passes. Washington, having overcome all obstacles, wears laurel that is indeed immortal. He is the Father of his Country. The hundredth anniversary of the evacuation of Valley Forge brings a crowd, including generals, orators, and, alas! poets, to the place. A few years later, and the Commonwealth of Pennsylvania acquires certain tracts of ground at Valley Forge, "to be reserved for a public park." From this small beginning grew the present large and beautiful reservation maintained by the Commonwealth of Pennsylvania in honor of Washington and the Continental Army forever.

At the time of the celebration of the one-hundred-and-twenty-fifth anniversary of the departure of Washington and his "contemptibles" from these historic hills, there appears upon the scene a young clergyman, well known and loved by those who know him, by others considered visionary and likely to get himself into trouble. When a man is called visionary, it usually means that he sees further than his fellows. Such a visionary was the Reverend W. Herbert Burk. At the time I am now considering, he was the rector of a small church in Norristown, a town in no respect different from a thousand other small towns, except that it is just across the Schuylkill River from Valley Forge. In All Saints' Church at Norristown, on Washington's Birthday, 1903, Dr. Burk preached a sermon, in the course of which, speaking of Washington having been discovered at prayer, alone, on the hills across the river, he said: "Would that we might on those hills rear a wayside chapel, fit memorial of the Church's and the Nation's most honored son." From saying "Would that we might," to erecting, in enduring stone, the most beautiful ecclesiastical monument on this continent, is a long and bitterly exhausting

REV. W. HERBERT BURK, D.D.
from a bust by Beatrice Fox Griffith

proceeding; for, having dreamed his dream, **Dr. Burk**
awoke and proceeded to put it into effect.

Of what use is it to recount difficulties when they
have been so largely overcome? *Pour encourager les
autres*. The difficulties which beset Dr. Burk were
many and sundry. The bishop of the diocese could see
no reason for erecting a chapel in a place where there
were few people; and, above all things, a chapel which,
before it was finished, might cost — millions. He
smiled benevolently, as is the habit of bishops, and
put his ecclesiastical foot down. Both feet. So did
everyone else whom Dr. Burk consulted, that is to
say, everyone who could by any chance have assisted
him in his undertaking, among them the writer of this
paper. Then people having neither judgment, experience, nor money came to his assistance — and made
his work more difficult. It is altogether possible that,
without the example of Washington himself, Dr. Burk
might never have overcome the obstacles which
confronted him.

Have I suggested that he is a marvelously fluent
talker; that he knows what he wants; that he is a
psychoanalyst, if that commits him to a study of the
weaknesses of others and to the development of his
own strength; or that he has the energy of half a
dozen men? Little by little, men, and women too,
came to believe in him. From having everyone against
him, everyone was for him. He went steadily on.
He was careful to make no mistakes. Finally, after
some years' preparation, a committee was formed,

and architects' plans were invited, which, at the suggestion of Dr. Charles C. Harrison, at that time Provost of the University of Pennsylvania, were referred to Professor Warren P. Laird, the present Dean of the School of Fine Arts of that University, whose trained judgment led him to select the plans of Milton B. Medary, Jr.

This architect had, after careful study, decided that Perpendicular Gothic architecture was best adapted for the building; and Professor Laird in his report said: "The chapel dominates the group" — for the chapel that one sees at present is only the first of a series of buildings connected together by cloisters, galleries, and the like, and, "while not overpowering, it is sufficient for its purpose and is placed at the right point to complete and balance the mass. . . . The chapel, while pure in historic character and fine in proportion, has an expression of dignity, repose, and strength, which it would be difficult to carry further."

In due time the cornerstone of this fabric was laid by the Bishop of the diocese, assisted by some two hundred clergy and choristers, who then marched away, leaving Dr. Burk with the plans for a fine building and a well-laid cornerstone on his hands. But Dr. Burk had only begun to fight. "Prayer and advertising" is his slogan. Every patriotic society in the country was appealed to: Colonial Dames and Daughters and Sons and Descendants of Sons were invited to contribute, and most of them did. The

WASHINGTON MEMORIAL CHAPEL AT VALLEY FORGE

from the cloister

thirteen original states were shown how they could honor themselves by joining in the undertaking, which, by this time, had become national in its scope. By slow degrees the building rose out of the ground. What was done was well done; and after a time the stone walls reached to the bottom of the sills of the great Gothic windows. Then temporary walls and a roof were erected, so arranged that the final structure could be carried up to its full height without interfering with the use of the chapel, in which the first service was held on Washington's Birthday, 1905.

About ten years, years of struggle against obstacles almost insuperable, were to pass before the full beauty of the Washington Memorial Chapel could be seen and understood by persons not in the confidence of those who were privileged to undertake the work. Now that the chapel is practically complete, its beauty is patent to all. Whose creation is it? Dr. Burk's, whose dream it was, or the talented architect's? — who, I am sure, has been inadequately paid, if indeed he has been paid at all, for his services. I venture to give the palm to Dr. Burk. It was his idea; to it he has dedicated his life, to the exclusion of all else. And if you were to ask him from whom he had received the greatest assistance and encouragement, he would say, "From Dr. and Mrs. Charles Custis Harrison, without a doubt." It is possible that without their efforts the beautiful chapel would still be far from completion. As it is, the tower only remains to be erected. This work, it is hoped, will shortly be undertaken, at the expense of the bankers of the country, in honor of Robert Morris, the nation's first financier. In it will be placed a chime of thirteen bells, which will be rung upon special occasions, and special occasions are of almost daily occurrence at Valley Forge.

As we come suddenly upon this finely proportioned cathedral in miniature, — I am inclined to think that its site could have been better chosen, but bishops are only men with frocks on, and must have their way, — lifting itself up along the roadside among the trees, we rub our eyes in amazement; and when one is told that the completed scheme calls for a museum, a library, a large assembly-room and dining-rooms, where learned, patriotic, and other societies can be suitably entertained, one is astounded at the scope of the plan, and increasingly respectful of the man whose life-work it is.

Leaving our motor by the roadside, we approach the chapel on foot; immediately our attention is challenged by a fine cloister which, we are told, is the "cloister of the Colonies." It consists of thirteen bays, adjoining the chapel, immediately to the west; all of these are at present completed, with the exception of those named after the States of Georgia and North Carolina. New Jersey has the honor of being the first State to erect its bay.

It has frequently been my privilege to watch the reaction of visitors upon entering the chapel, especially those coming from Europe, most of whom

WASHINGTON MEMORIAL CHAPEL AT VALLEY FORGE

from the road

never heard of Valley Forge. One leaves the glare
of day and of the present, and enters a shrine of
exquisite, if subdued color. Everything is in perfect
taste; the ceiling is of paneled oak, each panel revealing in carving and in colors the coat-of arms of one of
the States of the Union. The pews are oak, with beautifully carved ends, in which color has been used, with
great discretion, to heighten the effect. The stained-
glass windows are of almost overpowering beauty.
My friend E. V. Lucas, that sympathetic wanderer
in Paris and elsewhere, on seeing them, immediately
exclaimed: "They are as lovely as the windows of
Sainte Chapelle." It gave me pleasure to tell him
that they were made by an Italian artist of great distinction in Philadelphia. The wrought-iron work
might have come from the hammer and chisel of
Benvenuto Cellini; it also came from Philadelphia.
No detail has been slighted, nothing has been over-
looked; everything means something; everything has
some historical significance. The visitor will not fail
to notice the beauty of the wrought-iron work, and
the three beautifully illuminated prayers, — if Lincoln's address at Gettysburg may be considered a
prayer, — on parchment, by a talented Philadelphia
lady, Beatrice Fox Griffith, who is also the sculptor
of the excellent bronze bust of Dr. Burk.

In the chancel is an organ, a fine instrument, the
keyboard of which is never locked. Some day, someone will come forward and give a sum sufficient to
provide an organist who shall for an hour or more

every day make that organ peal forth its glorious music to those who may wish, in the delicious beauty of that chapel, to forget the cares and perplexities which press so constantly upon us. I have often heard the martial strains of the "Battle Hymn of the Republic" or "Onward, Christian Soldiers," wafted through the open door on a Sunday afternoon. What a delight it would be to feel that such hymns are to be played daily on that instrument — for ever!

In the cloister and forming a part of it is an open-air pulpit and beyond it a large grove of trees; among these have been planted a number of small elms from Washington's home at Mount Vernon. A century hence, when they shall have attained their full growth, they will become pillars or columns supporting an arching roof of leaves, and long before that time it will be seen that they have been set out in the form of a great cross two hundred feet long and one hundred and fifty feet wide. The stone walls of the chapel serve as a sounding-board and, there being no sides to this cathedral of trees to limit the crowd which can gather therein, one may imagine at some great service a congregation of thousands: indeed, as Professor Laird once remarked to me when we were speaking of Dr. Burk and his marvelous achievements, the time may come when the woodland cathedral may rival in interest the chapel which now seems so beautiful. What are Joyce Kilmer's lines?

> Poems are made by fools like me,
> But only God can make a tree.

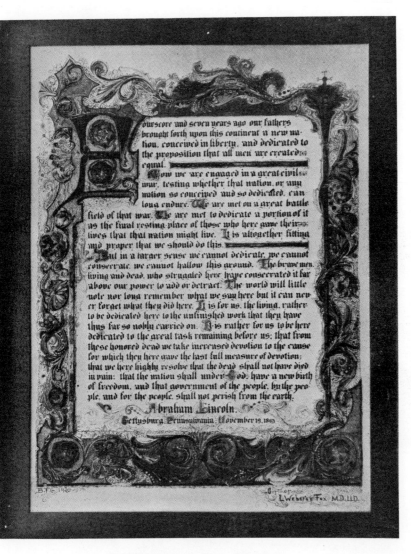

LINCOLN'S GETTYSBURG ADDRESS

illuminated on vellum

It was a glorious vision that appeared to **Dr. Burk** so many years ago! How thankful he should be that he was permitted to see his dream-chapel take form and substance. He has worked hard, he has overcome difficulties understood only by those in his confidence; and he has been permitted — not to complete his work; a century or more may elapse before "finis" can be written; but — to set a standard for what remains to be done. We quickly discover, as we listen to him, why he has accomplished so much. He is positively irresistible: one must do as he wills. If he wants the President of the United States to make an address, he goes to Washington and gets him. In this way Roosevelt was brought here some years ago; and since then President Harding, who, having said that he could not and would not leave Washington on account of important business, nevertheless came, and upon his departure had increased his admirers by the eight or ten thousand people who saw him enter the chapel, and who later heard him address them from the pulpit under the trees. President Harding was the first President to occupy the pew set aside for the nation's ruler.

A visit to the Washington Memorial Chapel at Valley Forge is a patriotic duty; for, as Lord Bryce, that great Englishman who understood us and our institutions so well, said in a letter to Dr. Burk, written only a day or two before his death: "No memory ever deserved more universal honor than

Washington's; we have, as you know, recently erected a statue of him in Trafalgar Square, one of the best positions in London."

We leave the chapel and look around us: near by, just beyond a grove of trees, on the hillside overlooking the Schuylkill, is to be a large cemetery. It is sparsely populated at present — we are hardy folk out here in the country; but some day it will be densely crowded. Farther on are well-kept roads sweeping over the hills, giving vistas of beauty; while here and there are little cabins which serve as guardhouses, erected in the same manner and of the same proportions as, if more substantially than, those built by Washington's soldiers. The lines of intrenchments, earthworks thrown up by the soldiers, as much to occupy their time as to afford protection, are still to be seen skirting the hillside; while down by the river is the little stone house which served as Washington's Headquarters, very much as it was when he occupied it. The monuments and markers here and there might detain us, were not time flying.

In reply to your question as to who attends this chapel, I would call attention to the little hamlets through which we have passed, and may tell you that there is more quiet comfort and unostentatious elegance between Paoli and Philadelphia than anywhere else I know. Consider the immense extent of this suburban country — not taken up by a few magnificent estates, but occupied by tens of thousands of

WASHINGTON'S HEADQUARTERS AT VALLEY FORGE

prosperous citizens, whose motors bring the chapel easily within reach. Besides which, there is a constant stream of visitors from all over the world.

May I recount an experience I had at the chapel several years ago? It was at a time when we had been highly stimulated by propaganda to hate the Germans and love the French, — the natural reaction from which we are now undergoing, — that someone had the happy idea of celebrating Bastille Day, which fell upon a Sunday, at Valley Forge. A company of marines was to be brought from the Navy Yard at Philadelphia, whose patriotism was to be stimulated with sandwiches, cake, ice cream, and coffee. It fell to my lot to preside at this part of the function. The services of a local band were requisitioned, and later there was to be a presentation of flags. Dr. Burk agreed to preach a patriotic sermon; I suspect that he would rather preach a sermon than listen to one.

If preaching is a lost art, as some maintain, undoubtedly Dr. Burk has found it. May I give proof of it? Some months ago, a fashionable, flapperlike person, B. G., spending the week-end with us, wanting to see the chapel, was taken to it one Sunday morning but warned that if there was service going on when she entered, she was to make no disturbance. She entered the chapel while I remained in the motor, but she did not return. Finally I went after her and found her listening in rapt attention to Dr. Burk. "Why, the man can preach!" she said. "Lend me ten dollars." "What for?" said I. "To put in the money box as I go out." I gave her the money with some reluctance, feeling that I should never see it again; and I was right. As a consequence I passed a sleepless night, and early the next morning I motored to Valley Forge and told Dr. Burk how I had slipped a ten-dollar bill into his money box by mistake; it was a pathetic story but it failed to move the rector. "Edward," he said, "your story is not convincing; come back with a better one if you think it worth while to come at all," and turning his back on me, he went on with his work, for he is a busy man. But to return.

"Bastille Day at Valley Forge" was well advertised; people for many miles about came in their motors; never before had there been such a crowd. It was midsummer, July 14; the weather — typical Philadelphia weather for that time of year — as hot as blazes. As the crowd gathered, it was decided that it would be best for Dr. Burk to make his remarks to as many as could hear him under the trees, from the open-air pulpit, an architectural feature of the cloister. The marines arrived; at a word of command they charged upon and overcame the refreshments, while the band played French and other national airs with involuntary variations.

The crowd increased; it grew hotter; the sky became overcast; it looked like rain; and I began to fear for the success of the meeting. The chapel might hold two hundred people; there was an attendance esti-

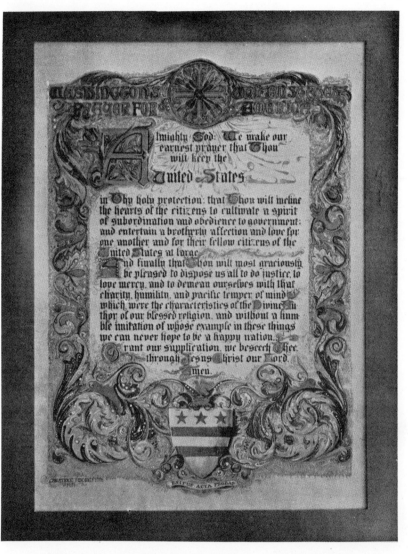

WASHINGTON'S PRAYER FOR THE UNITED STATES OF AMERICA

illuminated on vellum

mated at twenty times that number, most of
whom had come in motors which had been parked
on the roadside for a distance of a mile or more:
no one had thought of the necessity of regulating the
traffic.

At the appointed hour, Dr. Burk began to speak.
"The trees were God's first temples," he said. There
was a flash of forked lightning, followed by a crash of
thunder which suggested that God's first temples
were being torn up by the roots. Then it rained as it
rains only in Mr. Conrad's stories. Instantly, there
was a rush for the chapel, which had already been
sought by the wise ones; then there was a counter-
rush for the motors, and the ceremony was at an end.
Sauve qui peut became the order of the afternoon —
but few could.

I had been given five words to say: "La Fayette,
we have went," or some such matter; but there was
none to listen. It poured in torrents for twenty minutes, until we were all wet to the skin; then the rain
ceased, the sun came out, and it was hotter than
ever. There were a hundred cars between me and
my motor; my wife, having been despoiled of her
refreshments, was trying to save her china in a cabin
far away, crowded to suffocation. I saw that it was
from the circumference that help must come; I was
at the centre and could no nothing. Weary and wet,
I opened the door of somebody's limousine, entered,
and sat down, determined that nature should take
its course — which it did, in the direction of a heavy

cold. I may be mistaken, but I have always thought that my wife blamed me for that thunderstorm.

Before finally taking leave of Dr. Burk and his glorious creation, I must refer to an order I received from a lady several years ago, to write a paper calling attention to the beauties of the chapel — an order which I am only now tardily obeying. It was during the war, shortly before her death, that Mrs. Cassatt, the widow of the President of the Pennsylvania Railroad — we are back to the railroad, you see — sent for me and said: "Are you aware of the greatness of the work that Dr. Burk is doing in your community, and of how shamefully you are neglecting him? Do you know that he is depriving himself of the comforts, of the very necessities of life, in order that his work at Valley Forge may go on? A physical breakdown is imminent. I have sent him away for a month or so; when he returns I wish to hear" — she was an autocratic old lady — "that some of you men, prominent in your community, have agreed that in the future he shall be properly looked after. Are you one of his vestrymen? You should be: you live not far away."

"But," I replied, "how about your son? He lives nearer Valley Forge than I do."

There was just the merest trace of a smile on the face of the old lady as I referred to Colonel Edward Buchanan Cassatt, the most picturesque gentleman in our neighborhood, a distinguished sportsman, pos-

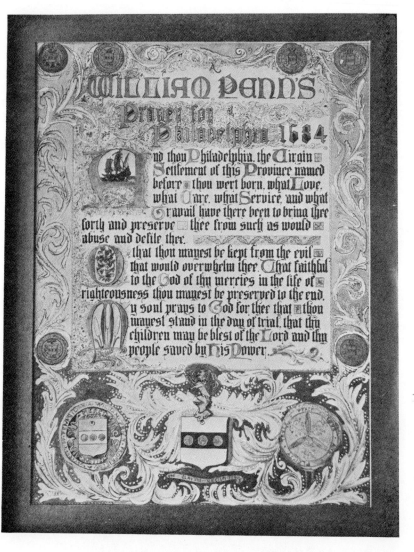

WILLIAM PENN'S PRAYER FOR PHILADELPHIA
illuminated on vellum

sessed of every charm that one would *not* expect to find in a vestryman. — How he laughed when I told him of my encounter with his mother! — "The fact is, madam," I went on to say, "Dr. Burk selects his Board of Directors with the same care with which your husband used to select his; and neither of us, I fancy, sizes up to his requirements, although I dare say — " But no, I must not write it.

I got one hearty laugh out of the old lady when, in reply to her question as to how money could be raised, I asked if she was willing to take shares in Dr. Burk's newly planned graveyard and make it a live concern. The enterprise had just been started, and I had bought a lot to help the scheme along; but this was not enough. What Dr. Burk wanted was interments, and so he told me very plainly. "You're little or no use to me," he said, "except under a handsome monument — something I can point to." I verily believe that he would cheerfully bury his best friend, if by so doing he thought he could add to the beauty or interest of the landscape. Such are the workings of his enthusiasm. It was quite a relief when, the last time I saw him, he told me I might go on and live forever, for all he cared: things had been coming his way very satisfactorily.

And now, unless you are considering investing in cemetery lots, I need detain you no longer at Valley Forge. Let the impression of what you have seen sink in, and you will wish to come again. As you roll along the well-kept roads leading to Philadelphia, you will pass through the country of which we Philadelphians are so proud: those towers belong to Bryn Mawr College — an institution with which I have not been in entire sympathy. At the risk of being taken for the old man who said, "If a girl is young and pretty she don't need no college education, and if she ain't it it ain't adequate," let me confess my belief that a college which tends to unfit a woman for becoming a wife and mother falls short of its obligations. "A man is, in general, better pleased when he has a good dinner upon his table than when his wife talks Greek. My friend Mrs. Elizabeth Carter could make a pudding as well as translate 'Epictetus.'" So said Dr. Johnson. The Brynmartyr would reply that it is not important for the man to be pleased; but the world must be peopled, and not by illiterates. Perhaps those who now control the destinies of Bryn Mawr will see to it that it does not lack, altogether, the spiritual radiance that Alice Freeman Palmer shed upon Wellesley.

Speaking of colleges, yonder is Haverford, for which curiously, I have a feeling of great affection and respect. I say "curiously" because I have no college affiliations whatever, and am not more than quarter Quaker. Haverford still preserves the traditions of its founders and runs not after that false god, Size, so earnestly sought by most institutions nowadays. If I were sending a boy to college, I would choose Haverford, but it may be just as well that I am not. There are too many college students as it is: it is quite as important that a college education should

DEAR MRS. ELIZABETH CARTER
the translator of Epictetus and equally good at a pudding

be deserved as that it should be available. I venture to say that, if half the men and women in every college in the country quit, they, the college and the country, would be better off.

That is the Merion Cricket Club. Philadelphia is the only place in the country where cricket is played with enthusiasm. In a few moments you will cross the city line and enter our justly famous Fairmount Park, disfigured here and there with some bad statuary, but otherwise very beautiful. You are approaching a specimen now. I never see a bit of bad statuary without thinking of that supremely wise and witty essay by George Moore, "Royalty in Art," in his volume, *Modern Painting*. Take it from your shelves, reader, get it from a library, better still, buy it; if you do not enjoy it, I will take it off your hands. The statue before you is of a soldier of our Civil War; he is of life-size, doubtless, but he is mounted on a tall, granite pedestal, so heavy that the figure which surmounts it looks like an implement with which to seal a letter. What can it be? The man is in the uniform of a private; he has a drooping moustache of granite, and he leans upon a rifle of the same. Curiosity will cause you to read:

DEDICATED

TO THE

SOLDIERS AND SAILORS

OF THE

CIVIL WAR

Did they succeed?

Let this monument be their answer

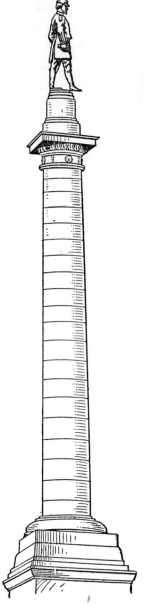

Do not laugh, dear reader; you probably have something quite as ridiculous at home.

As you pass the Memorial Hall, a relic of the Centennial Exposition, you will come upon and pass through a meaningless architectural bit, a sort of glorified gateway leading nowhere. On either side is a very tall granite shaft, something over one hundred feet high, and on the top of each shaft is a statue; but observe that one of the figures is *walking*. One foot is raised; should he do the obvious thing and put his foot down, he would plunge headlong into the shrubbery a hundred feet below. I wish that he might.

I have passed this artistic abomination half a dozen times a week for years. Has no one on the Fairmount Park Art Commission, or whoever it is that has authority in such matters, a sense of humor? Surely everyone must see how absurd it is. A man with courage and a rope could bring that statue to the ground in a jiffy — I have the rope. What is it that Max Beerbohm says? "Only a sculptor and his mother would maintain that sculpture is not a lost art."

Yonder is Philadelphia. Of its citizens a famous traveler once said: "they are a finer, taller race than the Chinese but less progressive." Be this as it may, they no longer live in their city, but in the suburbs, which are of enormous extent and easily accessible. Once Philadelphia was said to be a "clever green town built by Quakers," but it is now an enormous manufacturing wen which calls itself the Workshop of the World. Perhaps it is. Certainly it is a city of foreigners; the Quaker has disappeared, the American is submerged. There are whole districts where, for blocks, — squares we call them, — only Yiddish or Polish or Italian is spoken; where a newspaper published in the English language cannot be had.

Philadelphia is the city in which the Declaration of Independence was written: a document composed by an astute politician who knew quite as well as we do that he was writing nonsense when he referred to the "self-evident truth that all men are created free and equal." The Declaration is a masterpiece of political invective, which served its purpose, but I venture to say that the men who signed it would be bitterly disappointed if they could see the government it established in operation. When a competent and modest gentleman attempts to take part in it, his life is made so miserable and he is subjected to so many humiliations that he finally gives up in despair. On the other hand, an ignorant blatherskite finds himself in clover; no office is beyond his reach. Democracy is a beautiful theory; it provides a splendid subject for the orator on a Fourth of July, and for the demagogue at all times; the only trouble with it is that it works badly. It is a truism to say that there is a power behind every throne; we freed ourselves from the tyranny of a king only to place ourselves in the grip of a corrupt political machine, without which representative government stalls.

Occasionally we have what are called reform administrations; then everything stops until the machine — without which democracy will not function — gets into control again. When it is subjected to a strain, as in the late war, democracy instantly becomes a dictatorship.

The material prosperity which we enjoy is due to our good fortune in being possessed of a continent of unscratched resources, rather than to the form of government we have adopted. In all essentials the nation whose yoke we threw off enjoys greater liberty than we; the English people, as much as we, profited by the Declaration of Independence. It is altogether fitting that there should be a statue of Washington in London.

We have recently had a silly, if well-meaning, mayor, the most lasting achievement of whose administration was the erection of a poor statue to a

A RIDICULOUS STATUE

a type all too common in this country

fake philanthropist. Now we are grieving at the
antics of a governor who was wished on us by the
women of the state — to their regret and ours. Involved in a maze of personal quarrels with other
members of his administration, he is endeavoring to
use his present office as a stopping-stone to higher
political preferment; meantime, reform stands still.
Who was it that remarked, so aptly, "When Dr.
Johnson observed that patriotism was the last refuge
of a scoundrel, he was unaware of the immense power
for evil that lay in the word 'reform'?"

I wish that we might pause and take stock of ourselves. Is it not time for us to go slow, to "stop,
look, and listen," as the railway signs have it, at
dangerous crossings? I wish that we might descend
to a higher order of living. I wish that we might not
fell all our trees, burn all our coal, exhaust all our
mines. Let us leave something for our children. As
I look about, I see two great political parties, bank-
rupt of ideals, led by rival demagogues interested only
in securing or retaining power. I see one gigantic
"Main Street," a Corso along which is a reckless
race for wealth. I wish that we might close our doors
and keep them closed until we have assimilated our
enormous foreign population.

I remember Goldsmith's lines: —

> Ill fares the land, to hastening ills a prey,
> Where wealth accumulates, and men decay.

I wish that an intellectual and property qualification
limited the franchise, which politicians refer to as our

most precious possession. I suppose that it is for this reason they have given it to men who do not speak our language or understand our institutions; who are permitted to vote practically upon their arrival on our shores. Will "votes for women" remedy this condition, or aggravate it?

Emerson says somewhere that when God thinks of kings, he smiles. May He not also sigh as, looking at us over the rim of the world, He says to Himself: "My children down there are always going to extremes"?

VI

A ROYAL BOOK–COLLECTOR

LET us suppose, dear reader, that we are wandering about London together, and that you, thinking to please me, would say, "In the words of Doctor Johnson, 'Sir, let us take a walk down Fleet Street.'" I, thinking to enlighten you, would reply: "Sir, Doctor Johnson never said that; that is a Johnsonian 'tecla,' an imitation, but an excellent one"; and would continue, "George Augustus Sala, wanting a slogan for a magazine, invented it. Nevertheless, as you say, 'let us take a walk down Fleet.'"

Approaching that famous street, after pausing for a moment to comment upon the artistic demerits of the monument that marks the spot where Temple Bar once stood, your eye would be taken by a narrow timbered house on the south side, wedged in between fine modern banking-buildings. You would inquire, "What is that bit of old London?" Instantly you would regret asking me the question, for after that I should do all the talking.

That solitary fragment of old London dates from about three hundred years ago; it is supposed to have been the office or council-chamber of the Duchy of Cornwall in the time of Prince Henry, the elder son of James First. Some twenty years since it was the intention to remove it to make way for a modern building, but the people of London raised such a hue and cry against its destruction that the London County Council stepped in, bought, and as far as possible restored it. There is nothing to be seen on the ground floor, but above there is a fine old room with a plaster ceiling with the Prince of Wales's crest in the middle and wooden paneling of a later date. The room can be hired for public meetings of a select character, and a little-used visitors' book inspected, if you are so inclined.

Henry, Prince of Wales, with whose name this room is associated, has always had a peculiar interest for book-fanciers. Had he lived to come to the throne he would have been Henry Ninth. It was inevitable that his popularity with the people, who were none too fond of that Scotch pedant, his father, should lead to a good deal of friction between King and Prince, but the King took the keenest interest in the education of the young lad, and among other things, set out to make a book-collector of him. That he failed is no fault of the father; we fathers have to work, sometimes, upon the most refractory material.

Henry's grandmother was Mary Stuart; we do not often think of the beautiful Mary Queen of Scots as a grandmother, but she had a son by Lord Darnley, who became James Sixth of Scotland, and, after the death of Queen Elizabeth, James First of England. Quarrels in royal families were not unusual in those days; James made an alliance with Elizabeth against his mother, and even after Elizabeth removed his

A BIT OF OLD LONDON
The gateway leads to the Temple

mother's head with an axe, he did not break with the Queen, his chief business being to secure her throne. In due time he married Anne of Denmark, and when, several years later, a son was born, there was great rejoicing. This interesting event took place in Stirling Castle in Scotland on the nineteenth of February 1593. The boy grew up under his father's eye; a letter obviously composed by the boy's tutor, but written in the hand of the pupil, brought forth the royal command that in future his son's letters were to be his own composition, "in form as well as fingers."

On the death of Elizabeth, James came to London to be crowned King of England, and his son automatically became Duke of Cornwall. Subsequently the title "Prince of Wales" was conferred upon him, whereupon his father wrote to him not to let it make him proud or insolent; for, said he, "a king's son and heir were ye before, and no mair are ye now."

King James had an itch for authorship; he wrote much, including a treatise still to be seen in manuscript in the British Museum, wholly written in the royal hand, entitled "Book of Instruction of a Prince," which shows with how much care the father surveyed the son's education; and a sonnet from the same hand, addressed to him, is not without merit. Let me quote it.

> God gives not kings the stile of Gods in vaine,
>   For on his throne his sceptor do they swey:
>   And as their subjects ought them to obey,
> So kings should feare and serve their God againe.

> If then ye would enjoy a happie reigne,
>> Observe the statutes of our heavenly King;
>> And from his law make all your laws to spring;
> Since his lieutenant here ye should remaine,
> Rewarde the just, be stedfast, true and plaine;
>> Represse the proud, maintayning aye the right;
>> Walke always so, as ever in His sight,
> Who guards the godly, plaguing the prophane.
>> And so ye shall in princely vertues shine,
>> Resembling right your mightie King divine.

Admit that the lines are not very good, — I am no judge in such matters, — the sentiment is unexceptionable, and we could forgive James for much worse verses, remembering that it is to him that we owe the selection of the scholars who translated our English Bible. When kings are no more, the King James Version will remain a thing of beauty and a joy forever.

Meanwhile the lad grew up with a reputation for being decorous in behavior, but he was, according to his father's idea, too fond of sport. He played much with a small ball — that would be golf, no doubt — and "tossed the pike and rode the horse with dogs" when his father thought he should have been at his studies. It was to stimulate his taste for books that the King, upon the death of Lord Lumley, an antiquarian statesman of Elizabeth's time, bought his library *en bloc* and gave it to the Prince, with excellent advice as to its use. It was a fine collection of books, but the bindings were old and rusty and did not appeal to the eye of the young sportsman, who

JAMES FIRST AND HIS SON, HENRY PRINCE OF WALES
from a rare print

had them all removed and the books rebound in accordance with his own boyish notions of elegance. Royal coats-of-arms, Prince of Wales's plumes, and I know not what else appeared in gold, silver, and thread on costly leather and satin bindings in bewildering profusion. Not once or twice only, but in some cases as many as eight times on a single volume, were lions rampant, stamped in gold, which seemed to say, "I have taken this extraordinary attitude to please a Prince; don't touch me."

There are, of course, a large number of books in the British Museum associated with Prince Henry, but I was particularly happy when I once stumbled upon (if one can be said to stumble upon a book on a top shelf) the dedication copy of Coryat's *Crudities, Hastily Gobled Up in Five Moneths Travells*, with an inscription in the author's hand. Reader, dost know the book? It is one of my special favorites, is the earliest book of travel — as distinguished from explorations — in English, and is as readable to-day as when it was first published, more than three centuries ago. Tom Coryat was a favorite of the Prince, who allowed him a small pension. Holding in my hand the book, which is bound in crimson velvet on which H. P. OF WALES is stamped in gold, I could, in imagination, see the scamp — for he was no less — on bended knee presenting it to the young Prince, whom he likened to an "Orient Pearle." Fed on flattery royalty was in those days; little wonder is it that kings came to believe that they could do no wrong, but "hastily gobbled up" this polite fiction, mistaking it for a law of nature, not to be disputed.

Listen to a contemporary description of the person of the Prince.

He was of a comely, tall, middle stature, about five feet eight inches; of a strong, straight, well-made body, as if Nature had used all her cunning in making him. He had broad shoulders, a small waste, with a majestickal countenance, a piercing grave eye, a most gracious smile and a terrible frown. His favor like the Sunne shown upon all indifferently. He was, in spite of these qualities, shamefaced, modest, and patient, slow to anger, ardent in his love of Religion and above all things abhorring flattery, and never was he heard to take God's name in vaine. Being asked one day why he did not sweare in play as well as others, he replied that he knew no game worthy of an oath. Nor did he desire nor aspire to live long, many times saying that it was to small purpose for a gallant man to live when the prime of his days were past, until he were full of aiches, paines, and soares and that for his part he hoped that when he should be sick, three of four daies together, then God would take him away.

Popery, with all the adjuncks thereof, he hated to the death, yet he would now and then use Papists very kindly showing that he hated not their persons but their opinions. Not less careful was he to obey the King, his Father in everything, being also very diligent to honour the Queene, his Mother, so much as in him lay. Wonderful also was his wisdom and care in governing of his house, giving orders and seeing for himself everything to be done so that scarce were there any of his household servants that he knew not by name, amongst whom there was not one known or yet suspected to be a Papist.

BOOK FROM THE LIBRARY OF LORD LUMLEY,
rebound for the Royal Book-Collector

The world is not harsh in its judgment of princes, and Prince Henry enjoyed enormous popularity; he was young, he was gracious, handsome, and he was

a sportsman. Upon his death every man who could wield a pen, and many who could not, wrote an ode. These were, after the fashion of the time, fulsome to the last degree; of the many that have come down to us, the best, certainly the best known, is "The Epicede," a funeral song by George Chapman, a copy of which, bound up with a little pamphlet giving a full account of the royal obsequies, is before me. The little volume is made additionally interesting by a beautifully engraved book-plate of "William Penn, Esq. of Pennsylvania," to whom it formerly belonged. It was an impressive funeral, over two thousand nobles, gentlemen, and their servants taking part, with the dead prince's brother Charles as chief mourner; for some reason the King does not appear to have been present.

Only one of the details of the great function need now detain us. It is recorded that after the body was embalmed, "it was closed up in lead." Instantly there came to my mind the lines of Thomas Flatman to his "ingenious Friend, Mr. Faithorne," the celebrated engraver, in which he says that it were more enduring to have one's portrait engraved on copper by that artist than to have one's body wrapped in lead. The poet writes: —

> For my part, I prefer (to guard the Dead)
> A Copper Plate, before a sheet of Lead.
> So long as Brasse, so long as Books endure,
> So long as neat-wrought Pieces, Thou 'rt secure.
> A Faithorne sculpsit is a Charm can save
> From dull Oblivion, and a gaping Grave.

It seems to have been the custom to enclose the dead body of a royal — or other distinguished — person, before placing it in its coffin, in a covering of

a sheet of lead, which, being thin and plastic, could
be made to conform very closely to the outlines of
the body, so that it amounted to an indestructible

AN
EPICEDE
OR
Funerall Song:
On the moſt diſaſtrous Death, of the
High-borne *Prince* of Men, *HENRY*
Prince of W A L E S, &c.
With
The Funeralls, and Repreſentation of
the Herſe of the ſame High and mighty Prince;
Prince of *Wales*, Duke of *Cornewaile* and *Rothſay*,
Count Palatine of *Cheſter*, Earle of *Carick*,
and late Knight of the moſt Noble
Order of the G A R T E R.

Which Noble *Prince* deceaſed at Sᵗ.
James, the ſixt day of *Nouember*, 1 6 1 2.
and was moſt Princely interred the ſeuenth
day of *December* following, within the
Abbey of *Weſtminſter*, in the Eighteenth yeere of his Age.

LONDON:
Printed by *T. S.* for *Iohn Budge*, and are to bee
ſould at his ſhop at the great ſouth dore of
Paules, and at Brittanes Burſſe. 1 6 1 2.

metal sheathing. How old this custom is, no one seems able to tell me, but I have ascertained that the body of the Duke of Wellington was the last to be treated in this manner.

The "corps" of the young Prince was finally placed in a vault in Westminster Abbey. It is a sad commentary upon the brevity of human greatness that although a large number of royal burials have since taken place in Westminster Abbey, not a single royal tomb later than that of Queen Elizabeth had been indicated or inscribed, until 1869, when, under the direction of Dean Stanley, an effort was made to mark the places where royal personages have been placed with so much ceremony. "Out of sight, out of mind" would seem to have been the guiding motto of royalty. Three weeks were spent in locating the burial place of James First, — for the records were contradictory, — in the course of which the coffin of Henry Frederick, Prince of Wales, was discovered. It was found among a vast pile of leaden coffins, in a large vault obliquely under the tomb of his grandmother, Mary Queen of Scots, in Henry Seventh's Chapel, the entrance to which had been walled up.

King James has been called "the wisest fool in Christendom." If weak and incapable, he was learned; but great things had been expected of his son, who was keenly interested in all that went on around him — and much was going on. Hardly a day passed without the news of some important dis-

MARY QUEEN OF SCOTS
from a portrait in the National Portrait Gallery

covery. Henry wished to learn of them at first
hand, and became intimate with all the great men
of his time. He knew Francis Bacon and Sir Walter
Raleigh, and was much disgusted when the latter
was thrown into the Tower. "No man," he said,
"but my father would keep such a bird in such a
cage." This is the first time on record when a man
of Sir Walter's importance was called "a bird"; the
custom has prevailed to the present time. English
history would probably have been very different had
Henry lived. As a result of his death, his younger
brother came to the throne as Charles First, and
what Cromwell did to him is well known.

In due time after the young Prince's death his
library was appropriated by his father, and was
removed from St. James's Palace, where he lived and
died, to Windsor. The Royal Library may be said
to have dated from Henry Seventh's time. All the
kings and queens added to it except George Second,
in whose reign the British Museum was founded,
when it was represented to him that it would be a
fine thing for him to give to the Museum the library
which served no useful purpose at Windsor. Thackeray has said that the very sight of a book threw the
King into a rage. What a joke he thought it — to
buy popularity by a gift of books! The idea appealed
to him. He never opened one and could not have read
one in any language other than German. So to the
Museum came the first collection of royal books,
"with the compliments of the King," and when

George Third came to the throne there was a royal library at Windsor with no books in it. Under the guidance of wise men, including my friend Dr. Johnson, the Third George set about forming a fine library, and being a persistent man, right or wrong, before he died he had a splendid collection of books, perhaps the finest ever brought together by one individual. When his scapegrace son, George Fourth, came to the throne he was deeply in debt, and looking this way and that for the wherewithal to raise the wind, his eye fell upon his father's library and forthwith he began a search for a purchaser. Negotiations were completed and the books were about to pass to the Emperor of Russia when his devoted subjects heard of the royal intention. Immediately there was an outcry, and an arrangement was quickly arrived at. It was agreed in Parliament that, in exchange for the extinguishment of some of the King's most pressing debts, his books should go to the nation. In this manner the British Museum became possessed of the second Royal Library, and the transaction is commemorated by a not strictly truthful marble tablet let into the wall of the magnificent room in which so many and such priceless books are housed, reading:

This library
collected by King George III
was given to the British Nation
by his most gracious majesty
King George IV
in the third year of his reign
A.D. MDCCCXXIII

QUEEN ELIZABETH
from a painting in the National Portrait Gallery

What is it that Dr. Johnson says? "In lapidary work a man is not under oath." So it appears. Let us continue.

When in the course of human events George Fourth was gathered to his fathers, King William came to the throne, and once again there was a royal library at Windsor with no books in it; and once again a king set about forming one. And wisely he decided that never again should an English sovereign be without books. In his will, written in his own hand, displayed in one of the glass cases to the left as one enters the room in which the royal documents are exhibited in the British Museum, may be read a paragraph to the effect that his books, collected at his own expense, are to be regarded as heirlooms and are to be preserved at Windsor for the use of royalty forever. "Forever" is a long word, but it will take an act of Parliament, or something worse, to frustrate the royal will.

Prince Henry's books are, therefore, preserved in the British Museum, and a number of them, with his arms upon them, were in exhibition cases when I was last there. As years passed, the Museum received many important gifts, and in 1787 an alphabetical catalogue of all the books then in the library was begun, and it was found, quite naturally, that there were many duplicates. These duplicates were sold — unwisely, as I think, but happily for me. Several years ago, a fancy for possessing some volumes from royal libraries seizing me, I began to look around for them, and after a time found I had a nice little cluster of volumes bearing the arms of Henry Eighth, Elizabeth, James, and his son Prince Henry, whose brief life I have endeavored to sketch, Charles First and Second, and many more. Not the most valuable, but the one I treasure most, is a famous work on geography and astronomy published in 1541 by Claudius Ptolemy — an error in whose mathematics led Columbus to believe that the world was much smaller than it really is. It is one of the volumes Prince Henry had rebound. In addition to an elaborate coat of arms in the centre, on each side it has lions rampant, one in each of its eight corners. The signature "Lumley" adds to its value, and the duplicate-stamp which was put in all copies sold by the Museum in 1787 makes its provenance complete.

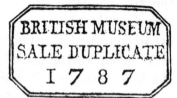

I would ask of what use in the world is this Museum, and to whom, and to what class of persons is it useful? It may do good to some who go to it, but to nobody else. Let those who lounge in it, and make it a place of amusement, contribute to its support. Why should tradesmen and farmers be called upon to pay for the support of a place which is intended only for the amusement of the curious and the rich, and not for the benefit or for the instruction of the poor? If the aristocracy want a museum as a lounging place, let them pay for it. For my part, I do not know where it is, nor do I know much of the contents of it; but from the little I have heard of it, even if I knew where it was, I would not take the trouble of going to see it. I should like to have a list of the salaried persons; I should like to know who they are; I should like above all things to see whether they are not some dependents of Government — some of the aristocratic fry. I want their names — the names of the maids who sweep out the rooms, to see whose daughters they are; whether they are the daughters of the heads of the establishment, or what other relation they bear to them. This Museum job is one of the most scandalous that ever disgraced a Government, and when I have said that, I have said all that is within my power to say.

Does the above burst of eloquence remind you of anything that you have recently heard? Can you not, in imagination, hear a mayor of Philadelphia talking about an Art Museum, or a former Secretary of State clearing the way (at so much per hour) for a blasting attack upon any form of education which destroys the belief that the world was created in six days of twenty-four hours each? Can you not, in imagination, see the Senator from Wisconsin, indignantly rising to demand an inquiry as to why our prisons do not attract a better class of patrons, or the mighty Magnus of Minnesota, eager to represent the "peepul," and anxious to make a noise on any subject?

But what you actually hear is a fragment of a speech made in the House of Commons by William Cobbett just a hundred years ago, opposing the proposition that a small sum of money should be voted by Parliament for the maintenance of the

Museum, which has been called the most important centre of public instruction in the British Isles. Its average daily attendance is now between four and five thousand, and on special occasions a much larger number of visitors have been counted. Its treasures are beyond price, and its library is the greatest in the world. It is open, practically without restrictions and without fees, to citizens of every country on earth. No wonder that the Germans, being what they are, sought, by every means in their power during the Great War, to destroy this monument to the wisdom and greatness of England.

And now I am going to ask you to imagine that you are reading from a number of little tracts published in London some time after the death of Henry. The form in which I present an account of the life and death and burial of the Prince is much abbreviated, repetitions are eliminated, and the spelling has been made a trifle less archaic than in the originals; but the spirit has not, I hope, altogether evaporated.

Our Late most Incomparable and Heroique Prince Henry, Prince of Wales, was born about three o'clock in the morning of the 19th of February, 1593, to the joy of the whole world but chiefly (next to their Majesties, his father and mother) to the Phoenix of her age, the matchless Elizabeth. At the early age of four he found no toyes so acceptable as gunnes and drummes and canyon, so that (had he lived) Mars himself would not have dared to look him in the face. But at the age of seven, he began to delight in manly exercises, so that at nine he could not only ride, sing, dance, and leap, but shoot

HENRY PRINCE OF WALES
from a rare print

at a mark and toss his pike. At ten he began to show sparkes of Pietie, Majestie, Gravite, as is the custom of Princes of this Royal House.

Meanewhile swift wingèd time pittying that Elizabeth, now overcloy'd with earthly joyes, decreed that she should not any longer be detained in this vale of teares did send the blessed Angels to change her corruptable for an incorruptable Crowne. Yet amid the lamentations which ensued, there could be heard the voyces of the Peeres of England, begging that for the great love they bore him, that James the Sixth of Scotland, the First of England, would come to London with hastie despatch that they might the sooner enjoy His Royal Presence. And James, hearing from afar off the cries of his so greatly distress'd subjects, did set out from Edinburgh on the first day of June, 1602 and did so expeditiously travel that upon the last day of the said month he did greet the Lords of Her Late Majestie's most Honorable Privy Councell, at Windsor. And what joy was at so loving a meeting I leave it for you to imagine.

Then began the young Prince to ply his bookes harde, continuing all the while his Princely sportes, so that he came to have a very strong and active body; and being come to his fourteenth yeare he began to feel himself indeed a Prince, and, unlike most boys of his age, be became very judicious, drawing neer to a majesticall gravite, a delighter in Sermons, and so attentive to them that at his three separate seats (of St. James's and Richmond and Nunsuch) set apart by his father for him, he caused money-boxes to be set up into which all who did sweare, in his hearing, should deposit coyne which was after given to the poor.

At sixteen yeares his Royal Father confer'd upon him the title of Prince of Wales, and he began seriously to advance himself so far as with modestie he might do in the affairs of the Kingdom which would one day be his, desiring to know of everything something and delighting all by his martial bearing.

The magnificence of his Creation [as Prince of Wales] will never be forgot: the proud river for two or three miles together was covered with pinnaces, barges, and boates: the Lord Mayor accompanied by thirty-six several livery companies rowing up the silver stream twords Richmond, where the Prince lay, accompanying him into Whitehall, where he was received by his Majestie, his Father, and welcomed by the High Court of Parliament and the Lords Spiritual and Temporall, with the joy and approbation of all.

And now he began to be a man, not only in stature but also in courage and wisdom, to the admiration of all, surveying with pride the mightie Inheritance of which he was the Heire Apparant and especially he did straine in the time of peace to prepare for Warre,[1] chiefly in ships accounted the brazen Wall of this Ile, intreating his Majestie to build him a ship called the Prince. And not content therewith he did also practise Tilting, Charging on Horseback after the manner of warre, with all other like inventions.

Then came talk of his marriage, to which he paid no heed, only that for Britaine's eternal felicity he would follow the streame of the King his Father's settled affection so that he would marry no Papist, being fully resolved that no bed was wide enough for two religions to lye in.

After the turmoil of previous reigns, a peace-loving Prince could not fail to be popular.

When it was observed that he had become thin and payle, general anxiety was felt by those about him: then he complayned of headache, yet when his father did send

[1] It is generally supposed that this is Washington's idea. The phrase is taken from a pamphlet published in 1618.

for him to come to him at Beaver Castle in Notingham-
shire, he did go, attending there one of the greatest and
best ordered feasts that was ever seen, at which he was
welcomed like a Princely Bridegroom, and but little
knew that this was his great farewel to his Father, Mother,
Sister, indeed unto the whole Court.

Returning to his home at Richmond he sent for his
physician, but he not daring to be too bold with his
Highness's body did only give unto him a Glister or purge.

Of what use is it to tell of the squabbles of the physicians who disagreed and whose drugs counteracted
each other?

Then came he to his Palace of St. James's where, feeling somewhat better and there being no one to say him
nay, he did on Saturday the 25th of October play at
tennis in his shirt only as though his body had been made
of brasse, and as if it were in the heat of summer, and
upon going to bed he complayned more than usual of
laziness and headache: from that bed he never rose.

The books from which I have been freely quoting
recite day by day the symptoms of his disease, and
the remedies which were applied: "Glisters" and
bleeding and fiery cordials and soothing lotions —

externall and internall, were tried and in vaine. Prayers
were prayed and sermons preached; finally the Archbishop
of Canterbury was sent for and he made so much the more
haste hearing that such great care had been taken of the
mortal body to the neglect of the immortal soul. The
same day a live cock was cloven into two parts by the
back and applied smoaking hot unto the soules of his
feet, also the cordials were redoubled in number and
quantity but all without profit.

The grief of all no tongues could expresse: several

times the news that he was dead passed into the city. People spent days and nights in the fields and lanes around St. James's Palace weeping and crying aloud in their agony: the doctors were at their wittes endes. His Majestie, the King, being unable to stand the strayne longer went to his hunting lodge, Tibbal's (Theobald's) twelve miles north from London, there to await the doleful tydeinges.

No one could be found who would assume final authority and responsibility: Dr. Mayerne, the Prince's chief physician, would not venture to do anything of himself without the consent of all the others, saying that it should never be said, in after ages, that he had killed the King's eldest sonne. At last someone greatly daring closed the door of the Prince's room in which he lay adying, keeping thereby the rabble out, so that there was comparative quiet therein, but nevertheless did the Prince's convulsions continue. . . . Sir Walter Raleigh, lying under sentence of death in the Tower, with the leave and advice of the Lords in Counsell sent to him a powerfull cordiall which, after it had been tasted and proved harmless, was given him, but in vaine as were also the most exceeding powerful and passionate prayers of Archbishops, Bishops, and Deanes.

And now, there being no remedy, death must needs strike the cruyl blow. Many times did he offer to shoot his dart and then draw back a little as if loath to kill so great a Prince, or perhaps awaiting the Angell to convey his Soule quick to Heaven, upon whose appearance he thrust his dart quite thorow, after which his Highness quietly, gently, and patiently half a quarter or thereabouts before eight of the clock at night yielded up his Spirit unto his Immortal Maker with as many Prayers, Teares, and strong cries as ever Soule was on Friday, the Sixt of November 1612.

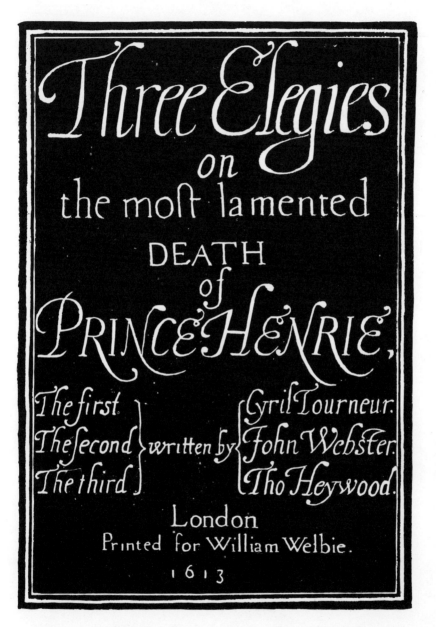

TITLE-PAGE OF THREE ELEGIES ON THE DEATH OF PRINCE HENRY

That the subject still retains its interest is shown by the fact that a few years ago no less a physician than Sir Norman Moore of St. Bartholomew's Hospital made, from published and unpublished sources, a careful study of the disease which caused the death of Prince Henry, and decided that it was typhoid fever, but at the time —

it was suspected that poison was the cause, administered either by his father out of jealousy or by papists, out of fear. Nor were these suspicions set entirely to rest by the opening of the body, which was effected in the presence of an immense number of Physicians, and Chirargions, Knights and Gentlemen,

who found — what they found: pages of noisome detail; after which the body was prepared for the funerals.

I use the word "funerals" advisedly, for they were many. From one room to another in the old Palace of St. James's, in that picturesque pile of buildings, only a stone's throw from where I write, now in the very heart of London, but then situated at the bottom of a shady lane, in broad green meadows, the corpse was carried first this way, and then that —

set down and took up againe, until the seventh day of December was come, a full month and a day after his death, when the final ceremonies were begun. The gentlemen of his Majestie's Chappell made woefull musick, singing mournefull ditties, commingled with prayers, until the night before the last funeral when his representation, that is to say, a waxen image made as like to him as possible could be, apparelled in his own cloathes and having over them the same Princelie robes he wore when his father, the King, created him Prince of Wales, with his crown upon his head, and his Garter, and his Collar, with a St. George about his neck, and his golden staff in his right hand lying crossed a little. In all thinges and in every way he was apparell'd as at the time of his creation, which being done his representation was laid on the top of the coffin containing his Royal body, and fast bound to the same, the head being supported by two cushions just as it was to be when it was drawne along the streets in the funeral charyot by eight black horses in black trapynges.

And now the most mournefull day of all being come the funerall set forth about ten in the morning and consumed about four hours in marshalling and marching the distance of one mile from St. James's Palace to Westminster Abbey being followed, as was thought, by two thousand mourners in black, the names whereof were now to no purpose, since together with their ranks and orders they are already printed in a book by all men to be seene.

As the funerall cortege passed along, the whole world sensible and insensible seemed to mourne. Innumberable men and women and children holding of their heads in their hands not being able to endure so sorrowful a sight, others holding up their hands passionately bewayling their great loss with Rivers, nay with Oceans of teares streeming from their eyes. At last to Westminster Abbey they came where, after much dolefull musick of all sortes being ended, the coffin was set under a great stately hearse, and the Archbishop of Canterbury, after a little pause and prayer, did with exceeding great passion make the Funerall Sermon of which I am loath to say anything, fearing to wrong so great and grave a person. Which being ended, the Earles, Lords, Barons, etc., retired, having each given up their several banners and honours which they carried. The Officers of his Household broke

HEARSE OF HENRY PRINCE OF WALES,
showing the "representation" on the coffin

their white staves and rods and placed them crosswise over the coffin, sygnyfying thereby the resigning of their places, after which the Greate Assembly dissolved.

At the end of these many and mournful proceedings, probably at night, the corpse, enclosed in a coffin of lead, was placed in a vault.

But the representation remained still under the Hearse to be seen of all for yet two weeks longer when decked and trimmed with cloathes as when he was alive; Robes, Collar, Crowne, and Golden Rodde in his hand, it was set up in a Chapell amongst the Representations of many Kings and Queens, his famous Predecessors, where it remainth forever to be seen.

Have I not said that "forever" is a long word? All that remains of all this glory is an empty box and a manikin in a crypt of the Abbey. I took much too much trouble to find it.

It is perhaps difficult for us to understand the great love that England had for this young man. His father was a slovenly, slobbering Scotch pedant, imported into England chiefly to keep peace between two powerful religious factions, which threatened at any moment to war upon one another. The common people had had enough of religious turmoil, with its bickerings, burnings, and beheadings; the constant fear in which men lived had made them willing to pay any price for peace. They were prepared to accept the Stuarts, and later the German House of Hanover — in short, anything, for the privilege of life unmolested.

Men had looked forward to being ruled by an Englishman — as they regarded Henry — rather than
by a woman, however great. King James was more
properly James the Sixth of Scotland than James
First of England, but Prince Henry, while he had
been born in Stirling, had grown up in or near
London. The people adored him: when men met in
the city they told one another how fortunate they
were in their Prince. Never before in the history of
England, and perhaps never since, have the people
been so loyal; never has the heir to the throne given

rise to such hopes or inspired every class of his coun-
trymen with such love and admiration as Henry,
Prince of Wales.

Upward of fifty books or pamphlets were published immediately or shortly after the lad's death. Most of them are unreadable to-day, but many possess peculiarities which are interesting to the book-collector. Some pages contain no words whatever, but are printed in solid black, as if to suggest that words fail to describe the grief of the author. In others the text appears in white against a black background, while the ornamentation and decoration of other pages consist of designs composed of skeletons, skulls, coffins, tombstones, and the like.

And it is to be remembered that, while most of these eulogies were written shortly after his death, some did not appear until after the death of his father, when there could have been but little hope of reward "for an unexpected fresh and violent outpouring of teares." Making due allowance for the wildly extravagant and bombastic language of poets and courtiers, his death was more sincerely mourned than the death of any sovereign. The prince was summed up by Bacon, the great Verulam, as being slow of speech, pertinent in question, patient in listening, and strong in understanding.

Let us close our eyes to the world around us for a moment and speculate as to what would have happened had Prince Henry lived to come to the throne instead of his brother, Charles First. Let us assume that he was not any of the things we have been told that he was, but that he had sense enough to keep his head upon his shoulders and his crown upon his head.

There would certainly have been no Cromwell, no stupid and cowardly James the Second, no four German Georges, perhaps no George Washington. Is it too much to say that no death in modern history has so influenced and changed the course of the whole world?

VII

A "DIVINE" AND HIS WORKS

That "one man's meat is another man's poison" is an old adage, and there must be truth tucked up in these old sayings or they would not become old; or to put the matter in Sancho Panza's words, "there is no proverb but what is true, because they are all drawn from experience." This thought, if it be a thought, came to me the other day when I read in a magazine that Professor Phelps was willing to "jeopardize what little good reputation" he had, — I am quoting his own words, — but that he wanted it distinctly understood that *Don Quixote* and *Tristram Shandy*, two books which the world has been applauding for some time, "are bores, colossal bores." He then went on to state that he knew that "the Don tilted against windmills; hence I wish he had tilted against the author of his being, who was one of the greatest windmills of all time"; and "as for *Tristam Shandy*," he says, "I might enjoy it if it were not so infernally dull."

This estimate does not sound exactly judicial to me. Certainly both books are to be skipped — most books are — and Professor Phelps must have the art of skipping, otherwise he would never get through the amount of reading he credits himself with. Or perhaps the amount accounts for his rather brash judg-

ment; he will not have forgotten the lines of another
famous professor who wrote: —

> Now there happened to be among Phoebus's followers,
> A gentleman, one of the omnivorous swallowers,
> Who bolt every book that comes out of the press,
> Without the least question of larger or less,
> Whose stomachs are strong at the expense of their head;
> For reading new books is like eating new bread —
> One can bear it at first, but by gradual steps he
> Is brought to death's door of a mental dyspepsy.

There we have, I think, the key to the situation:
"mental dyspepsy" is the complaint that Professor
Phelps is suffering from, and it is, I fear, too deeply
rooted for him to take the advice of a mere layman
like myself. Perhaps, however, he could be induced
to listen to a wise and sometimes caustic old gentleman, Augustine Birrell, who says somewhere that
"if one reads for any better purpose than to waste
time, the great thing is to keep pegging away at
masterpieces in cheap editions." This advice sounds
so good to me that I took it before I heard it.

A book that has survived the changes and chances
of this mortal life for three centuries, — the first
part of *Don Quixote* was published in 1605, — needs
no defense, and Sancho Panza and his master are
about as sure of living as any men in a book can be.
It comes down to the question, what constitutes
immortality in a book? A book appears and, if successful, is read for a time, enormously it may be, and
then, like Burns's snow-flake in a river, is gone forever.
This is the fate of most books: oblivion will overtake

this volume that you are reading, almost before you put it down. But occasionally — very rarely — there comes a book that makes its way slowly at first, and then with gradual increasing momentum, until at last it is read, or at least skimmed, by all the world. And after a century or so it takes its place as a "classic," by which we mean that "most men know it as they know a lord, by name, and then boast of its acquaintance." But if we look narrowly into the matter, we shall discover that these classics are full of the merit that Shakespeare has: in a word, of phrases or words that have become a part of our inheritance — and this is fame. There are names, and high names, too, that survive chiefly by reason of a single couplet; Lovelace, for example, whose

> I could not love thee, dear, so much,
> Loved I not honor more,

and

> Stone walls do not a prison make,
> Nor iron bars a cage,

are enough to keep him in the honor class.

In *Don Quixote*, however, we have much more than couplets; we have stories, and sayings, and words by the score, perhaps by the hundred, that pass current in all languages, certainly at least in English; proverbs which save time and add spice to conversation. All this is "as plain as the nose on a man's face." "Let us not mince matters"; if the Professor had "looked before he leapt," he would not now be making a "laughingstock of himself"; but "the least said the soonest mended." Here is a sentence composed almost at random out of sayings from a book that Professor Phelps roundly condemns. If, as Dr. Johnson says, "classical quotation is the parole of literary men all over the world," the ordinary man in conversation clinches his argument with a saying — taken from he knows not what.

And while *Tristram Shandy* is by no means a *Don Quixote*, it is a book that is not "infernally dull," as I hope to show — except in spots; and the wise reader will know what to do when he comes to them. I have read at it many times, indeed, I am not sure that it was not intended to be read that way; but I never read it right straight through — skipping the hard words is my custom — until a year or two ago, when, just as I was closing the door of my library for a journey abroad, my eye lighted on a first edition of the book, which had just come in from London, and I said to myself, "Where is that little India-paper edition complete in one volume, which will slip so handily into my pocket?" It was not far to seek, and it beguiled delightfully many a half hour on the deck of an ocean steamer or in the smoking-compartment of a railway train, or while waiting at stations in Italy, and once for an entire afternoon, when my wife forgot to keep an appointment and left me sitting for three mortal hours on a bench under a tree in the Giardino Garibaldi in Palermo — but of this anon.

Tristram Shandy was written by a witty clergyman; that is to say, by a man who after being born in Ireland, — English wits are almost invariably born in Ireland, — and being pushed through Jesus College, Cambridge, was pulled into the Church, where he had as little right to be as I have; and that made him a "divine."

Let us consider for a moment the ribald jester who died just one hundred and fifty-six years ago. He came of preaching stock; had an uncle who was a dean or something in York Minster — something with good pay attached to it, and pull. Those were the days — they're almost over now — when one "entered" the church very much as one now enters the theatre, just to see what was going on. If he got a good seat, a stall, he saw and took part in a fine performance; if he did not, he ate with the servants at second table.

I have said that Laurence Sterne had little calling for the Church; that he wrote a lot of sermons and preached them and published them and made money out of them, is nothing to the point. I have them in that case over there by the door, in boards uncut, and unopened too — and, by gad, they shall stay that way for me. And next to the sermons stands *Letters by Yorick* — Sterne's pen name: "Alas, poor Yorick! I knew him, Horatio: a fellow of infinite jest, of most excellent fancy" — and *Eliza* in two volumes, boards, also uncut; and three volumes more of letters published by his daughter after his death, "an elegant, accomplished little slut" (if the truth must be known, the words are her father's). These letters are badly edited, if indeed they can be said to be edited at all. The only holograph that I have been able to compare with the printed text shows sad ignorance of an editor's duty, which is either to print a letter verbatim or to let it alone.

And next to it is *Tristram Shandy*, a rather complicated bibliographical study. The first edition is in nine volumes, dainty little volumes such as were then the fashion, and they usually come bound in full morocco by Bedford or Riviere. Old calf sets occur occasionally, but they are scarce, and I suppose someone has a set in boards uncut, but this is an unheard-of rarity. The first pair of volumes has no printer's or publisher's name, and no place on the title-page. Probably the volumes were printed at York; the date is 1760. R. and J. Dodsley — London, the year following — are responsible for the second pair, the first volume of which has an engraved frontispiece after Hogarth, referring, however, to an incident which occurs in the fourth volume. The next pair of volumes have the imprint of Becket and Dehondt, London, 1762, who were also responsible for the completion of the work, the last volume of which appeared in 1767. Long before the story was told, pirated editions printed in Dublin and fake conclusions printed anywhere made their appearance, much to Sterne's disgust, for he was as keen as mustard for royalties, which were usually spent before they were received. Probably to inform his patrons that they were buying the authorized edition, it was usual for him to sign his name, "L. Stern," on the half-titles of volumes 5, 7, and 9. I have heard of booksellers taking advantage of their customers' ignorance to suggest that volumes so signed were Sterne's own copies; there are tricks in all trades, we are told.

Last, and perhaps best of all, is *A Sentimental Journey through France and Italy*, in two volumes, my copy of which, "entirely uncut, a fine unpressed copy" in original paper wrappers, was published in 1768, only a few weeks before the author's death.

What a life he led! Married to a woman whom he hated, — but whom he treated not so very badly, all things considered, — of too fragile a frame for robust vice, he managed by sly innuendo and a smile to suggest it wherever he went, and he went far and wide. No literary man in England was better known on the Continent than he, and he was welcomed and petted and fêted everywhere. And this was at a time when to be petted meant something: another parish, with no duties attached, if you were in the clerical line; or a post of honor or profit or both, if you caught the fancy of a reigning statesman; at the very least, a handsome purse from the noble lord, your host, as you stepped into your "chair." One wishes one could have more respect for a man who has given so much pleasure to the world, but in Sterne's case it is difficult.

Professor Wilbur L. Cross published some years ago *The Life and Times of Laurence Sterne,* one of the best books of its kind that I have ever read: he knows his subject thoroughly, and had the use of some fine hitherto unpublished material in the Pierpont Morgan library; I am glad to know that a new edition of this excellent work is impending.

Of Sterne's own books, the *Sentimental Journey* is better known than *Tristram;* it is much shorter, more delicate, more coherent, and less inspired, if one can use that word about anything Sterne wrote. In it occurs the phrase which has a Biblical ring and which the unknowing sometimes think comes from the Bible: "God tempers the wind to the shorn lamb."

Less than a month after its publication Sterne passed away in lodgings in Bond Street, London, and was buried in the burial ground of the fashionable church, St. George's, Hanover Square. But this was not the end. The graveyard was new; it was in what was then the suburbs; and shortly after his interment the grave was rifled and the corpse, that "bale of cadaverous goods," as he called his body, was sold to an anatomical professor at Cambridge. The gruesome story continues: the professor of anatomy invited two friends to view the dissection of the nameless corpse, and by chance, after the work was nearly over, out of curiosity one of them removed the covering from the face and then were revealed the features of the Reverend Laurence Sterne, a man whom he had known and seen in London not long before. The story goes that the skull reposes in the anatomical museum of the university. "Alas, poor Yorick!" in very deed.

In his heyday Sir Joshua Reynolds painted him, with his wig slightly awry and with what Thackeray — who hated him — calls a satyr's leer upon his face. The portrait now hangs in Lansdowne House in Berkeley Square. It was purchased by the third Lord Lansdowne just a century ago, for five hundred guineas. Sir Joshua has a note relative to the sitting: "Sterne is the lion of the town; engaged fourteen deep to dinner . . . his head topsy-turvy with his success and fame." Sterne rather than Gay should have been the author of the lines: —

> Life is a jest and all things show it;
> I thought so once and now I know it.

Let it be said that *The Life and Opinions of Tristram Shandy* is not a book for a child; not that a child is likely to — or indeed could — read it, and I think that few women do; at least I have never met but one who could confess to having done so. It is a book for men: that is to say, no man old enough to read it could be harmed by its smut, for it is admittedly a coarse book, and not with the robust coarseness of Fielding, say, which makes one laugh a good hearty laugh, but rather with the subtle slime which makes the knowing smile. But a book which has kept its vogue for one hundred and sixty-five years, and which is constantly being reprinted in popular editions and

LAURENCE STERNE
after a portrait by Sir Joshua Reynolds, now in Lansdowne House

read, notwithstanding its inordinate length and discursiveness, must have merit. It should not — indeed it cannot — be read in a hurry, and it must be skipped; but one must have the art of skipping; if this art is lacking, it should be read word by word, or many of its witticisms and beauties and naughtinesses, which are very subtle, will be lost. It is a book to read in bed: in a bed in which you sleep diagonally and in which you may chuckle or talk quietly to yourself without being told it is time to put out the light.

   Sooner or later I shall be asked who Tristram Shandy was and what sort of

THE

L   I   F   E

AND

O P I N I O N S

OF

TRISTRAM SHANDY,
GENTLEMAN.

Ταρασσει τὺς Ἀνθρώπὺς ϐ τὰ Πράγμαϊα,
αλλα τὰ περι τῶν Πραγμαϊων, Δογμαϊα.

VOL. I.

1760.

opinions he held, and I shall reply that I do not know; that it makes no difference, anyhow; and will talk of Uncle Toby and of his man, Corporal Trim. Uncle Toby! Who does not love him? Was there ever a finer gentleman? Think of all the gentlemen you know in flesh or fiction; they pale into insignificance beside my Uncle Toby; and for devotion, where shall you find the like of Corporal Trim's?

It is, I believe, generally admitted that the most charming letters are about nothing — much. But they must have style — style, humor, wit; it is wit that has kept *Tristram Shandy* not pure and sweet, — that it never was, — but alive after all these years. It is as verbose and rambling as an ill-constructed sermon. Much of it is stolen from Burton's *Anatomy*, which Dr. Johnson said was the only book that ever took him out of bed two hours earlier than he wished to rise (I have never understood this). But the best of it is Sterne himself. If anyone insists upon knowing who Tristram was, I shall reply that he was the nephew of Uncle Toby — and that is honor enough. Uncle Toby! "His character is one of the finest compliments ever paid to the human race," says Hazlitt. Uncle Toby is the hero; the "opinions" are those of his nephew.

In *Tristram Shandy* are some of the loveliest, some of the raciest, some of the wittiest stories ever written in English. The story of Le Fever is in every prose anthology, as it deserves to be, and made volumes five and six of the first edition go like wildfire when they appeared. In the account of the approaching death of Le Fever, a brother officer, Uncle Toby is so moved, although he has never seen the man, that he swears, "He shall not die, by G——." Then comes the supreme passage: "The accusing spirit, which flew up to Heaven's chancery with the oath, blush'd as he gave it in; and the recording angel as he wrote it down dropp'd a tear upon the word and blotted it out forever." Praise is superfluous; and in the face of this Thackeray says, "There is not a page of Sterne's writing but has something that were better away, a latent corruption — a hint as of an impure presence." What was it that General Wolfe said about Gray's "Elegy," the night before the attack on Quebec? "Now, gentlemen, I would rather be the author of those lines than take Quebec to-morrow." There is not a finer or more famous phrase in all literature than this.

In quite another vein is the story of the Abbess of Andoüillets and Margareta, which may be related briefly. It seems that the knees of the Abbess had become stiff and rheumatic from long kneeling on hard stones at her convent, and her efforts to secure relief from oils and fats, "smoak" and poultices, ointments and fomentations, having been unavailing, she was persuaded to try the hot baths of Bourdon. The Abbess could not, of course, go to the baths alone; she might indeed have taken a poor old sciatical nun with her, but she concluded that a novice of seventeen, fresh from the world outside, would be better company; and after many preparations they set out, having an under-gardener for their muleteer. How the muleteer, getting drunk during a pause in their journey, starts the donkeys off without his guidance, which was well-nigh useless anyhow, and how the donkeys, once stopped, cannot by any means be made to resume their travel, is told at length and with many a sly innuendo.

Finally, their efforts to start the donkey being unavailing, Margareta says she knows a word, two words in fact, which have never failed to start donkeys, however recalcitrant; but they are naughty words and must not be used except as a last resource. "Certainly not; what are they?" says the Abbess. "They are sinful in the last degree," replies Margareta. "Never mind, better that I should hear them than die unabsolved," says the Abbess, and at last Margareta whispers them into her ear. "You say one half the word and I the other," and Margareta cries her half and the Abbess the other, but the donkeys refuse to move. "Night is coming on: we shall be ruin'd and undone, we shall be ravished!" cries the Abbess in a voice of terror. "Ravished as sure as a gun," says Margareta, in a note in which no terror is discernible. "Louder and faster," cries the Abbess. The mules acknowledged their understanding by twitching their tails, but they declined to move. "Much louder and much faster," cries the Abbess. "Quicker still," cries Margareta.

"And did they reach the Baths of Bourdon?" asked my uncle Toby.

"That is more than I know," said Mr. Shandy.

There is another donkey story in the author's most characteristic vein. A donkey with two large baskets lashed to his back gets jammed in a doorway, so that he can neither go forward nor retreat. When

in doubt, a donkey eats. Sterne's donkey, fully
realizing his trouble, began munching the bitter
stem of an artichoke —

and in the peevish contentions of nature between hunger
and unsavoriness let it drop out of his mouth and picked
it up again . . . whatever life is to others 't is all bitterness
to thee . . . and now thy mouth is all bitterness . . . for
he had cast aside the stem . . . and thou hast not a friend
perhaps in all this world that will give thee a macaroon,

which our author proceeded to do. Now his enemies
say, — for he had enemies, — and his friends almost
admit, that Sterne would have been better employed
in taking care of a termagant wife dying of a con-
sumption in England than in sentimentally feeding
macaroons to a jackass in France; but there is the
story, writ for all time.

I have said that I found *Tristram Shandy* excellent
in the Giardino Garibaldi in Palermo. It came about
in this way. My wife and I had a rendezvous with a
lady in the English tea-rooms in the Piazza Marina;
when we got there I was confronted with a cascade
of steps. Now I can climb when required. I had
recently been to the top of Mont Saint Michel; but
I have been warned not to climb unnecessarily and,
a cup of Italian tea not being sufficiently alluring,
and having *Tristram* in my pocket, I determined
to await my lady in the garden. I read the story of
the donkey, and I waited, and read again, and
finally, looking up, I noticed that just in front of me
were two tiny donkeys, each hitched to a little

two-wheeled cart in such a way that if one donkey started for home he would pull the other donkey after him backward. Now 't is well known that a donkey can be made to do little against his will. One beast was tugging against the other, but the progress of each could be measured in inches. The carts, which had been driven into town early in the morning, loaded high with green vegetables, — on each of which reclined, doubtless, a lazy Sicilian, — were now empty, and the masters, the business of the day over, were now certainly drinking cheap Chianti, talking and gesticulating in one of those dark, evil-smelling caverns which opened across the street.

Suddenly the thought came to me: in what respect was I unlike the donkeys before me? I had been tethered with a word by my mistress, who had gone off to tea and talk, forgetful of my very existence. "We are asses," I said, "three of a kind"; and the donkeys nodded their heads in complete agreement. But was I not wiser than they, after all? I asked myself. They would have trotted home if they could and would have been well cudgeled for it; to avoid a beating I would stay on till my mistress came and released me.

A bell in a near-by steeple struck: it was five o'clock; it struck again: it was half past. It struck six: in imagination I began to chew the bitter stem of an artichoke. I had been left till called for — and forgotten. I hated those donkeys and was glad when something after six their masters came with high words, and in a threatening manner, I thought, but doubtless it was friendly, parted for the night, going in opposite directions. Leaving my bench in the street I went over to where a high-power automobile was standing and took my seat upon the running-board, intending to ask for a lift when its owner, whom I knew to be a gracious lady, came out — which she soon did.

"Why, you poor man!" she cried, when I told my pitiful story. "Let me go back and get you a cup of tea and some macaroons."

"No macaroons for me," I replied; "they will assuage my hunger; and I want to be hungry as well as angry when I get home."

We started, and in fifteen minutes we swung into a long tunnel of flowers which divides the fairyland gardens of my hotel from the rather sordid town of Palermo. In the Villa Igiea, mounted on terraced cliffs jutting into the blue Italian sky out of a still bluer Mediterranean Sea, I found my wife, sitting out a dance with a handsome young officer in the Italian army.

"Why, where have you been?" said she.

"And what did you say?" said Shandy.

"Some things are better left unsaid," replied my Uncle Toby.

But I suppose the story of the Widow Wadman's capture of my Uncle Toby is the great, long-drawn-out event of the book. If ever you, reader, are called upon to take part in a discussion as to what widow in fiction did her work with the greatest adroitness, don't forget the Widow Wadman, and remember that it was Uncle Toby's habit to court danger. Was he not an officer? Had he not faced peril unflinch-- ingly in the wars of the great Marlborough? And as the Austrian generals said of the conduct of Napoleon, that it was magnificent but it was not war, so Uncle Toby might have described the method of the widow: it was not intended to be a battle, but a siege; and all was progressing surely, if slowly, when, overhear- ing the method by means of which Corporal Trim was secured by his lady, the widow determined to take the works by direct assault. And then the odds were a thousand to one in favor of the lady. Seeing Captain Toby one day with his pipe, sunning him- self on a bench, she squeezed herself down upon it, and turning up her face to his, said: "I am half dis- tracted, Captain Shandy; something, a mote or sand, I know not what, has got into this eye of mine — do look into it." All is fair in love and war, we are told. There was neither mote nor sand, nor dust, nor chaff, nor speck, nor particle, but Uncle Toby would have been safer looking into the mouth of a cannon than into that lady's eye. My Uncle Toby could see absolutely nothing, and so said, but he could feel something: it was the widow spraying him with love and fire. The searching look into Mrs. Wadman's eye did the business; after that it was merely a question of when the surrender would take place. Success was

announced fifteen days before the event took place.
Uncle Toby's sister-in-law had the news conveyed
to her by Susannah, her maid, she having had it from
Corporal Trim, who had it from Miss Bridget, Mrs.
Wadman's servant, who, by putting two and two to-
gether repeatedly, arrived at the correct conclusion.

Tristram Shandy moves deliberately— sometimes it hardly moves at all — but it is a great book. And if the lesser book can be called the greater, *A Sentimental Journey* may be so described. I had it in my pocket during a recent journey in France and Italy, and almost came to the conclu-

A

SENTIMENTAL JOURNEY

THROUGH

FRANCE AND ITALY.

BY

MR. YORICK.

VOL. I.

LONDON:

Printed for T. BECKET and P. A. DE HONDT, in the Strand. MDCCLXVIII.

sion that I would prefer to read *A Sentimental Journey* rather than to make one. I am not a good
traveler; new sights and experiences weary me. It
is the same old problem that vexed the philosophers: whether it were better to kiss one girl a
hundred times or a hundred girls once. "I have
sixty years," and I have "seen Carcassonne" and

those interesting old Roman cities of Arles and Nîmes
and Avignon. At Avignon I thought of what Dr.
Johnson said to Boswell when asked by that interro-
gating genius whether he did not think the Giant's
Causeway worth seeing. "Worth seeing! yes, sir,
but not worth going to see." And upon another
occasion, when they had spent half a guinea to see
something which had disappointed them, he said,
"But, sir, we have half a guinea's worth of superior-
ity over those who have not seen it." That satisfaction, at least, is mine.

In Avignon a mistral was blowing. It was bitter
cold, and as we had been seduced into going over the
old palace, or prison, or fortress, occupied by the
Popes from thirteen hundred and something to thirteen hundred and something else, I swore gently but
firmly to myself that never again would I start out
upon the examination of an old barracks which would
necessitate my climbing interminable flights of stone
steps leading to cold and vaultlike chambers containing exactly — nothing. "Just like my father's
cow barns at home," remarked a Scotch girl who
had grafted herself on to our party, "only they
are cleaner."

Cold and hungry, I looked forward to my dinner.
The hour arrived; eagerly I sought the table and
gazed for a moment contemplatively upon a plate
of tepid water, slightly discolored, on the bosom of
which a fragment of cauliflower floated. It was soon
whisked away, being replaced by a small fish about

the size of a mature sardine, of the consistency of
rubber. I was reminded of the Raines' Law sandwich,
which in happier years one had to buy in New York
when one wanted to get a drink on a Sunday. Following the fish was the heart of an African artichoke
covered with a thick brown gravy, as though the hotel
authorities were ashamed to show it in its nakedness.
It in turn was followed by the *pièce de résistance* of
the dinner: two English sparrows, reclining upon their
backs on a small "canopy" of toast, with a dozen or
two canned peas rolling about the plate. A few leaves
of plantain, served with oil and vinegar, half a lady-
finger, set upright in a small cone of ice cream made
of condensed milk, a cup of a black and bitter mix-
ture called coffee, and the repast was complete. As I
left the dining-room, trying to dislodge my dinner, —
which had located itself in a 'ollow tooth, as the music-
hall artist has it, — my thoughts were of London. I
thought of the steaming basins of real turtle soup I
had devoured at Birch's in the City; of the saddles of
mutton with currant jelly at Simpson's; of the turbot
at Scott's; and the birds at Hatchett's. I thought of
the corned-beef hash with a poached egg and the delicious hot cakes and coffee that they serve you at
Child's in New York,—and elsewhere,—and I prayed,
fervently, that I might never again be obliged to eat
a table d'hote dinner, at least not in France. I was
aroused from meditation by confronting a sign:—

THIS HOTEL IS SOUGHT BY ROYALTY

If they don't find it, they really don't lose much.

In the drawing-room a double semicircle of ladies of varying degrees of spinsterhood sat around what had once been a small wood-fire; it was a room in which thought, reading, and conversation were impossible on account of two young persons' — each of the opposite sex — performance upon musical instruments: she upon the remains of a piano, he upon a fiddle. I recognized the artists; she earlier in the day had tried to inveigle me into hiring an automobile; he had showed us to our rooms upon our arrival. It was a desolating experience.

Slowly we made our way through the French and Italian Riviera to Genoa, where we spent a day or two at one of the finest and most expensive hotels in Europe, the Miramar, the destinies of which seem to be directed by a man whose resemblance to John L. Stewart, professor of economics at Lehigh University, was disconcerting. He, too, is an economist in his way: I believe him to be the lightning short-change artist of the world.

Who that knows him would not spend a day or two with Max Beerbohm, if he could? He lives in one of the loveliest places in the world, Rapallo. From the deck of the villino Chiaro he watches, year after year, the ever-changing and always beautiful Mediterranean, heedless that the world passes his door: let it pass. His talk is as whimsical as his writing, and his writing is — must I say, was? — the most subtle of his day and mine. "Collect" him; "And Even

Now" there is time. "No. 2. The Pines" is one of
the best essays of our generation. Far be it from me
to say that Max, "the incomparable Max," is no
longer young; he is not so young as he was thirty
years ago, when I first met him, but he is — in a way
— immortal. So much for my Sentimental Journey
through France and Italy.

Rome! And then London, my spiritual home,
which I made, as the Swede made the ferryboat, in
two yumps. In three days I was sauntering comfortably up Bond Street; my thought was of Laurence
Sterne. He died in lodgings in this street, "over the
silk-bag shop." Messrs. Agnew, the picture-dealers,
have built their premises upon the spot. He lived and
died a jester, and his end was pathetic. It is a serious
world, my masters.

VIII

LONDON IN THE EIGHTEEN-EIGHTIES

DINING once with a charming woman, and matching minds, as was our habit, about London, she asked me: "If you kept a public house in London, what would you name it?"

"Well," I replied, after a moment's thought, "if my 'pub' had a good connection — meaning thereby, if every old soak in the neighborhood preferred to buy his drink of me rather than of another — I should keep the old name, whatever it was. If, on the other hand, I had to name it myself, I should call it the 'Bunch of Grapes,' suggesting thereby expensive wines rather than cheap malt liquor; then also it would be called by the cockney the 'Bunch of Gripes' — and that would delight me. What would you call yours?"

"'The Marquis of Granby,'" she replied promptly; "I've always thought that a very elegant name. You'd call it 'Markis,' of course."

"Certainly I should," I replied. "What's your favorite railway-station?"

"Victoria, Brighton Line," she said. "And yours?"

"Oh, there's only one for me," I answered, "Euston, the station by which I first entered the great town, one evening in June, just forty years ago."

We drifted on to other subjects and the matter

went out of my mind until the other day, when, hap-
pening to pass the great granite portals of that station, I thought of the joy that was mine when I first
realized that I was actually in London.

I was traveling entirely by myself, and my chief
preparation for my tour had been a course of the
Rollo Books — I can hardly imagine a better. By
them I was in some measure prepared for whatever
came my way, whether "Upon the Atlantic," "In
London," or elsewhere. When my boat — the British
Prince, a small tub that sailed from Philadelphia —
touched at Queenstown, greatly to my surprise a
letter was put into my hand. It was from a young
lad, a distant cousin whom I had heard of only
remotely; but it welcomed me to English shores.

"If I knew what you looked like," he said, "I would
meet you at Euston." (I wondered where Euston
was.) But as my cousin was not prepared to recog-
nize me, his letter went on to say that perhaps I
would take a cab at the station and come along to
Number 2 Rupert Street, where I could live with
him, very cheaply, if I wanted to. When, upon arrival, I stepped out into the almost unspeakable
confusion of Euston, I wondered how ever was I to
make my way to my destination; but the difficulties
vanished as I approached them, and half an hour
later I was being welcomed by a boy about my own
age into a cheap and dingy boarding-house where
he was living, and found I could secure a tiny room, —
a mere closet in which I could sleep, — and that bed

and breakfast would be thirty shillings a week. The bargain was soon struck. I liked the price, even if I did not care for the accommodation, and we sallied forth into the streets.

I have, I suppose, been happier since — but not much. And London always makes the same appeal to me. I enter with a feeling of elation — supremely happy; I leave it with a feeling of depression. Some day I shall leave London and never see it again. Well, be it so; we can die but once.

The London of the eighteen-eighties was a much noisier and a far more crowded city than now. The streets were narrower and fewer; the great thoroughfares of Shaftesbury Avenue and the Charing Cross Road were not cut through; Kingsway and Aldwych were undreamed of; and above all, there were no tubes — only one underground railway, into which it was worth one's life to enter, so filled was it with filthy smoke and sulphurous gases, the accumulation of years. The noise of tens of thousands of horse-drawn vehicles made a confused and ceaseless roar, as of distant waves breaking upon a rocky shore. The streets were brilliantly lighted with gas lamps and alive with people surging in every direction; most men wore silk hats and carried canes; the poorer class looked very poor indeed and wore caps; soldiers, gayly dressed, with tiny round caps about the size of pill boxes, held on over one ear by a narrow strap, carrying canes about as thick as a lead pencil and two feet long, were everywhere in evidence.

"So this is London," I said to myself.

We ate something, somewhere; I have no idea where or what, for my friend had said to me, "I have half a sovereign, let's go to the theatre. Florence St. John [pronounced "Sinjin"] is playing in *Olivette*. She's a beauty! I don't suppose you have ever heard of *Olivette*."

"Don't you?" I cried. "If Florence St. John can beat Catharine Lewis singing and dancing in *Olivette*, she must be a good one. I know it, every bit of it, words and music. Let's go to the theatre by all means."

I wonder how many, if any, of my readers will remember Audran's merry comic opera? And if they do, whether they can sing the interpolated "Torpedo and the Whale" song? The chorus, which came in the middle of each verse and was supposed to be the murmur of a seashell, nothing but "Oh-o-o-", continued until all the pretty girls were out of breath, when the song went on again. These are the words as I remember them:

> In the North Sea lived a whale,
> Big in bone and large in tail,
> CHORUS: *Oh-o-o-o-o-o-o-o-o-o-o-o,*
> This whale used unduly
> To swagger and bully,
> And oh, and oh,
> The ladies loved him so!
>
> All went well until one day
> Came a strange fish in the bay;

CHORUS: *Oh-o-o-o-o-o-o-o-o-o,*
This fish was indeed, oh,
A Woolwich torpedo —
But oh, but oh,
The ladies loved him so!

"Just you make tracks," cried the whale,
Then he lashed out his tail;
CHORUS: *Oh-o-o-o-o-o-o-o-o,*
The fish, being loaded,
Then and there exploded —
And oh, and oh,
That whale was seen no mo'!

These words I sang softly to myself (I was always singing in those days, and silly music still has great charm for me) as I walked through the streets to the old Gaiety Theatre. It was, if my memory serves me, Louise Baudet, a French soubrette, who gave this song its vogue, and I can yet hear her fetching delivery of the words, "Ze ladie' luv heem zo." Anyhow, this particular song was not well sung at the Gaiety, but on the whole I was forced to admit that never before had I seen such a wonderful performance. Florence St. John was superb; she danced and sang all the songs I knew so well, and I was in the seventh heaven of delight. I was told that she was a very naughty woman and that that wealth of golden hair was her own — or was n't — I forget which. I vowed it made no difference, and it hardly seemed possible that anyone so beautiful — in tights — could be so very bad. Plainer women had set such rumors afloat out of mere jealousy. If anything could make me happier than I was it would be to meet Florence St. John in the flesh — there was a good deal of it.

"Wait till you see Marie Tempest," said my friend.

We went to bed. In five minutes I was asleep, in another five, seemingly, I was awake, and, if I ever knew that London was a late riser, I had forgotten it. There was much to be seen. I would get up and see it. It was almost seven o'clock. Dressing quietly, — for not a sound was to be heard in the house, — I went downstairs and let myself out into the street. Not a soul was in sight. Of the roar of the traffic, which had so impressed me the night before, nothing was to be heard. It seemed very strange that the pulse of London should have ceased beating. I did not know which to see first: the Tower or Westminster Abbey. Consulting my map, I found the Abbey to be the nearer and I quickly found my way into Trafalgar Square and walked rapidly on through Whitehall, stopping for a moment opposite the Horse Guards. Reaching the Abbey, I tried the door. I might just as well have tried the door of the Bank of England. It was a little better than half past seven. I think I had not passed a single person on my walk. I walked by and admired Westminster Hall and the Houses of Parliament, and crossed over Westminster Bridge.

Then I began to feel hungry, very. I tried the doors of several restaurants — finally one yielded to my hand. I went in; on the bare wooden tables were stacked equally bare wooden chairs; harpies were on their hands and knees, scrubbing with an ecstasy I had never seen before. I asked for coffee and a roll. I might just as well have asked for canvasback duck and champagne. This occurred at Lockhart's; these establishments are gone now — if I remember correctly, they have been swallowed up by the A. B. C.'s. I then decided to return to Rupert Street, trying restaurant doors as I did so, always with one result. Entering the house, — I had a key, — I went to my friend's room and saw him preparing for his ablutions in about a quart of very hot water in a small basin. He asked me where I had been. I told him. "My word! you are early," he said. "Go downstairs. I'll join you in a few minutes. You'll find my newspaper at my place in the breakfast-room — I take in the *Chronicle*." In England a man never merely takes a newspaper; he always takes it in.

I had a very bad cup of tea, an egg that had met with an accident, bread, butter, and something that was called marmalade — but I was in London and I was very happy.

My mind is on the theatre; why should I stop the quick flow of recollection to speak of the major sights of London? They remain for all to see. The theatre, the music hall, are changing out of all recognition. Where are our comic songs? And our comic singers? And our fun-makers generally? The movie, the cinema, has destroyed them. I sing the songs of yesteryear.

Number 2 Rupert Street is next to the corner of

Coventry, and just across, on the opposite corner of what would still be Rupert Street if that thoroughfare had not tired of its name, was the Prince of Wales's theatre. At that theatre a young and beautiful girl, as exquisite as a Dresden-china shepherdess, — her name Marie Tempest, — was playing the name part in an operetta called *Dorothy*. The score was composed by Alfred Cellier, *chef d'orchestre* at the Savoy Theatre, who also did the music for Gilbert's *Mountebanks* after his falling out with Sullivan, but *Dorothy* was his great success.[1] Over the gulf of years I remember it as a sort of combination of *Erminie* and *Robin Hood*. It was lovely! There was a fine song, "Be wise in time, O Phyllis mine," and another, "Queen of my heart," sung by Hayden Coffin, then in his prime, that I thought one of the finest songs I had ever heard. They might seem rather flat to-day, but at the time — it was forty years ago, dear reader, and I was twenty — I thought nothing more melodious had ever been written. And there was a hunting-song that almost turned me into a sportsman. The chorus, sung by the Squire, went like this: —

> Here's to the man that's content with his lot,
> Who never sits sighing for what he has not,
> Who's peaceful and happy with what he has got!
> Here's a welcome for all to Chanticleer Hall!

I liked the sentiment and I liked the music. Night

[1] As originally published, I said I did not think that *Dorothy* had been played in the United States. A hundred people rose up to correct me, including a man, now a college professor, who said, "I can swear that it was played in the opera house in Peoria, Illinois, in 1891, for I sang in the chorus!"

after night I used to climb to the gallery of the Prince of Wales's, until I knew the words and music so well that I could have taken any part, on short notice.

And in after years, whenever and wherever Marie Tempest was playing, I always used to see her and with all the enthusiasm of youth. She played Kitty Carroll in *The Red Hussar* and subsequently toured the country in *The Fencing Master*. The Lord has so constituted men that a pretty woman in tights is not an unattractive sight. How charming and graceful she was with the foils! And did she not make our hearts beat when she sang her fine song: —

> If the heart of the maid you 'll win and wear
> You must carry your sword in air,
> Throw down the gauntlet then and there;
> You must fight for her,
> You must die for her,
> Give up life at her command.

I was ready to do so; in Belle Greene's words, "I 'll tell the world."

Finally she gave up comic opera and became a comedy actress of charm and grace, occasionally singing some simple song with such skill as only a cultivated musician can, playing her own accompaniment. Once I saw her as Polly Eccles in Robertson's old-fashioned but amusing play, *Caste*, and more recently — but Marie Tempest is only of yesterday — or is it to-morrow? — and the whole world is at her feet.

The last time I saw her I did what I had always

been threatening to do: I told her that I loved her. But many men have told her so, and my declaration occasioned her no surprise. It came about in this way: it was during the war, and for economy's sake we had closed our house in the country and were living at a hotel in Philadelphia. One evening, after the play, she came into the supper-room with her husband, Graham Browne, and seated herself at a table not far from where my wife and I were sitting. On the spur of the moment I got up, and telling my wife that something very pleasant, or very unpleasant, was almost immediately going to happen to me, I went over to where she sat and, holding out my hand after the manner of an old friend, I said, "Miss Tempest, I cannot suppose that you remember me; but we have met many times in London."

She gave me her little hand with the merest trace of bewilderment, and asked me to sit down. As I did so, I observed that it was in 1884, when she was playing in *Dorothy* at the Prince of Wales's, and that I had never forgotten and never should forget how unspeakably lovely she was. Instantly she became the actress again and, holding my hand to detain me, said, "Run away, my boy, run away; there was no such year!"

"I have left my wife over there," I went on, pointing to my table, "to come and sing to you 'Be wise in time.' It may be a little late, but — "

"It is, it is!" she cried, with a laugh. "But do you know my husband?" Then followed about the merriest ten minutes' talk I have ever had, when, telling her that I should love her to my dying day, I returned to the wife of my bosom, whom I have always suspected of hoping that I would meet with a rebuff.

A few minutes later Graham Browne got up and coming to my table, held out his hand to my wife, saying that as I had been making love to his lady he thought it only fair that he should be allowed the same privilege. So the honors were even, and I am waiting anxiously for our next encounter. Please Heaven it may soon come!

Theatrical reminiscence is rarely interesting. The stage from the front is all motion and light and color; one would say that an actor's life could not fail to be delightful; but in reality it is not so. It is a life of difficulty, drudgery, and jealousy; and when one comes to read of it, one is confronted by a maze of names, real and fictitious, and dates which are useful but not inspiriting. In writing about the success of this actor in that part, or the failure of another in some other part, one finds one's self indulging in exclamations rather than explanations. Indeed, how is one to suggest the power of a glance, a gesture, and a voice, by a written word? The actor's is a fleeting art. Perhaps it is only fair that this should be so, for what other artist enjoys such immediate and tumultuous applause? The author produces his effect in his study, alone; the artist paints his picture, wondering whether the public will accept it; the successful actor is instantly rewarded — and almost as instantly forgotten. Confronting these difficulties, I want to speak of Irving and Terry.

Charles Lamb once wrote, "I have no ear"; and then went on to explain. In like manner, I have no eye. When by chance I remember a face, I rarely fasten the proper name to it. But I have "ear," and after a lapse of years I can yet hear, in imagination, Ellen Terry as Beatrice say to Henry Irving as Benedick, "I wonder that you will still be talking, Signior Benedick. Nobody marks you"; and I can still see the lift of his eyebrows as he replies, "What, my dear Lady Disdain! Are you yet living?" and a moment later, when she says she would rather hear a dog bark than a man swear he loves her, he replies, "God keep your ladyship still in that mind! So some gentleman or other shall 'scape a predestinate scratch'd face."

These words, uttered in the Chestnut Street Opera House in Philadelphia in 1883, still ring in my ears; from that moment the great theatrical passion of my life has been Irving and Terry. All the scenes of *Much Ado* — it was the first of Shakespeare's comedies that I had seen — come before me as I write. How electrified I was when Beatrice in the church scene cries out to Benedick to "kill Claudio!" And who that has heard it can forget Benedick's soliloquy in the garden, in which he details the charms a woman must have ere he marry her, ending, "and her hair — her hair shall be of what color it please God."

I have heard it said that Irving could neither talk, walk, nor act: that his mannerisms were offensive, that he was "always Irving." I am willing for the sake of the argument to admit all that may be said in his despite; but no actor in my day had such intellectuality, was so full of that quality we call magnetism, without which an actor cannot reach the top of his profession. Call to mind Creston Clarke: he had a fine stage presence; a beautiful voice; he was conscientious and painstaking; yet he left one cold. Irving was electrical; one knew him for a great man. Who that has seen him can forget his noble brow, his piercing eye, his long and graceful hands? And as for Ellen Terry ("dear Ellen Terry," as Irving always called her in the little speeches which he used to make before the curtain), her delicious voice is still ringing in your ears if, unluckily, your ears are as old as mine. Shall you ever forget her fascinating, if irregular, beauty?

When and where and in what I saw these complementary and supplementary actors, what matters it? Suffice it to say I saw them in all or almost all their great parts: in *Romeo* — in which I confess Irving was awful but Terry lovely; in *Lear* and *The Merchant;* in *Macbeth*, in *Hamlet* — which was, I think, Irving's greatest part; in *The Vicar of Wakefield*, during one scene of which every man, woman, and child in the audience cried as frankly and openly as one does at a funeral. How well he played Charles the First! Certainly no actor ever looked the part more perfectly

SIR HENRY IRVING

than Irving: I can see him now in the leave-taking scene, with Ellen Terry crying quite as much as Henrietta Maria in real life could have done.

Then there were those fine plays in which Irving acted without Terry — *Louis XI*, *Waterloo*, and *The Bells*. In these, especially in *Waterloo*, Irving was supreme. As a character study it remains unsurpassed. *The Bells* I first saw in Philadelphia one winter's night, when there was so much snow on the ground that the street cars were not running, and I had to walk home after midnight, a distance of several miles. I had never seen such acting before. The bells continued to ring in my ears as I trudged along, and occasionally actual sleigh-bells could be heard. To this day, I never hear sleigh-bells of a winter's night without thinking of Irving in the death scene where, as Mathias, he cries, "Why is not Christian here?" Sound seems to have for me the reminiscent quality that smell has for others.

In the early productions the part of Christian was taken by the gifted young actor William Terris: who ever saw a better lover than he? What a matinee idol he would have made! Only they hardly had matinee idols in those days. And what a handsome and reckless young villain he was as Thornhill in *The Vicar of Wakefield!* Poor fellow! When still a young man, not having an enemy in the world, he was stabbed by a lunatic at the stage-door of the Adelphi.

I saw Irving in *Ravenswood*, — a lugubrious dramatization of *The Bride of Lammermoor*, — which cannot, I think, be called one of his successes; in *The Amber Heart*, of which I remember nothing; and in *Madame Sans-Gêne*, of which what I remember I do not care for. What did, however, delight me, was Tennyson's *Becket*, produced in 1893, a few months after the great poet's death. Incidentally, in the years to which I am reverting I scarcely ever went into Westminster Abbey without treading upon the new-made grave of some great man whose name was so vital to me that it seemed as if I were treading on a living thing. The names of Tennyson, Browning, and Irving instantly occur to me. Great men don't die to-day — they are all dead.

But to return to *Becket*. It was a beautiful, dignified performance, for which Irving was by nature especially suited. With what exquisite care it was produced! How well one remembers the beauty of the first act. The curtain rises and reveals two men playing a game of chess; there is complete silence for a time; then moves are made; and at last the King, beaten, knocks over the chessboard, and Church and State in the persons of Becket and the King come actually to grips.

I never pass the Lyceum Theatre in Wellington Street — and I passed it no later than last night on my way to see a sporting melodrama, *Good Luck*, at Drury Lane — without thinking of the wonderful "first nights" when it was the most fashionable theatre in London. For full twenty years Irving was on the crest of the wave. Nightly people stood in line at the pit entrance for hours, waiting for the doors to open; and when, to save them from fatigue and exposure, Irving permitted them to secure reserved seats at the regular admission prices, they were so outraged that immediately they got in they tore up the seats and a riot was with difficulty averted. Who ever heard of the pit being reserved? A three-century-old tradition had been violated; the old order of things was quickly restored. What is the Lyceum now? It is given over to Hall Caine melodrama at popular prices; no theatre in London has fallen so low.

It is not, perhaps, surprising that Irving's greatest financial was not his greatest artistic success. *Faust,* the most melodramatic spectacle produced up to that time, has always seemed to me unworthy of the great traditions of the Lyceum — as better suited to Drury Lane, although Irving's physical gifts and peculiarities especially fitted him for the part of Mephisto. In these days, when the production of elaborate spectacles is a matter of such ordinary event as to call for no comment whatever, a run of six hundred nights and "takings" of a million dollars seem nothing remarkable; but in 1885 the world gasped. And well it might. Irving employed the best artists and spared neither pains nor expense to secure the most wonderful effects. The scene in the Brocken was really marvelous: elaborate electrical effects were used for the first time in a theatre; electrically charged iron plates were so placed upon the stage that, when one stood upon two of them, an electric circuit was completed. In the fight between Faust and Valentine, when their swords clashed, sparks flashed therefrom, as occasionally they did from Irving as Mephisto; and when he, in a scarlet robe, with red lights playing on him, raised his tall figure to its full height and hurled his curse at all and sundry — well, the audience fairly gasped. Ellen Terry as Marguerite was lovely, as always; but my own feeling was that the play was not worthy of the powers of the actors. Irving was at his best in subtly intellectual parts — parts in which the workings of his refined and melancholy face and, above all, of his wonderful eyes, could be seen to better advantage than during the play of colored lights, in clouds of steam, and amid the crash of stage thunder. I always regretted that I did not see him as Alfred Jingle, for in eccentric comedy Irving was as remarkable as in tragedy. And in my time, there never was, I think, a better melodrama than *The Lyons Mail*, in which Irving played the double rôle which gave peculiar scope to his ability. His quick change from sardonic ferocity to repressed pathos was marvelous.

Alas! that there is always an apex to an actor's career — to any career. Why can we not, having been present at the glorious ascent, be spared the pain of witnessing the declension of our idols! Ellen Terry, the lovely and lovable, whose voice was music and whose smile a reward for a day's labor, began to grow old; after twenty-five years together she and Irving

ELLEN TERRY

parted. There was no quarrel; as has been said, their separation was due to the fact that she was no longer suited to play young girls' parts, and to redeem financial losses Irving became more and more inclined to melodramatic rôles in plays in which there was no part for Terry. Could she, who had delighted the town as Juliet, come to play the Nurse? Irving, never a robust man, toward the last played against great physical weariness, and he died in harness. Becket was his last part, and his last words spoken on the stage were: —

"Into Thy hands, O Lord — into Thy hands!"

At the bottom of St. Martin's Lane, not far from the world's worst statue, — that of Edith Cavell, — is a statue of Henry Irving, erected to his memory by friends in his profession. It shows Irving in academic robes, and is in a deplorable condition: anything long exposed to the damp air of London soon becomes covered, as with a veneer, with grime and dirt. The statue should be cleaned; a few buckets of hot water and soap would soon set things right. I must write a letter to the *Times* about it. In the Guildhall Art Gallery, perhaps the most incongruous collection of art objects in the world, is a beautiful marble statue of Irving as Hamlet by Onslow Ford, the talented sculptor, who died young. If it could have been produced in bronze it would have been a much finer monument to the great actor than the one which now represents him as an academician.

In the days I am reviewing, just round the corner from the Lyceum was the Gaiety Theatre. It was well named. The old building was swept away when the Strand was widened and Aldwych built; to me, the name of the present Gaiety is a misnomer. Music and mirth have departed from it; I have n't seen a good show there for years.

In the old days, as soon as I reached London I secured lodgings and then drove to the Strand and bought theatre tickets at the Lyceum and Gaiety for alternate evenings. Those were the days — or nights, rather — when they always ran a burlesque at the Gaiety. They were light and witty and took a lot of acting, and I think it will be admitted that never before or since, on the London stage or any other, has there been seen such beautiful dancing. Kate Vaughan is credited with having introduced a new style, which came to be called "skirt dancing." She was enormously popular, and at the height of her career is said to have received one pound per minute for her work upon the stage. "The poetry of motion" is a phrase which must have been invented to describe her exquisitely rhythmical movement. Later on came Sylvia Gray, Letty Lind, Marion Hood, and a host of others, all of whom danced divinely. There was no suggestion of vulgarity in the best dancing at the Gaiety; rather it seemed as though a number of singularly beautiful and refined, creamy, country girls, in long frocks, soft and fluffy, with innumerable colored-silk petticoats, had stumbled into the theatre

LETTY LIND
one-time queen of the Gaiety Theatre

while on their way to a very swagger garden-party and, having done so, decided to lark it a bit with some interesting men they had quite innocently discovered. Then the orchestra began a tune, as infectious as it was original, and in a moment the stage was a blaze of multicolored Liberty-silk petticoats, out of which would occasionally project a silk-stockinged leg and a dainty foot. In those days the *jeunesse dorée* of London might nightly be seen in the front rows of the stalls, picking out their brides — "reinvigorating the peerage," it was called.

How those Gaiety shows — *Miss Esmeralda, Faust up to Date, Ruy Blas or the Blasé Roué*, and the rest — caught the town! They were full of comedy — not too refined — and were as English as boiled beef and carrots. The English have always been great rhymers and punsters; puns were as common on the old Gaiety stage as flowers are in the country, to mutilate one of Oscar Wilde's best witticisms. What fun was made by that great comedian, Fred Leslie, so graceful and accomplished, who died when he was but thirty-seven, his ambition to play Hamlet unachieved! Fred Leslie! he was, I think, the most gifted comedian I have ever seen: he was tall, handsome, laugh-provoking, humorous, and he sang and danced to perfection. He usually played against Nellie Farren, "our Nelly," as she was popularly called. She played street-urchin parts mostly, and at sixty was divine in tights. In what did she sing that fetching song, "I'm a jolly little chap all round"? She had graduated from the Old Vic and was an accomplished actress before she became the star of the Gaiety — if the Gaiety can be said to have had any one bright particular star. She did not have an especially good singing voice, but she had wit, a rare thing in woman, and she was tireless in her efforts to please. I did not see all the Gaiety successes, and years have blunted somewhat my recollection, but looking backward I seem to remember best *Ruy Blas*. The music was by Meyer Lutz, and the words by the best librettists of the time. I wish to go on record as saying that never was such dancing. The "Pas de deux," "de quatre," and "de huit" were delightful, and as an eccentric dancer I never saw a better than Fred Story. Memory is assisted by my discovery not long ago, in a little-used desk, of a lot of photographs, among them one of Leslie and Nelly, both dressed as schoolgirls for a song, "Ma's Advice." The fascinating dance which followed each verse was danced on their slates; the patter of their feet still sounds in my ears. And in romantic vein was Leslie's "Whistling Lullaby," the while he did marvels with a sword. Then there was "The song that reached my heart," which drifted into "Home Sweet Home," and "Johnny Jones and His Sister Sue," interpolated — if anything can be said to be interpolated into a hodge-podge; and "Killaloe," which went something like this: —

>Now I happened to be born
>At the time they cut the corn
>Quite contagious to the town of Killaloe,

and I remember that it had a rattling good chorus.

FRED LESLIE AND NELLIE FARREN
in the Gaiety Burlesque: "Ruy Blas and the Blasé Roué"

I have mentioned Letty Lind: she was a tall, blonde, dangerously demure creature who early danced and sang — and not too well — her way into the hearts of her audience and stayed there; but my own passion was for Sylvia Gray, who is now the Mrs. Fenwick one reads about in the newspapers as a daring rider in the Quorn Hunt. I remember her as tall and slender; now she probably rides to keep down her weight.

And there was Arthur Roberts, another Gaiety wit! The spirit of comedy seems to have deserted the stage to-day. One form of amusement crowds out another. The Gaiety burlesques of my youth — themselves the followers of opera bouffe, an importation from the Continent — gave way to musical comedies, — *Morocco Bound* was the first of them, — as these have given way to vulgar and meaningless *revues.*

I was speaking of Arthur Roberts; I saw him at the Pavilion a year or two ago, playing the part of an octogenarian in a Bath chair at Brighton, and doing it very well too, talking to another old crony of his experiences in London before the war — with Napoleon. But Arthur Roberts was a wag off the stage as well as on: I remember a story of which he was the hero. They are always holding exhibitions of one kind or another in London; the Motor Show is the latest of them; but in the year I have in mind they had an exhibition of foodstuffs — they referred to it as the "Healtheries." Food, *en gros et en petit,* was exhibited and occasionally some samples would be given out. Well, one day Arthur Roberts had the bright idea of having a lot of cards printed: PLEASE TAKE ONE HOME. These he stuck freely over pyramids of exhibits, tins of sardines, bottles of olives, boxes of dates, and the like, with the result that, before the distracted exhibitors realized what had occasioned it, thousands of small parcels were set in motion as if by magic.

But good things must come to an end: Fred Leslie died, Nellie Farren retired wisely at the height of her fame, and the famous beauties married and lived happily ever after — let us hope! A new theatre, Daly's, opened to divide with the Gaiety the patronage of those in search of music and laughter. Musical comedies became the rage and four of them, *The Geisha, San Toy, A Country Girl,* and *The Merry Widow* ran for a total of ten years. One of the greatest successes of a slightly earlier period was *The Belle of New York,* an importation which succeeded in spite of a one-time prejudice against an American musical comedy. It ran somewhere over there for two years or more, thanks to its tuneful music, and the ability of that excellent comedian, Dan Daly, and the charms of the demure Salvation Army Girl, Edna May, who soon became a peeress and is now the widow of one of America's very rich men.

Shall we ever forget *Florodora*, with its famous double sextette, "Tell me, pretty maiden"? There are ladies, now firmly established in high places, who owe their rank largely to the fact that in the original sextette they were given a chance to display such charms as, in the past, have changed the course of empire. When I saw *Florodora* in London, Marie Tempest was no longer in the cast; therefore I never heard her sing "When I leave town." You remember it? One verse goes: —

> When I'm up, just for the day,
> London seems so bright and gay,
> Policemen smile,
> As I drive thro' the park in style!
> Busmen greet me from above,
> Cabmen drive me just for love,
> And every waiter says that he
> Waits exclusively for me.
> I'm known everywhere,
> From Bayswater to Berkeley Square,
> I've got that sort of an air,
> That positively knocks 'em over.

And she had, too.

With *The Arcadians*, musical-comedy shows came practically to an end. It ran over two years in London and then came to New York where I first saw it. I forget the name of the man who played the high-comedy part in London; but the lugubrious jockey with his song, "Always merry and bright," was the inimitable Alfred Lester. In it too was Connie Ediss, a vulgar cockney comedienne with a rasping voice, graduated from "the halls" — a great favorite of mine. And what was the name of the girl who was so tired of violets but not of roses? Oh! yes, I remember; it was Phyllis Dare in London and Julia

Sanderson in America. Blessings on them both for the joy they have given me!

But I must be careful not to mix my dates. I am verging upon the present. Most writing about the theatre is done by old men, who paint the past in radiant colors against the dull background of the present. I cannot think of myself as an exception to this rule, but before leaving this subject I want to remind my severest critic — my wife — that twenty-odd years ago, when we were enjoying to the full the wonderful shows then being given at Weber and Fields' in New York, I said that never before had there been and in all probability never again could there be assembled in any theatre such a brilliant cast as that which, in addition to those two clever comedians themselves, included Charles Ross, Peter Daly, and Dave Warfield among the men, and Lillian Russell — and here I fall into reverie from which I do not wish to be disturbed.

I could, if it were necessary, give the exact date upon which I took a young and charming lady — the lady aforesaid, indeed, now a grandmother and wearing glasses very becomingly — into a small music-hall in the Strand, and saw, through a haze of fog and tobacco smoke, a large fat man in ridiculous trousers, and listened to a song in which occurred words something to this effect: —

> They want a man for the Prince of Wales
> And they're after me, after me;
> I'm the individual they require.

"Isn't he wonderful!" I said to my little bride,

gasping for breath at my side. "That's Herbert Campbell, one of the most popular music-hall artists in London."

"Artists!" the girl cried, "I think he's disgusting!"

"Never mind," I replied, "that feeling is like sea-sickness; you'll get over it. Keep quiet and listen to the words and try to learn them"; and joining in the chorus, I sang at the top of my voice: —

I'm the individual they require!

Herbert Campbell was a large man with an unctuous voice, enormously popular with his audience and much in demand for pantomimes at Drury Lane, for which, on account of his size, he was particularly well adapted.

His once popular song would n't go now, for the present Prince of Wales is the most popular man in England.

Who shall explain the popularity of a song? What quality is it of words or music that gives it vitality? When I was last in Buffalo I visited the Grosvenor Library; I hope some day we shall have as fine an institution in Philadelphia; it is so quiet, yet gives the impression of being intensely alive. That it is so I am sure, else my friend Judge Louis B. Hart would not devote so much of his time to it. Under his direction an effort is being made to preserve for all time the once-popular songs of the nation, the abstract and brief chronicles of their time. Songs may be as important in a nation's history as its laws; frequently they are written by wiser men. I hope he will not overlook that recent lyric gem: "Does your spearmint lose its flavor on the bedpost over night?" And I wonder whether he would mind my referring to a little incident which occurred at the time of my visit. I shall take a chance and tell it. We were in the fine room devoted to music, in which is domesticated a grand piano, when Judge Hart asked me what was the first song I remembered hearing. Promptly I began to sing a song that I had heard a clown sing at a circus a hundred years before in Fort Scott, Kansas.

> "I'll never kiss my love again
>   Behind the kitchen door,
> I'll never pinch her funny-bone
>   Till it is growing sore,
> I'll never" . . .

do something else, I have forgotten just what; to my delight Judge Hart went to the piano, and picking out an accompaniment, finished the verse. He's the Judge for my money! The next time I'm tried for arson or petty thieving, it shall be before Judge Hart.

Let us join in singing "Grandfather's Clock," which swept over America in the Centennial year, 1876. And let us not forget "Silver Threads among the Gold," the author of which, a battered and destitute old man, was found some twenty years ago dead in a mean lodging-house in Philadelphia. Yet at one time, wherever he went, he might have heard someone singing: —

> But, my darling, you will be
> Always young and fair to me!

And only a few days ago the widow of this forgotten

genius, to whom the song had been the tribute of her youth, died after many years of poverty and unhappiness. She too was found alone in a desolate room. She had n't seen her husband for ten years before he died. On a copy of "Silver Threads," which the police found in the author's hands, was scribbled a line: "It's hard to grow old alone"; doubtless it is so. I find it hard to grow old in tandem.

Do you remember "After the Ball," which is the musical monument of the World's Fair in Chicago in 1893? These unconsidered trifles have, of course, no musical or literary value, but in after years they will be interesting as showing the varying sophistications of their day.

To return to London. In what year was it — upon the day when it had been discovered that Charles Stewart Parnell, the great Irish leader, had been indulging in· an illicit amour with Mrs. O'Shea — that a man came out on a music-hall stage and sang a song, the words and music of which had been written only a few hours before? I remember that the chorus went something like this: —

> Charley Parney, Charley Parney,
> Naughty, naughty boy,
> Who'd have thought you'd have interfered
> With another fellow's joy?

The next lines I forget, but the last lines were: —

> You want Home Rule for Ireland
> And you can't home-rule yoursel'.

Instantly there was a riot; when two or three Irishmen are gathered together there usually is. The Irish determined that the song should not be sung; the English wanted it badly. We were a hundred to one — but what are odds to an Irishman? While it lasted it was a very pretty scrap, but just as it was getting interesting the policemen came and put an end to it, just as firemen do to a fire — I could never understand why.

If I was not the first person in America to sing Lottie Collins's great song, —

Ta, ra, ra, boom de ay,

I don't want the credit for it; but certainly I was her most steadfast defender when anyone happened to say that that song was not designed to be sung by a perfect lady. No, I am mistaken; the song in that way challenged was not Lottie Collins's acrobatic song and dance, which swept round the world as it deserved to; it was another balladic masterpiece: "Her Golden Hair Was Hanging Down Her Back." It was the pathetic story of a beautiful young country girl who came to London to see the sights, with her golden hair "a-hanging down her back." It took many stanzas to tell of the experiences that befell her; her name was Flo; and the chorus went this way: —

> But O Flo! What a change, you know!
> When she left the village she was shy;
> But alas, and alack, she came back
> With a naughty little twinkle in her eye.

When I first told the pathetic story of Flo, in print,

from the indignation expressed in the letters I received one might have supposed that I had been reflecting on the character of the writer's mother. Her name was n't Flo, it was Jane, I was told. Now the fact is that there are almost as many versions of this song as there are girls "with a naughty little twinkle in [their] eye" in London. The Jane version is not universal: it is strictly "little old New York." Listen: Jane toddles into Broadway, a smile upon her face, where she meets an artless man to whom she imparts her secret — she is uncommonly thirsty, and not for milk.

He takes her to Delmonico's (of blessed memory) where —

They drank until the artless man so very weary grew, —
 And her golden hair was hanging down her back, —
She took his chain and ticker, and his diamond breast-pin too —
 And her golden hair was hanging down her back.
Then silently she left him as he slumbered in a chair,
Into the street she wandered with a very simple air,
She would have carried off the stove if there had been one there!
 And her golden hair was hanging down her back.
But, Oh Jane! is n't it a shame? *etc.*

I well remember the fate of my version of this song. My wife, growing tired of playing my accompaniments, once remarked to herself: "I wish someone would burn this song"; whereupon my daughter, then a girl of seven, before anyone could stop her, placed it upon the embers of a wood fire. But the words of most of it have been burnt into my brain.

Does anyone now remember the rattling chorus?

> Strolling round the town,
> Rolling up and down,
> Tasting every kind of wet,
> Having a h— of a time, you bet;
> Treating all the boys,
> Did n't care a sou,
> Fair old, rare old
> Ricketty-racketty crew.

If you have forgotten it, I would be pleased to sing it for a small remuneration. I learned it with lots of other songs in St. Bartholomew's Hospital, to which I was conveyed with a broken leg just thirty years ago to-morrow.

How can a lot of boys and men more harmlessly spend two or three hours of an evening, after a hard day's work, than in listening to and singing a lot of nonsensical and sometimes absurdly sentimental songs? Don't let us try too hard to "uplift" our fellows in the street. Life is a dull, unhappy business at best for them; before they were born the cards were stacked; the chances against them are ten thousand to one. Think of the homes that many of the patrons of the halls come from! Think of the streets into which they must go for recreation, and remember that

> Hearts just as pure and fair
> May beat in Belgrave Square,
> As in the lowly air
> Of Seven Dials.

The streets of London are ceaselessly interesting, and coster songs, as sung by Gus Ellen and above all by Albert Chevalier, have always had a powerful fascination for me. Chevalier was, I think, with the exception of Harry Lauder, the greatest music-hall artist I have ever seen; and when I say artist I mean it. Most of his songs I know by heart, but in a desultory paper like this one should not discuss him.

While not in the same class with "The Man That Broke the Bank at Monte Carlo" and "Waiting at the Church," sung with such success by Vesta Victoria (I keep the words and music of her pathetic ballad under lock and key, that it too may not find its way into the fire), the old song "Jack-the-Dandy Oh" always amused me. It was one of Arthur Roberts's best songs, and was sung in the Gaiety burlesque of *Joan of Arc*. Originally it was a skit on Lord Randolph Churchill, whose son, Winston, after a year's retirement, is again in the public eye. Lord Randolph had gone out to the Cape and elsewhere as a traveler for the London *Graphic*. In his absence the song appeared, holding him up to ridicule as "Randy-Pandy Oh," his political nickname. Lady Churchill objected and sought to have the proper authorities suppress the song. They asked her to point out the objectionable words; she did so and they were replaced by other words of the same general meaning and exactly the same rhyme. For example, instead of Randy-Pandy Oh, sailing away on the foaming main, "as a traveler for the *Graphic*," Jack-the-Dandy Oh sailed the same water as a "traveler geographic." Then the song caught on in earnest and swept the town; Lady Churchill, perhaps, was the only lady that did not go to the Gaiety that season to hear it. Here are a couple of stanzas: —

> I sailed away on the foaming main,
>   In the biggest possible hurry —
> For dinner we'd lots of dry champagne,
>   But everything else was curry!
> And the food was cooked on a wretched plan,
>   So I wrote the Captain a letter —
> I said it might do for the Grand Old Man,
>   But that I must have something better!

> CHORUS: I'm a regular Jack-the-Dandy, oh!
>   And a very complete gourmand-y, oh!
>   And I don't much care for the steamboat fare,
>   Washed down with soda and brandy, oh!
>   Although I'm as sweet as candy, oh!
>   It's more than I can stand-y, oh!
>   And to get no truffles extremely ruffles
>   The epicure Jack-the-Dandy, oh!

> To Mashona-land at last I got,
>   The girls came out to greet me;
> They fell in love with me on the spot,
>   As soon as they chanced to meet me!
> And some of them wore a cheerful smile,
>   And some but a string of coral —
> But I only looked for a little while,
>   For a nobleman must be moral!
> CHORUS: I'm a regular Jack-the-Dandy, oh!

It was good fun while it lasted.

What has become of Vesta Tilley — later to become Lady de Freece — who for years wore men's clothes, especially evening clothes, better than most men, and sang and danced in them to the distraction of the chappies about town? The "great Little Tilley" she was called, and she deserved both adjectives. She was christened Matilda and assumed the name of Vesta from a match box. Wherever she is, I hope she is happy. She ought to be, for she has given so much and such innocent pleasure. At one time she was earning, not merely being paid, as much as £500 a week.

Marie Lloyd! — another great favorite. I happened to be in London a year ago when she died, almost the last of her line, and a great to-do was made at her funeral. She was vulgar, but droll and enormously popular. At the time of her death she supposed herself to be very rich, and left a lot of money to charity; but she had lived rich and died as so many of her profession do, poor. Years ago, when she first became popular, the story goes of a man in London for the first time, being shown the sights by a friend who, although long a resident, was not over-sure of his facts. On top of a horse-drawn bus, the town innocent explained to the country innocent this building and that, not often giving the building its proper name. But the driver, who knew every inch of the road, was imperturbable. At last, nearing St. Paul's, the countryman inquired, "What is the name of that statur' there?" For several centuries it has been Queen Anne; but the cockney, at a loss, paused for a moment, whereupon the driver, with a face like a frost-bitten apple, turned round and, chuckling to himself, said: "Don't 'esitate, don't 'esitate; say it's Marie Lloyd."

Who that has seen him has forgotten Dan Leno? He was an exquisite artist, always in trouble — on the stage; poor fellow — if I am not mistaken he went insane. Genius is to insanity allied, and Dan Leno was a genius. He made you laugh inside rather than out; no smutty word or suggestion ever came from him. He was a little fellow and when, during the Christmas pantomime, Drury Lane claimed him, he was lost in the immensity of that huge stage; but at the Tivoli — gone now, alas! — he was in his element. I do not seem to remember any songs of his, but as a dancer he was superb. Fifty years ago, nearly, at Tony Pastor's in New York, I remember two black-faced comedians who used to sing and dance to words something like this: —

> Oh, we are a pair of mokes,
> And we're always full of jokes,
> And it's watch a nigger's educated feet,
>   Tah, rah, rah!

Then would come a patter of feet as faultlessly rhythmical as a verse by Swinburne. This forgotten jingle suggests one of Dan Leno's great accomplishments: with his educated feet, sometimes in shoes almost as long as he was tall, he would clog-dance with a grace and agility that I have never seen equaled. Even Royalty, and Royalty is hard to amuse, found him amusing.

But the old-fashioned music hall was not entirely

given over to song and dance. I have seen animals do incredible things; I have seen cyclists ride wheels until my heart was in my mouth; I have seen feats of strength; and I have heard "Datas," the man whose memory was so remarkable that he could, as he said, "give the correct answer to any question found in the following books of reference" — then followed a long list; and he could do it too. I primed myself to catch him, as others did, but always failed. Tumblers and acrobats too I have seen — they are still with us; but alas! Paul Cinquevalli is no more. He was an Austrian, — his right name was Kestner, — a sensitive gentleman; the war broke his heart. As a juggler I suppose he never had an equal. I have seen him keep in the air, at one time, a cannon ball, an egg, and a lighted lamp.

I mourn the passing of the old-fashioned music hall, a typically English form of amusement, with its constant supply of good and merry songs designed to lengthen life and banish care. Life has become too serious. I verily believe, if our reforms and refinements continue, that man will cease to be a laughing animal. There are those who can laugh at Charlie Chaplin, but I am not among the number; that he appeals equally to the Chinese and the Patagonian, does not interest me. Nor can I get my joy out of mechanical contrivances, no matter how marvelous they may be, and heaven knows they are positively awe-inspiring. For real fun we must have the human voice and the human face, not over a wire or extracted from the air or displayed upon a sheet.

Equally distasteful to me is the so-called Russian dancer, some ugly, half-clothed creature of mature years, leaping about the stage, plucking an imaginary butterfly from an imaginary bush; this entertainment is usually billed as "Summer"; or the same woman, disguised as an Egyptian, writhing and twisting herself about, imitating with long and scrawny arms the squirmings of a serpent; this is called "Old Nile." Contrast this with a young and graceful *danseuse:* a girl "after your own heart" in very deed, and speaking your own language, becomingly dressed in skirts or tights, who knows her art and her charms and how to display or conceal them, who can put you in an ecstasy of delight merely by the fluttering of her eyelid.

At a music hall, as long as I can smoke I can stand anything. "Jonathan Wild is not too low for me, nor Shaftesbury too genteel"; but I hate a contortionist. When a contortionist comes on, I always close my eyes and sometimes go to sleep. Many years ago, in the smoke-room of the old Teutonic, I fell into conversation with a man about "the halls."

"I am glad that you enjoy them," he said. "You have probably seen me."

I looked at him carefully and tried to place him, but could not, and I told him so.

"I am the 'Human Corkscrew'," he replied.

Then I remembered him with horror.

IX

EVERY once in so often someone sets a silly phrase in motion and it rolls and rolls, farther and farther, until one is powerless to catch up with it; such a phrase is "Comparisons are odious." It seems to mean that comparisons, in general, are unfair and should be avoided. Now I take it that in travel, if one is not going to make comparisons, one might as well stay at home. Comparison is the essence of travel. Sterne in his *Sentimental Journey* sets out with, "They order this matter better in France." In my experience what they order in France better than elsewhere is a dinner; I know of some things they order badly.

For example, let us compare the Bibliothèque Nationale with the British Museum. The English library is always open; its treasures are always on view, displayed to the best advantage in rooms well lighted, well heated, ventilated, and served by an intelligent and accommodating staff: in a word, everything is done for the comfort and convenience of the visitor. Enter now the great French library, one of the oldest and probably the richest in the world. Did I say "enter"? Say, rather, attempt to enter; on only two days a week is one permitted to break in upon the slumber of the attendants, who, resenting the intrusion, shrug their shoulders at your questions as to the whereabouts of the exhibits you especially want to see, and go to sleep again. Alone and unaided you wander through cold, dark chambers where, in cases so placed that at best only half of their contents can be seen, are displayed books so rare and bindings so magnificent that the book-lover, under happier surroundings, would wish to spend the rest of this life in their contemplation. As it is, he gives them a glance and is glad to get out into the hospitality of the streets.

Turn now to the Conciergerie, that famous prison, fairly reeking with history and especially reminiscent of Marie Antoinette and other figures of the French Revolution. It is not too easy to find, but at last you reach the portal only to learn that it is necessary to get an order of admission from M. le Préfet de Police. You write for it, taking care to assure that gentleman that you entertain for him feelings of consideration which simple words are powerless to express. In due course the permit arrives in the stamped and self-addressed envelope you have enclosed with your application. You receive with joy the small scrap of paper which is to open to you the portals of that gloomy prison, and once again present yourself at the door, ring the bell, and again the attendant declines to let you enter, pointing gleefully to a line of fine print on your permit which you had not before observed, which translates: "The visit may be made only on Friday." As the day is Sunday, that settles that.

Sunday in Paris being like all other days, only more so, you decide you will visit the Tomb of Napoleon, which was closed when you were last there. You look in your guidebook to be sure that it is a day upon which it is permitted to gaze upon the sarcophagus which contains the remains of the man who tore up and remade and tore up again the map of Europe. The day is the right one, and the hour twelve. You are lunching with a friend at Prunier's at a quarter to one; there is just time. Entering a taxi, you are in a few minutes descended before the great gates — which are closed. Upon one of them hangs a sign which informs visitors that they may enter at twelve o'clock. But hold! following the 12 someone has written .45, in small characters, in ink: twelve forty-five is the hour of admission. Just the hour when you should be discussing the particular variety of oyster you will be ordering at Prunier's. "They order these matters better in France, I don't think," you murmur to yourself as you turn away, at the same time applauding the ingenuity with which the French make sight-seeing in Paris an obstacle race. And when it comes to getting a passport visaed, it is certainly better to be robbed several times at your hotel than to subject yourself to the indignities you are likely to experience in the upper halls and chambers of the Bureau of Police.

How ever did the fiction arise that the French are a polite people? Their language is so, without doubt, and a Frenchman may be very polite to a lady with whom he is not too intimately acquainted; but polite as a nation! certainly not — except by comparison with the German. It is my honest belief, in spite of the fact that black eyes are frequently worn by ladies of the lower orders in London on Monday mornings, that the English are the politest and kindliest people in the world. Of the manners of the American, I refrain from speaking — some subjects are too painful.

As I loitered across the Place de la Concorde on my way to the restaurant, I thought of Napoleon's desire that his "cinders" should be interred on the banks of the Seine in the midst of the French people that he loved so well. Should I be unlucky enough to die in Paris, I wish my cinders placed elsewhere at the earliest possible moment. With their love of red tape, the French would be reluctant to permit them to be interred anywhere until my mother-in-law's marriage certificate and lots of other little certificates of this character were produced; this being difficult or impossible, a horde of governmental officials would have to be seen and placated: the thought is paralyzing. Love of bookkeeping is a national trait. I have no doubt that the age and sex of every oyster I have consumed at Prunier's is on file with the Chief of Police.

> If you go to France, you must speak the lingo,
> If you don't, by Jove, you'll be stuck, by jingo.

So sings an English poet: I speak the lingo fluently enough; the trouble is, no one understands it. I should be stuck anyhow; as an American I expect to be stuck wherever I go; if I don't like it, I can stay at home where I know how to take care of myself.

I realize that I am out of sympathy with the life of Paris. It is the most beautiful city in the world: the French have forgotten more about town-planning than we shall ever know. Its buildings are magnificent, and so perfectly placed that one superb vista opens after another. But it is too artificial; nothing fine ever happens by chance. And its atmosphere of gray-pink and violet, which so delights the artist, is indeed lovely, but I prefer the dull and frequently sunless streets of London, and occasionally, even, give me London in a fog. The English weather has been much maligned: it has produced the loveliest landscape in the world. Kit Morley once told me that the most pathetic thing he had ever seen was a sign in an Oxford Street clothing-shop: RAIN COATS FOR THE HOLIDAYS. That was n't pathos; that was humor.

Forty years ago I had but one ambition: to make enough money to retire from business and spend my declining years in England, preferably up the Thames in any one of the many beautiful houses which border either side of that historic river. To-day nothing would induce me to accept as a gift any cottage or mansion either on the Thames or elsewhere, if I had to live in it; not that I do not love England as much as ever, — as I know it better I love it more, — but I do not belong there; and so far as an Englishman would consent to express his opinion, I am not wanted there; few Americans are.

A moment's reflection will show why this is. For almost three centuries the English have been the richest and most powerful people on earth. Their laws permitted — indeed, they encouraged — the concentration of wealth and power in the hands of a few great families, who came to believe that wealth and power were their natural prerogatives. By one means or another they acquired great estates in the country, on which they built magnificent castles, and on the whole they used their wealth and power wisely. Then came the industrial era, and the wealth of the world began to pour into England. More palaces were built, and the Continent was ransacked for works of art for decoration. Pictures, statuary, and books were acquired; Italy became the happy hunting-ground of every Englishman of means. Then a German-English King forced Washington to become the Father of his Country, and after that country had successfully fought a civil war it dawned upon the Englishman that the United States had come to stay. He did not like the idea; up to that time he had been prophesying our speedy relapse into barbarism as a result of our having cut ourselves off from the humanizing influence of the Empire.

How many Englishmen know — or, knowing, care — that the Marquis of Hartington (subsequently the Duke of Devonshire) wore a secession badge at a public ball in New York during our Civil War? The matter was reported to Lincoln, who said nothing; but one of the neatest strokes of humor was his treatment of this gentleman when curiosity induced him to be presented to the President. The story goes that the President insisted on calling his guest "Mr. Partington"! And to be the husband of "Mrs. Partington," a ridiculous character in the fiction of those days, was not an honor to the noble lord. Lincoln was generally referred to as the President of the "Broken Bubble" by English aristocrats sixty years ago: this was their kindest reference to him. After this nation had looked death in the face, without flinching, for four years, England began to respect us, and when Lincoln died fine amends were made by *Punch*, who for years had been jeering at him, and England has atoned handsomely for her bad treatment of us during our time of trouble. Is there not a statue of Washington in Trafalgar Square, and one of Lincoln in Westminster?

When was the turning-point in England's greatness? No one knows exactly. It may have been when our iron production overtopped hers, for, as Gibbon has said, the control of iron soon gives a nation the control of gold; it may have been shortly after that dramatic moment when Disraeli hailed his Queen as Empress of India. Be that as it may, the United States became enormously rich, not only potentially but actually, and our wealth was not concentrated in a few hands, as in England, but was better distributed. Then Americans began to play in England the rôle that Englishmen had played a century or two before in Italy. They searched the country for art treasures, and many of them, falling in love with the well-ordered life of the people, began to take up their residence there, at least for a part of every year. In time they came to occupy some of the finest mansions in town and some of the most historic castles in the country. Then they became disliked. Many of these Americans were loud, vulgar, and ignorant, as well as rich; more and more they came, and more and more they flaunted their wealth, which was their only distinction, in the face of the English. The feeling of *noblesse oblige* is very real in England: the English understand and, I believe, respect the foreigner who settles there and goes to work — John Julius Angerstein, for example, the founder of a great British institution, "Lloyds," whose pictures formed the nucleus of the National Gallery, which is celebrating its centennial this year. Angerstein was a Russian, who became, as foreigners are apt to do, more English than the English themselves. What they do not want is to have Americans come over and sit down on them, taking up their town and country houses, and trying to get into their clubs, which are more difficult to enter than the Kingdom of Heaven.

When we ceased to be "the Colonies" we ceased to be interesting to the English. A century ago we had to work hard to subdue a continent; now that the continent is subdued, we keep on working from force of habit. This has given us the reputation of caring for nothing but money, whereas, actually, the Englishman cares far more for money than we do, because he knows the value of the leisure that money will buy and how to enjoy it. We work long after there is any necessity, because we do not know what else to do with our time: this makes us poor company for our wives, whom Europeans say we spoil, and I think we do. We are the most indulgent husbands in the world, but the most uninteresting men; hence it is that so many rich American girls go to England and, meeting men of a type that we do not breed over here, cast themselves and their fortunes at their feet — and usually live to regret it.

As sportsmen, the English — well, "despise" would hardly be too strong a word to use: they say we play to win, not for the sake of the sport. I am no sportsman, but I suspect that they are right. I believe that the Englishman is the best — I had almost said the only sportsman in the world. He plays for the fun of the game; we play to win, introducing into our sports the same efficiency that we pride ourselves upon in our business; and business with us is a kind of warfare.

A year ago I was going up in a lift to my little flat in Albemarle Street with two Englishmen; one worked the tiny lift, the other was a lodger like myself. Said the lodger to the liftman, "Well, the Americans have won again." I forget what the sport was, but the reply, which was made for my benefit, was, "Yes sir, by that low cunning which is so characteristic." Not wishing to pick a quarrel with a man who could easily have thrashed me, I said nothing, but on my next visit to London I did not return to Albemarle Street.

A peculiarity of the American is that he is never satisfied to leave well-enough alone. "There is no such thing as standing still." "Not to go forward is to go backward." Phrases like these we repeat to one another until we come to believe them. Conditions in England are static; here they are dynamic. An Englishman is content to follow in the line of his father. We are extravagant in our talk, and are always blowing our own trumpet. Have you read *Babbitt?* Well, there is much of Babbitt in many of us and some of Babbitt in all of us. But in the Englishman's modesty there is more arrogance than in our bluster. We are always trying to improve ourselves — especially our women are; hence their passion for attending lectures. The Englishman is quite certain that he cannot be improved.

The English are the most law-abiding people in the world: when they pass a law, they do so after a certain amount of thought; we pass laws in a spirit of levity, and hundreds of thousands of lawyers show us how to break them — with impunity. With us a very rich man almost never goes to prison for stealing; his crime is called something else, and having stolen millions he escapes with a small fine, at which he laughs. In 1921 there were twenty-two murders in

London; in New York, with a population almost two millions less, there were two hundred and thirty-seven. It would be interesting, and humiliating, to know how many of these suffered punishment for their crime. Of our laws prohibiting the sale and transportation of liquor I shall not now speak.

On the other hand, the efforts that our rich men make to justify their existence are the amazement of the world. In a new country of almost limitless resources money is easily made; there are no strings to these fortunes, and almost as soon as they are made they are dissipated — in charity. Colleges, schools, hospitals, and libraries are created and endowed upon a scale of magnificence which the Old World knows nothing of. America accepts as fundamental the doctrine of "the greatest good for the greatest number," and if Dr. Johnson was right when he said, "the state of the people is the state of the nation," it is much. With us mediocrity is the rule; on the other hand, England does not in the least interest herself in mediocrity. She is not interested in the "greatest number" but she takes the best possible care of the individual. Such has been her habit for centuries.

Does anyone suppose that when Dr. Nicholas Murray Butler goes to England and tells the Warden of New College, Oxford — founded in 1379, mark you — of the difficulties he has confronted or overcome, incidentally remarking that Columbia has enrolled over thirty thousand students in one year, does anyone suppose that the Warden of New is in the least degree interested? He is thinking of the great men who call Oxford "Mother"; and concealing a yawn, he wonders in what manner Dr. Butler's students will use their education when they get it — if they get it.

Those of us who love England do so not only because it is beautiful but because it is well ordered and comfortable to a degree that we, at home, know nothing of. Things fall naturally into their proper place; all is — perhaps it would be more exact to say all was — ordered for the best in the best of all possible worlds. By best, one means, of course, for the upper classes. One day in church during an appallingly stupid sermon, such a sermon as one can hear only in the Church as by law established, when all around me were asleep, I looked for and found in the Hymnal two silly verses which express not only the idea of the rich toward the poor, but also the idea of the English toward the rest of the world: —

> The rich man in his castle
> The poor man at the gate,
> God made them high or lowly,
> And ordered their estate.

> God has given each his station;
> Some have riches and high place;
> Some have lowly homes and labour;
> All may have His precious grace.

The idea, of course, comes from the Church of England Catechism. But this is not the silliest rhyme

ever penned: that distinction belongs to Lord John
Manners' famous couplet: —

> Let wealth and commerce, laws and learning die,
> But leave us still our old nobility.

When the American eagle, which the British lion
long persisted in regarding as a goose, ceased moult-
ing and when Englishmen discovered that we had
more money than we could wisely spend, they began
to descend upon us in hordes, "that the goose might
lay for them a golden egg in return for their cackle."
I do not refer to Mrs. Trollope's or Charles Dickens'
strictures upon us. I have no doubt that we deserved
all the criticisms we got and more. No: Matthew
Arnold is my Exhibit A. While here he made small
effort to conceal his contempt for us. He came
frankly for money and would have been greatly surprised if anyone supposed that he came for anything
else. "What else?" he would have said. Every year
British ships, and recently a few of our own, deliver
bounders by the thousand to English shores, but
never a man so raw at heart as this disciple of
"sweetness and light" who first came to this country
when I was a boy. Our exportations behave as well
as they know how; Arnold knew better; he sinned
against the light. Asked to make a few remarks at
a dinner given him in Boston, he replied that his fee
would be ten guineas, and that sum not being forth-
coming, he declined to speak.

"I am afraid we have hurried you," remarked a
charming western woman, with whom the lecturer

was staying as a guest; she had caught him at the top of a staircase as he was preparing to descend in baggy tweeds to grace a dinner that was being given in his honor. "I shall postpone the dinner for half an hour," said the lady sympathetically, "and that will give you time to change." And this to a gentleman who in his own country would not have thought of sitting down to a five-and-sixpenny ordinary at a country hotel without dressing.

At Swarthmore, a small town just outside Philadelphia, in which is located an excellent college, he was engaged to speak; before going upon the platform he asked for his fee and was told that a check would be sent to him in the care of his host — he had accepted the hospitality of a distinguished Philadelphia family. He replied that he preferred to have the money before giving his lecture. "Quite so, quite so," replied the embarrassed man he was addressing, "I shall immediately give you a check"; whereupon Arnold said he made it a rule never to accept checks. At that, a group of rich old Quaker trustees, any one of whom could have given away a sum greater than Arnold's lecture-takings of a lifetime and forgotten the incident, were seen going about borrowing twenty dollars here and thirty there, until the required sum was raised. Meanwhile Mr. Arnold sat upon the stage, curiously regarding his audience through his monocle. I personally had this story from the man who finally set the lecturer in motion. Yet, upon his return to England, Arnold said that what most impressed him in this country was our gross materialism.[1]

More recently we had an unhappy experience with the Honorable John William Fortescue, the scion of a noble house and the King's Librarian at Windsor. He had published a book in which he unbosomed himself thus: —

Americans esteem a good bargain, even if gained by dishonorable means, to mark the highest form of ability. The United States cannot engage in any form of competition with us, from athletics to diplomacy, without using foul play. They must win, if not by fair skill then by prearranged trickery or violence; if not by open negotiations, then by garbled maps and forged documents. There is the fact. It may be unpleasant, but it cannot be denied.

And holding these opinions, he came, quite naturally, to lecture us, among other places, at West Point. When the Secretary of War's attention was called to the offending passage, he at once telegraphed the Commandant that "an author entertaining these sentiments is not considered to be a proper person to address the students of a Government academy." This resulted in all his lecture dates being canceled, whereupon the Honorable John William, making an inadequate apology, returned home in high dudgeon. That his "apology was inadequate" is not a phrase

[1] Mrs. Florence Earle Coates, who entertained Mr. Arnold when he was in Philadelphia, tells me that I am mistaken in my judgment of Arnold. She insists that he was a gracious, genial, and witty gentleman. She ought to know. I voice, however, the general impression.

of my invention; I had it from an English newspaper.

Sometime ago I saw a picture in *Punch* which illustrates prettily this will to lecture: a callow youth
rushes into his mother's drawing-room and cries exult-
ingly, "Oh, mother, my novel has been accepted at
last!" "Splendid!" exclaims the mother. "Now you
will be able to go to New York and lecture." And has
anyone who heard "Margot" when she was with
us, forgotten the experience? She was dreadful! In
an effort to pack the houses, boxes were offered to
those likely to occupy them in evening dress, and one
of our newspapers described her lecture by saying
that "she pelted us with soiled feathers." And
Margot was not the wife of a raw, uneducated man
who had made his money packing pork during the
war, but one whose husband had been Prime Minister
of England and is now the Earl of Oxford!

But this lecture-habit is a European rather than
an exclusively English weakness. Maeterlinck came
to us speaking no English, yet after a few weeks'
intensive study, he essayed to address us in such a
language as was never heard before by mortal man.
Not a soul understood whereof he was speaking, and
he finally fled the platform and the country. And
when I was last in London I cut the following from
a newspaper: "A protest has been lodged with Dr.
Nicholas Murray Butler, the President of the Colum-
bian (*sic*) University, against the proposed course of
lectures at the University by Giovanni Papini, author

of *The Life of Christ*. The protest is based on Papini's definition, in his writings, of America as 'the home of millionaires and the birthplace of the nauseating Longfellow, the intolerable Washington, and the degenerate Whitman.'" Even as I write, Dr. Bridges, the Poet Laureate, a gentleman in his eightieth year, arrives a few months tardily, and draws down a substantial sum merely for making benign faces at the students of the University of Michigan: absurdity can go no further. But my quarrel is not with the lecturers: it is with those who hire them.

The more I ponder upon the resemblances of and differences between the English and ourselves, the more I am impressed by our dissimilarities, and these must be more obvious to them than to us. They are an old and conservative people, full of picturesque traditions, compared with whom we are young and raw. With them, social lines are strongly drawn; with us, they are almost nonexistent, though social lines are being broken down in England and are being created in this country. They are subtle, with a subtlety equaled only by the Oriental; we have no reticences, we are simple, outspoken, and direct. They talk in whispers; we talk at the top of our voices, and are so intensely interested in ourselves that we cannot understand people not being interested in us. But our unforgivable sin is that we are sleek, prosperous, well fed, and have to be reckoned with. Twenty years ago an English Prime Minister is quoted as saying: "Thirty per cent of our people are on the verge of starvation, doubtful from day to day of the sufficiency of their food." How much worse is their plight to-day after the strains to which they have been subjected in the last ten years!

I have searched in vain to discover any reason why the English should like us, or we them: in general, nations do not like one another, and likings artificially stimulated always suffer the inevitable reaction. My own admiration is for the English as a nation rather than for the individual. I am very fond of my English friends, but I have not very many, and I try hard not to exhaust the patience of those I have. My acquaintance with the English aristocracy is confined to books. I once spoke to a man on a transatlantic steamer, whom I took to be an American — a traveling salesman, I knew that by his manners. Judge of my amazement when I found I was addressing the Duke of Marlborough! I had spent so much time in the company of Trollope's Duke of Omnium — not Planty Pal but his uncle — that I thought I should know a duke when I saw one; but I was mistaken. I like to think that I understand the feelings of an English country gentleman, but best of all I know and like the London cockney. The men of our streets have no manners, and they are quite destitute of humor. To tell a man to go to hell, or to call him a foul name, as we do, is not wit, yet it is the only retort we know how to make. Did I hear or did I read this? A taxi-driver in London drove his motor too near a policeman who had raised his hand against the traffic; the policeman did not deign to speak, but with a look sought to extinguish the taxi-driver. "Why did you give me that hugly look?" said the taxi-driver. "I did n't; you were born with it," was the reply. It was the humor of the British Tommy that kept him going in the years of discouragement during the war. "Lions led by asses" was the opinion of Napoleon of an English army. The next time you are in the British Museum, look at the menu of an imaginary Christmas dinner made out by the starving and frozen men on the famous Scott Expedition to the South Pole. Nothing could be finer than this unconscious testimonial to English character.

For Men Only

At home I have little time for looking into shop windows: in London I spend hours tramping up one street and down another, gazing at the never-ending displays of old silver and jewelry, pictures, bric-a-brac, cheese, furniture, fish, and tailor shops. There are more tailor-shops in London than in all the rest of the world put together, and I am invariably struck with the beauty of the cloth displayed in them. Exquisite in weave and color and style, one is powerless to resist the temptation to enter and order one more suit. If you obey that impulse you are lost. Obsequiously the shopman listens while you tell him of the harrowing experiences you have had with the tailor in the next street. "You shall have no difficulty like that with h'us, sir, h'I h'assure you, sir."

Seduced by a fine line of talk and beautiful cloth, and a low price, — cloth suits are to-day the only cheap thing in England, — you order a suit, being very explicit in your instructions. Will you get what you ask for? Not within a mile of it. After the third trying-on, the suit, originally cut for a giant, begins to work down to within a few inches of your measure; that is to say, you can stuff only one large sofa-cushion in the seat of your trousers, not two. In vain do you tell the so-called fitter that you are not *enceinte*; that your figure is entirely under your control, if your temper is not. To your instructions he listens, it may be deferentially, or perhaps he tells you that his grandfather was responsible for the fit of the clothes worn by the Duke of Wellington; in any case he does his own way. Eventually, after several more "fittings," in disgust, or despair, or both, you pay for the suit, have it sent to your hotel, and some weeks or months later, when in the seclusion of your own room at home, this is what you find: The waistband of your trousers is three inches too large, and cut heart-shape in the back as though intended to be worn conspicuously on St. Valentine's Day. They are two inches too large in the leg, and either several inches too short or too long. Between vest and trousers there is a hiatus of an inch or more which reveals a strip of your shirt — or your trousers may come snugly up under your armpits. Recently a new species of trousers has been introduced with pleats around the waist, but I cannot

think that this "maternity" type will long endure.
The arms of your coat are too small: you smash
your cuffs getting it on; seemingly nothing fits anywhere. Cursing gently, you then begin to explore the
pockets. How wonderful they would be, were you a
shoplifter by profession! In each of your coat pockets
you could secrete a large dictionary; in your lower
vest pockets you can stick your hands comfortably,
as occasionally you have seen men do on the stage.
But hold! Here is a small pocket — two pockets in
fact, the upper vest-pockets, which you insisted upon
being made very narrow, as you carry in one only a
narrow leather case containing your commutation
ticket, and in the other a tiny cardcase or a lead
pencil. These pockets have indeed been made narrow,
in accordance with your specifications, but only at
the top; below they are so large that anything you
put therein drops down and extends itself lengthwise,
well out of reach. In the fob pocket of your trousers
you can carry an extra large Waterbury clock, while
in your hip pockets — which, out of deference to
your being an American, the cutter insists on calling
"pistol pockets," you can conceal cannon, such as
are a part of the equipment of a villain in a melodrama. How your tailor at home will enjoy your
discomfiture when you tell him of your experiences!
Can you blame him for stinging you: "For altera-
tions to English suits . . . "?

I mention no names; it is not necessary; but I have
in mind certain shops in the West End, over the

doors of which heraldic animals prance dangerously, as though to suggest they are prepared to give their lives in defense of those within from the assaults of outraged customers. And lest these remarks be considered too sweeping, I might except the "Toga" works of Studd and Millington in Conduit Street, famous for topcoats the world over.[1]

I chanced to be in England one year when she was undergoing what was called the "throes of a general election." Mr. Baldwin, as Prime Minister, had a majority in Parliament of about one hundred and fifty, when suddenly he decided upon a general election and the issue which he presented to the country for its consideration was Protection. Instantly every politician in the country, with the exception of Lord Curzon, who was at the Foreign Office, which has many problems these days, was dashing madly about the country making speeches. The issue was one which an American could understand. Business in Britain was and still is very bad. There were, it is said, almost a million and a half people out of work. Many of those who are working are insufficiently paid — are earning just barely enough to keep body

---

[1] This paragraph was originally published in the *Atlantic Monthly* several years ago, whereupon a number of men wrote me that I had done the subject scant justice. A few evenings since, re-reading Fielding's *Joseph Andrews*, I came across this: Bellarmine, the gay gentleman, displaying his well-fitting apparel to his ladylove, exclaims: "I defy the best English tailor to imitate it: not one of them can cut, Madam, they can't cut, I assure you — except great-coats. I never trust anything more than a greatcoat to an Englishman." And *Joseph Andrews* was published one hundred and eighty-three years ago!

and soul together. Taxes are very high. "The dukes," as Lloyd George called the tremendously rich land-owning class, have been practically extinguished. Two or three deaths in a certain succession almost wipe out an estate. I am not sure that this is not good business. Why should one man have half a dozen palaces, each surrounded by a magnificent park, in a tiny, overpopulated country like England, in which there is not enough of anything to go 'round? But the dukes' cake is dough, and I must say they take what is coming to them uncomplainingly. Not so, however, the manufacturers of the country: they see themselves deprived of foreign markets that they have for a long time been enjoying, and see their own domestic markets being taken away from them by Germany, France, Belgium, and the United States. Something has to be done quickly, they say. Such were conditions when Lloyd George left home to make his whirlwind tour through Canada and the United States, during which, according to a cartoon in a French paper, he was seen standing reverently before the tomb of P. T. Barnum — the picture bearing the legend: "Barnum, I am here!" While he was on the high seas the Prime Minister came out for Protection. Mr. Baldwin is an ironmaster on a large scale, swept into politics by the war. His rise has been a rapid one; an honest and educated gentleman, he is hardly adroit enough to be a successful politician. Had he been content to extend little by little the power that he had, — by which motor-cars and talking machines and certain other things are made to pay a heavy duty, — all might have been well; instead of which he asked for a mandate from the people to put into effect such tariffs as would in the judgment of a board of experts afford protection to certain trades and better employ labor. For the great question in England to-day is the question of unemployment. But to expect an Englishman, and above all things an English yokel, suddenly, in less than a month, to reverse the policy of a century, was expecting too much.

Personally, I have no doubt that Lloyd George, who was on the sea when Mr. Baldwin threw his bombshell, having seen the prosperity of America under a protective tariff, was going home with a full determination to do another sudden "about face" for which he is so famous, and himself come out for Protection. If so, when he found Mr. Baldwin had beaten him to it, he said not a word — rather, it would be truer to say that he said a great many. Of course Lloyd George had been advised of the trend of affairs by wireless, but nevertheless upon the arrival of the steamer he expressed amazement at the news and was in fighting trim in an instant. "And so," he said, "they are going to feed starving Labor with the mouldy straw of the last century, are they? Well, nothing that Mr. Baldwin does surprises me. He does n't know his own mind from one hour to another" — thus firmly establishing himself on horses going in opposite directions.

It was a whirlwind campaign: in less than a month it was over and Labor was in power. I followed the speeches as they were reported in the *Times;* important addresses on both sides were reported, almost all at full length, and Free Trade was all but demolished every day in a long and carefully reasoned editorial. Certainly, if an outsider could judge, — and the players do not always see the game to the best advantage, — Mr. Baldwin had the better argument. He spoke with great simplicity and directness, but I believe, had he consulted his own personal wishes, he would have prayed to be let out of the difficulty of governing England during those troublesome times. Lloyd George, on the other hand, gave his hearers an hour's free entertainment; he joshed his audience and jazzed the subject until all, except the judicious, were convulsed with laughter.

After Labor got in, nothing was done about the most important plank in its platform, the "capital levy." Labor sought or was said to seek the confiscation by Government of an immense amount of the wealth of the nation. Asked how many times they intended to put this plan in operation, they said "once only" — which was clever; for having once done so, what wealth was left would have flown away. Listen to Lloyd George's rhetoric on this subject: "At the mere possibility of a Labor Government the western skies become black with the flight of capital seeking safety beyond the Atlantic. The fright is real: there has been nothing like it since horror filled the streets of Rome at the approach of Attila." Such is rhetoric. What actually happened was that the five-per-cent war loan, the premier security of England, went off about three points at the possibility of Ramsay MacDonald's election, and promptly recovered them upon his coming into office.

During the war MacDonald was a "passivist," a "conscientious objector," an "internationalist," and I know not what. He made what trouble for the Government he could and a passport was denied him when he sought to visit his friends in Russia. Then, by a turn of the political wheel, he became Prime Minister of England; yet at a "Victory Meeting," held at the Albert Hall after his election, the proceeding commenced with the singing of the Marseillaise and concluded with The Red Flag. This was not a good beginning; but there is nothing so sobering as responsibility, and before MacDonald, who proved to be a whiner, was ejected from office, he became more Tory than the Tories.

In less than a year another election was held and Mr. Baldwin was returned with an enormous majority. The two great questions which press upon the English are taxes and unemployment. How long can England stand the terrific taxation she has imposed upon herself? How can she become prosperous with so large a part of her population unemployed or, if employed, underpaid? Mr. Baldwin was a protectionist and probably still is. The question was not brought to the fore at the last election, but it will come up again. England cannot forever allow the nations of the world to dump their surplus manufactures upon her. It was Lloyd George and not logic that once defeated Mr. Baldwin. Within ten years, I prophesy, England will have a protective tariff; she may, she probably will, call it something else; no doubt she will be told it is something else; and possibly the man who will do the telling is that verbal acrobat — Lloyd George.

Before Mr. Baldwin became Prime Minister for the first time, he came to this country with the Governor of the Bank of England, Sir Montagu Norman, to arrange for the payment of Britain's debt to the United States. If the question had been solely a financial one, the interallied debts should have been canceled for the good of all, including ourselves. This suggestion was publicly made toward the end of the war by the Honorable James M. Beck, and it was generally applauded by the press of the country, but Mr. Wilson, constitutionally unable to see good in any idea which did not originate with him, came out strongly against the plan and killed it; as a result, the debts stand. I believe that an unwise agreement was reached with our Secretary of the Treasury. France and Italy should have been brought into line at that time, and England allowed to quiet her conscience by an expression of her willingness to pay when she had collected the moneys due her — or pro rata, for the money had been spent upon what was practically a joint account. The group of men who came from England were of a class whose word was as good as a bond. The result was that we were able to freeze into concrete form our claims against England, not only for the sums that we advanced her during the war, but also for the money that through her we loaned to France and Italy. These obligations were given a due date, a rate of interest was fixed, and payments were made.

Meanwhile, what of France? To-day she is richer than ever before — that is, the people are. The Government is "busted" and the people want it that way, because they have no idea of paying their debts to us, to England, or to anyone else — if they can get out of it. Taxes in France are low as compared to England's or to our own. The wealth of the French people is enormous but it is out of sight — in the country — and it is not of a kind that makes exchange. They pay a lot of what we would call nuisance taxes — that is to say, they tax windows, and closets, and four-wheel carts (twice as much as two wheel carts), and horses, and donkeys, and dogs; but the idea is not so much to raise money as to employ a host of bookkeepers. The Government gets its chief income from the cities; to attempt to raise real money from the peasantry of France would bring about a revolution. We are accustomed to speak applaudingly of the thrift of the French; avarice is the word we should employ.

But sooner or later England will ask us what we intend to do with France. Are we to have our money

before or after England gets hers — for France owes
England almost as much as she owes us — or at the
same time? Are we going to take all or only a part?
When will the payments begin, and what will the rate
of interest be? And if we grant France better terms
than we gave England, she will ask "Why?" It will
hardly do for us to say, "Because you were an honorable debtor and were willing to pay." The debts of
France and Italy occasion those countries just as
much concern as you would feel, dear reader, if Mr.
Rockefeller had an outlawed claim against you for a
hundred million dollars. If they have any feeling in
the matter it is regret that they did not get more
from us while the getting was good.

It certainly was good getting. From the day the
Armistice was signed until the day when Mr. Harding
was inaugurated, it was a case of "nobody home"
in Washington. The Government ran itself; anybody
could have money that would take it. Let us be
thankful that more was not taken. Before we entered
the war France had borrowed from us six hundred
millions; after the war she bought material left
behind, food, buildings, docks, railways, and the like,
— which cost us several billion, — for four hundred
million. We shall never see a penny of this money
and shall be called extortionate if we ask for it.
England will pay if she can, not for the fun of paying,
but to keep her credit good; and she won't love us
much after the strain is over. France and Italy won't
pay, won't even make an effort to pay, and will hate

us as a man always hates another to whom he is under an obligation. The fact is that the debts can be neither collected nor canceled. They will, however, be made to serve the purpose of silly politicians who will scream at one another across the ocean — and across the years — until the subject is worn threadbare.

These are my views; I have published them before, and I adhere to them notwithstanding the receipt of a letter of protest from a friend of mine in which occurs this paragraph: —

Do not say that England should not pay her debts: a promise was made, and the word of a great people given by their elected representatives — therefore by the people themselves — must be kept and honoured in the spirit and to the letter. England and Englishmen will never be popular, they are too cold, too self-contained, too self-satisfied: let them at least be, as ever, respected.

This is not the magnificent gesture of an orator at a futile English Speaking Union dinner; it is from a London bookseller, Charles J. Sawyer, and does him honor.

Of our social and political problems the English know little and they care less. Why should they care? They have their own, and they are very real. When we blunder, they rejoice; this is human nature. They are mildly curious in regard to the rapidity with which Henry Ford has amassed his fortune, and what we call "prohibition" amuses them as much as it distresses us. We at least have made an effort to

deal with the question of drink, which some people
consider the curse of England, where the liquor interest seems more strongly intrenched than the Crown.
Only a short time ago the Bishop of Durham, in a
speech in the House of Lords, killed a measure
affecting the sale of alcoholic beverages in England.
The great brewers and distillers have taken such
steps as were necessary to enlist the Established
Church and many leaders of public opinion on their
side, and reforms in the use of liquor are going to be
difficult.

In no city in the world does poverty so impinge
upon wealth as in London. The rewards for eminence
in any business or profession in England are immense,
but mediocrity has a hard time of it, and failure is
punished severely. One is constantly impressed with
the magnificence of the fashionable districts and the
misery of the slums, and they exist almost side by
side. "The rich man in his castle, the poor man at
the gate" — with a vengeance.

One cold raw Saturday night in December I put
on a cap and a heavy coat and tramped from my little
flat near Piccadilly to the Elephant and Castle, "in
the south suburbs" where, says Shakespeare, "it is
best to lodge." Three or four centuries ago elephants
were usually represented with pagodas or castles on
their backs, and such a tavern sign must once have
hung before a tiny tavern at a place where a number
of roads met leading to important towns in Kent and
Surrey. But no longer is the Elephant in the suburbs:

it is now a great public-house in one of the most densely populated districts in South London, a centre as crowded as Piccadilly Circus, but very different in character.

Walking through the magnificence of Whitehall, stopping to look at the Abbey and the Houses of Parliament as they rose out of the night over Westminster Bridge and skirting — almost — Lambeth Palace, the official residence of the Archbishop of Canterbury, I passed from splendor to scenes of poverty and misery almost beyond belief. The streets of London are probably safer than the streets of any other large city in the world: the police are not in politics, as with us, and although many were drinking and a few were drunk, there was no disorder; I have never seen any, though a London mob, no doubt, when aroused can be as terrible as any other. The public houses are now closed for several hours in the middle of the day and earlier than formerly at night, and an effort is being made to close them at 8 P. M.; it may be successful for, as the music-hall artist replied, when asked to sign a petition to that end, "Cert'nly, cert'nly; if a man's not drunk by eight o'clock, he's not tryin' to get drunk."

In England a man is not afraid to express his opinions. With us, no man holding public office can express his honest beliefs: we prefer platitudes. Some time ago I attended a dinner at which a politician of a western state, when called upon for a speech, replied that he would like to recite a poem.

Permission was granted upon the understanding that the poem was to be short; and this is it:—

> A thousand Jews
> Are selling booze
> Against my state's permission,
> To supply the needs
> Of a million Swedes
> Who voted for prohibition.

Following our usual course of leaping first and looking afterward, we wrote into our Constitution what should have been a police — or at most a State — regulation. What a tragedy it is that people with honest convictions against the use of liquor should be supported and abetted by the worst element in our community. Our state and city officials see to it that prohibition officers are constantly being changed, ostensibly in the interest of efficiency, but actually because such a post is regarded as too rich a political plum long to be held by one man. So what may be described as the best and worst elements in the community are agreed that the absurd law shall not under any circumstances be repealed. The whole corpus of the law has been brought into disrepute, for people will not have their innocent pleasures interfered with — not to enrich a lot of crooks. Temperance was making enormous strides in this country. Now drunkenness is hardly disgraceful. Legally I cannot enjoy a glass of Burgundy with my dinner or "a large cold bottle and a small hot bird" after the theatre, because some farmer in the South or West conceives that a beefsteak smothered in onions, with hashed brown potatoes, washed down with iced water, is a feast for Lucullus. "Who was Lucullus?" What profiteth it me if my gardener can no longer get a drink of decent whiskey for fifteen cents, if my daughter can go to a party with a young man in a Ford coupe — not coupé, mind you — chaperoned by a bottle of raw spirits?

On the other hand: I spent a week in Liverpool, on a Gilbert and Sullivan pilgrimage, staying at the best hotel in England, the Adelphi, built for the American trade just before the war came and diverted all the traffic to Southampton, where they rob you and give you nothing. The poverty, the squalor, the misery, the wretchedness, the vice of Liverpool — largely due to drink — is something beyond words.

"But it is a seaport," they tell you; "seaports are always like that." Two weeks later I spent a few days in Marseilles — also a seaport; everyone sober, busy, happy, seemingly contented.

We are just where we set out, dear Reader. "They order this matter better in France."

X

COLORED–PLATE BOOKS

THIS essay and the one immediately following grew out of a paper on English Colored Plate Books, read before the Print Club of Philadelphia.

The event came about in this way: two ladies, light-blue-stockinged women, in a manner of speaking, asked me to prepare and deliver this paper. They were charming women, or I would none of them: moreover, one was the wife of the Chief Justice of the Commonwealth of Pennsylvania, and the other, the wife of a Superior Court Judge. Now, in these days when traffic rules and regulations change every hour, one spends a good deal of his time before a Chief Justice, and, as it is a well-known legal axiom that the fines imposed by a Chief Justice are subject to review by a Judge of the Superior Court, I thought it well to accede to their request. Everyone is aware that there are not enough lawyers to go round, and that it is almost an impossibility to get a lawyer to go square: hence it is my invariable custom to throw myself on the mercy of the judge. At such times it is always well to have a friend at court — preferably two friends.

By nature a sedentary man, color-plate books changed the whole course of my life. I have become a sportsman, an authority on horseflesh; I breed dogs and ride to hounds. I have learned to swear, roundly, with Jack Mytton, — not difficult, — and to drink, deeply, with Jack Jorrocks, who claims, with some reason, that drinking will soon become a lost art. My friend Mr. Frank Raby was by my side when we stood with bowed heads at the grave of Mr. Mytton. "Take him for all in all, we shall not look upon his like again."

In all the realm of English bibliography there is nothing, I think, more interesting and more perplexing than the subject which we usually refer to as colored-plate books. First, we must begin with defining what a book is. Obviously, letterpress bound, with or without illustrations, is a book. If it is a few leaves unbound, with or without illustrations, it is a pamphlet; but a certain number of plates or illustrations unbound is not a book. Does the binding of them make it a book? I should say, strictly speaking, that it does not. Where are we then? Frankly, I do not know. If I labor the point, it is because there are certain items — I do not know what we collectors would do without that handy word "items" — very important and costly in themselves, which when bound together look like books, but which, having no letterpress, are not books; or, if we must call them books, we add some qualifying words, as when we say, "a book of drawings by Cruikshank," or "A book of plates by Alken."

I am going to eliminate from present consideration

anything which cannot fairly and squarely be called
a book, for the reason that to do otherwise would
extend this paper unduly. I shall have little or nothing to say upon that fascinating subject of sporting-
prints, but there are certain works of art which are
usually bound and look like books, which on account
of their beauty and importance I must briefly refer
to; Wheatley's *Cries of London*, for example, thirteen
plates engraved in untouched mezzotint by Schia-
vonetti and others, is a superb example of one kind
of colored-plate book; and Orme's *British Field
Sports*, the plates of which, drawn by Howitt and
engraved by Clark, Merke, and others and subsequently colored by hand, so exquisitely as to look like
water-color drawings, is another. The arts to which
we owe these items, that is to say, mezzotinting and
aquatinting, I shall refer to in more detail later.

But when we have decided what is and what is
not, properly speaking, a book, when we have decided
to eliminate certain important works of art as not
within our range, we meet with other difficulties.
There are no bibliographies of colored-plate books.
Perhaps no one with a reputation would care to
jeopardize it by attempting to make one: the subject
is intensely difficult. Colored-plate books were frequently first published in monthly parts, and when
it is remembered that it is the plates and not the text
that are of chief importance, it will be seen there is
a fine chance for a difference of opinion. Plates were
printed separately, not in sheets, and inserted in the

text in a more or less haphazard manner. Sometimes there are "instructions to binder," more frequently there are not; and what is to prevent an artist or a publisher from changing his mind after he has made his announcement? For example, this very day, as I write, there drifts to my desk a catalogue from Harry Stone, a New York dealer. Glancing at it, under the head "Colored Plates," I read this: —

Rowlandson (Thomas). *Journal of Sentimental Travels in the Southern Provinces of France.* Illustrated with 18 full-page beautifully aquatint-colored plates. First edition in book form; the title calls for 17 plates, but the list calls for 18, all of which this copy contains. In pristine condition. London, Ackermann, 1821, price $50.00.

And we have further to remember that the artists who have done most to make colored plates famous have also done most to make them perplexing. Perhaps the greatest name in English book-illustration is Cruikshank. It is important to remember there were three Cruikshanks, a father and two sons. Of Rowlandson there was, thank Heaven, but one. Of Alken there were four: two Henrys, a father and a son, to say nothing of Samuel and George, and they all made sporting-prints. "With plates by Alken," then, does not necessarily mean much. There was, of course, one great Alken, the father, as there was one great Cruikshank, the son.

And now that I have suggested some of the difficulties that confront me in speaking of English colored-plate books, let me begin.

A good place to begin is with William Blake. His *Songs of Innocence* (1789) was the first of a number of books published by him, — "created" would be a better word, — which have become famous alike for their literary and their artistic merit. The story is well known of how Blake, his first volume of verse having proved a failure, decided to become his own publisher and, being by trade an engraver, elected to try a new method of production and reproduction. Taking small pieces of copper, he wrote upon them the text and drew the designs and embellishments in an impervious varnish, and after he had by this means covered that portion of the plate which was *to appear in relief*, he ate away the rest of the surface with acid such as etchers use, and by this means secured a result that somewhat resembled a stereotype, from which he could print a reasonable number of impressions in any color he desired. This method, original with Blake, served him admirably until the end of his life. Pulling prints from his plates in dull browns or greens or grays, he colored and elaborated them by hand, the outlines serving him somewhat in the manner of a stencil. Almost never were two plates colored in the same manner, with the result that all of them are, practically, original paintings. In this manner Blake produced his *America, Europe, Milton, Urizen,* and other works. As we shall not return to this particular method of publication and illustration, we may say here that fine examples of Blake's work are now excessively rare: probably not more than two hundred examples of all of his different books were made in this manner, and most of these, having passed into great public libraries and museums, are not available for the collector. But they will ever remain a monument to the skill and originality of one of England's greatest artists. As Blake had no forerunner, so he has had no successor, for this reason: while his work was important, it had little or no influence upon the article of commerce usually referred to as the colored-plate book.

We have referred to Wheatley's *Cries of London;* another good example of mezzotint is the volume known as *Imitations of Original Drawings of Hans Holbein*, engraved in stipple and printed in colors by Bartolozzi. The plates in this monumental work were first published in folio, in 1792, under the direction of "John Chamberlaine, Keeper of the King's Drawings and Medals." The original drawings are in the library of Windsor Castle. The work was so exquisitely done and proved so popular that twenty years later they were again reproduced, this time in quarto. The large volume is now rare from having been broken up to provide portraits suitable for framing. The subjects are illustrious personages of the court of Henry VIII.

There were, too, a large number of books of colored engravings, that is to say, of plates only, in stipple, without letterpress, which were subsequently colored by hand, on a variety of subjects: architecture, views of places, natural history, and the costumes of

various nations at different periods. These last are
not very interesting in themselves and do not greatly
attract amateurs; they are chiefly to be found in
public libraries, where they are frequently referred to
by members of the theatrical profession and by others
who have in mind making an appearance at a fancy-
dress ball.

Pictures are books which we can read without turning the leaves. We who live in an age when the news
of the day is told in pictures, can hardly understand
a world in which there was no photography. At the
beginning of the nineteenth century the only way in
which a subject treated in a book could be represented
to the eye was by a drawing or by some kind of
engraving. Lithography, which for a time lent itself
admirably to book illustration, had not yet come into
existence, and publishers of books of travel and natural history all had recourse to engravings. These
engravings, whatever their character, whether subsequently tinted by hand "after nature" or allowed to
remain as they came from the plate-printer, supplied
a want as inexpensively as was necessary, at a time
when only people of means indulged their taste for
books.

But when we say that a man is collecting colored-
plate books, we do not mean that he is collecting the
works of either Blake or Bartolozzi, or costume books,
or books on birds or butterflies; we usually mean that
he is threading his way through the fascinating maze
laid out originally by Rudolph Ackermann, and added

to and made more bewildering by his contemporaries and their successors. Ackermann was born in Germany in 1764; he was the son of a coach-builder and was, himself, originally a designer of equipages of state — such as we now see in museums or occasionally on the streets of London when the Lord Mayor gives himself an airing, or the King attends some great function. After a thorough training under the eye of his father he went to Paris, and afterward to London, where he married and became a rich, influential, and public-spirited citizen.

He began by teaching drawing. From the first his progress was rapid; his drawing-school soon became an "academy"; and finally, when he added to it a print-shop, it became a "Repository of Arts." Soon he became a publisher of colored-plate books, and we may be sure that from among his former pupils he recruited the small army of colorists he was subsequently to employ upon the books with which his name is identified. Incidentally we may say that throughout his life — he died in 1834 and was buried in the Church of St. Clement Danes — Ackermann interested himself in whatever was new and useful. He was one of the first men in London to illuminate his place of business with gas; he introduced the art of lithography into England; he took out patents for a number of useful devices; and he was famous for his efforts on behalf of foreigners in England, who during the Napoleonic period arrived in shoals.

The art of illustration which Ackermann did so

much to advance appears to have been of French origin; all methods of engraving were employed, but stipple with line seems to have been the usual method. The engraving or etching, — which was subsequently hand-colored, — when pulled from the plate, looked as though it might be a drawing in sepia. As the art progressed, impressions were sometimes pulled in two colors, usually brown for the foreground and blue for distance, and as beneath the brush of skillful work-men these printed lines practically disappeared, no great care was necessary in the printing.

It must always be kept in mind that a colored mezzotint indicates a very different process from that of a colored aquatint. A colored mezzotint is the result of an impression pulled from a warm copper plate upon which the colors have been directly applied either by brush or by hand, or both, and in its perfect state it should not require touching up after the im-pression has been pulled. The plate is heated to keep the oil colors from becoming dry. In the case of very large and very fine impressions, — such, for example, as the exquisite work of Macbeth-Raeburn, in such demand to-day — one or at most two prints is a day's work, for the engraver is sometimes the printer also. Obviously such impressions are much too expensive for book illustration, especially as the plate begins to show signs of wear after a hundred or two impressions are pulled. Aquatints, on the other hand, could be printed by the hundred and colored by hand by men who were glad of the opportunity of earning their ten or fifteen shillings a week. Several great artists are said to have supported themselves at the outset of their careers by "tinting," as it was called, for publishers, among them Girtin and Turner, later to become very famous.

Before taking up Ackermann's more important work I must refer to two slender oblong books, the illustrations of which are typical of the period we are discussing. The first is *An Excursion to Brighthelmstone* (1790) by Henry Wigstead and Thomas Rowlandson. The text is of slight value, but the plates, eight in number, in aquatint, are fascinating and give an excellent idea of the experiences and scenes through which would pass the traveler in a post chaise on a journey from London to what is now Brighton. The book begins at Westminster Bridge and ends in the famous Pavilion of His Royal Highness the Prince of Wales, to whom the book is dedicated. The Marine Pavilion is a most striking object, we are told. It certainly is; it strikes us dead; and the statement that "all who are not biassed by Party, blinded by Prejudice or hostile to dignified Merit will agree that the *tout ensemble* of the building is in perfect Harmony," suggests that even a hundred and fifty years ago there was some question as to the taste of the architectural nightmare in which the Prince spent many happy hours with the beautiful Mrs. Fitzherbert, subsequently discovered to have been his wife, and whom, after the manner of Royalty, he used abominably.

The other "book" is the story of *Dick Turpin's*

Ride to York, (1835), told out of Harrison Ainsworth's romance of *Rookwood*, in six pictures drawn on stone — that is, lithographed — by Edward Hull, and subsequently "colored by hand and varnished." The incidents chosen are full of action: the famous highwayman, after having robbed a gentleman at Kilburn Wells, escaped on his famous mare to York, a distance of almost two hundred miles. The journey is packed with incident, and at the end the noble horse, who has carried its master to safety, drops dead just outside the gate of the cathedral city. The destruction of books of this character is clearly suggested by a note of the publishers, the well-known firm of Colnaghi, that "few sportsmen will not deem this set of prints a valuable addition to their collection, and as an ornament to Sporting Parlours we know of none which so well deserve a conspicuous situation."

Come we now to a number of unimportant ventures by Ackermann, which will not detain us long, as he was at work upon a book which would compel the attention of the world, — his world, that is, — the *Microcosm of London*. The interest of the Prince Regent, afterward George IV, was enlisted, and this fine work was dedicated to him in an engraved title-page of great beauty. To paraphrase the words of Austin Dobson, it was

> Humbly inscribed with curls and tails
> To His Royal Highness, the Prince of Wales,

and was certainly worthy of Beau Brummell's "fat

friend," who liked to think of himself as the first gentleman of Europe.

It was in 1808–10 that the *Microcosm of London* or *London in Miniature* was given to the world, or rather sold to gentlemen of literary and artistic tastes. The first idea was to publish the book in twenty-four numbers, at seven shillings and sixpence a number, but this was found to leave little or no margin for the publisher, and the price was subsequently increased to half a guinea. When the book finally appeared in three large volumes the price was fixed at fifteen guineas, and the set is now worth three or four times that sum.

I have said that there are very few sources to which one can turn for exact information as to colored-plate books. We should indeed be lost without the data contained in the sale catalogues of such concerns as the Anderson Auction Company and the American Art Association of New York, and the descriptions published in the secondhand dealers' price lists, among which I rate most highly those of my friend, Ernest R. Gee of New York. Occasionally, too, we have excellent descriptions of such books as are shown from time to time at the Grolier Club exhibitions. At the moment I have in mind the admirable, beautiful, and now scarce "Catalogue of Books Illustrated by Thomas Rowlandson." This last bears evidence of the care and skill of its painstaking librarian, Miss Ruth S. Granniss, to whom most of us collectors are personally indebted. There are also two other books which should be carefully studied by all collectors of colored-plate books: *English Colored Books* by Martin Hardie, and *Aquatint Engraving* by Miss S. T. Prideaux. All subsequent writers on the subject must draw largely on these.

The *Microcosm*, as everyone knows, consists of about two hundred pages of letterpress to each volume, describing, rather prosily, over one hundred famous buildings, most of which have now disappeared. The beauty and interest of the work lie in the illustrations, as Ackermann suggested in his introduction. The great objection hitherto made to engravings of architectural subjects was that buildings and figures were almost invariably made by the same artist, to the great disadvantage of the plates. To do justice to both the buildings and the figures our publisher employed two artists on the same plate: Rowlandson for the figures, and Pugin for the architectural part of the work. The result was eminently successful; the buildings were shown in their proper perspective, and the figures, too, were excellently drawn. The magnitude of the work will be best realized by considering that the book contains one hundred and four engraved plates, and one thousand copies of the book were published. This means that for this book 104,000 perfect impressions were made and separately colored by hand, and anyone who has studied Ackermann's books knows with what uniform excellence this coloring was done and what a high degree of finish was frequently obtained.

When this work was undertaken, Rowlandson was in the height of his fame. He was a talented artist, and had he been able to repress his humor and his love of caricature, he might have had great success in portraits, but his vagabond nature led him to turn to the streets and the scenes around him for inspiration. His eye was like the lens of a camera: it caught and retained all that passed before it, while his love of the grotesque and his intimacy with Gillray and other caricaturists gave a lasting bent to his genius. He had inexhaustible humor, extraordinary imagination; and he worked with the utmost rapidity. Life in London at the end of the eighteenth century was full of color and motion: taverns and places of public amusement supplied him with all that he needed in the way of "copy," for he was, in a way, what the camera man on a newspaper is to-day. English art is largely photographic; the Englishman loves to look at pictures which tell him stories that he knows already. This is one reason for Rowlandson's great popularity. So much for the man that Ackermann selected to do the figures for his *Microcosm*. As we turn the pages of this great work, London, the world in miniature, unfolds itself before us: we see the courts of justice and the great exchanges where men most do congregate; we visit in turn hospitals and prisons, churches and theatres; we move in the exclusive precincts of St. James's, or spend a night wedged in between peer and pickpocket at a cockfight. In brief, the plates in the *Microcosm* are documents essential to anyone who would understand life in London a hundred and fifty years ago.

It was inevitable that the success of this work should lead to several other undertakings of a similar kind. A volume on the Abbey Church of Westminster, one on the colleges of Oxford, and another on those of Cambridge, quickly followed; these appealed to a limited audience and need not detain us. In 1816 a volume usually spoken of as *The Schools* was published. It is a book of great beauty, one of the best of colored-plate books. It is a history of the great public — actually the very exclusive and private — schools of Eton, Winchester, Harrow, and. others. This volume contains much better work than the "Colleges"; it is more generally popular, and fetches a much higher price. It consists of forty-eight plates by Pugin, Westall, and others; W. H. Pyne wrote a portion of the text. The mention of Pyne's name, relatively unknown, reminds us that, if Rowlandson's fame depended upon the work so far done, his name would mean no more to us than Gillray's; for in the last analysis his fame depends chiefly upon the *Tours of Dr. Syntax* and the *Dance of Death*.

Ackermann was now embarking in a new venture: he decided to publish a magazine which should contain nothing but poetry. I am not by nature well fitted to judge of its merits, holding with the elder Weller that "poetry's unnat'ral." Be this as it may, in the editor's Introduction he stated that the pages of the *Poetical Magazine* would be open to all comers, provided their productions were in verse; even advertisements were to be rhymed. I quote — with omissions: —

We solicit the attention of advertisers, provided their advertisements have the passport of Parnassus. We shall be happy to receive any interesting accounts of public events or domestic occurrences, but they must be given in verse. A Bulletin of Bonaparte, or an official letter from a British Admiral or General, will be inserted, if any poetical politician will give it rhyme. Marriages, Births, and Deaths will be accurately registered, if they are poetically stated. The Critic who will favor us with measured opinions of a book, a picture, a play, or an opera ballet, will be considered as a valuable Correspondent.

Needless to say, it was soon seen that something was required to enliven such dreary pages as resulted, and Rowlandson was asked to supply a humorous plate for each monthly issue. The tour of a whimsical clergyman-schoolmaster, who was always getting himself into all kinds of scrapes, was the result. "Fine," said Ackermann, when he saw the highly humorous sketches, "but we must have verses to accompany the plates." Now it so happened that there was in London a man as great a genius in his way as Rowlandson: that man was William Combe. And here a considerable digression is necessary.

William Combe was the typical product of his time. By birth a gentleman, by training a scholar, he had inherited from his father a fortune which he dissipated by the magnificence of his living, and by his thirtieth year he was a ruined man. To retrieve his

fortunes he married the discarded mistress of a nobleman who had promised him an annuity with her,
but such promises are frequently broken; so it was in
his case and he lost no time in "shaking" the lady.
Reduced to penury, he became a teacher of elocution,
and finally went to France and enlisted as a soldier.
But soldiering not being to his taste, he returned to
England and became an author, ready and willing
to do any odd job in authoring. He wrote with extraordinary ease: verses, political pamphlets, or sermons,
as required, dripped rapidly from his pen, but he
always retained a certain amount of elegance and
distinction. In those days it was inevitable that such
a man should be arrested for debt, and by the time
he was forty he had settled down to living very
comfortably within the "rules" of the King's Bench
Prison, where he remained till his death at the age
of eighty-two. He had a man to attend him, half
servant, half companion; he knew the best people
in London, and was an intimate friend of Walter
of the *Times*, for which he wrote what we would
now call editorials. Such was the author to whom
Ackermann turned for the poems, verses, lines, text,
— call it what you will, — to accompany Rowlandson's humorous drawings in the *Poetical Magazine*.
He, too, even more than the artist, owes his fame to
his publisher.

The remarkable thing about the joint work of artist
and poet, as they shall now be called, is that they did
not meet personally for several years, and the artist

may be said — and indeed he claimed — to have originated the story, for Combe had no idea what he was to write about until the artist supplied him with the picture. By the time that the "Schoolmaster's Tour," as it was originally called, was completed, both artist and poet were famous, for its popularity had saved the magazine from an early death. The first number of the *Poetical Magazine* appeared in May 1809, and it carried on until April 1811, when, the "Tour" having been completed, the magazine succumbed. A complete set in four volumes is before me, and I venture to say that it contains some of the worst poetry ever written. As Dr. Johnson once said, "I expect this statement to be accepted without proof." But the "Tour," a poem of ten thousand lines, can still be read by the hardy reader and, accompanied as it is by the highly humorous plates of Rowlandson, can be read with pleasure, if perhaps not with the keen delight that it gave the reader a century ago.

Upon the extinction of the magazine, Ackermann at once announced that he was preparing an edition of *The Tour of Dr. Syntax in Search of the Picturesque* — a new name for the "Schoolmaster's Tour." A new set of plates was made, and their number was increased by three new subjects. These were a frontispiece showing "Dr. Syntax in Meditation" at his desk, an engraved title-page, and "The Doctor's Dream of the Battle of Books," one of the most charming plates Rowlandson ever did. Successful in the magazine, in book form Dr. Syntax became the rage: everything useful to man or horse became "Syntax." There were "Syntax" wigs and hats and coats and saddles, and when finally a race horse named "Syntax" began to win money for his backers, the triumph of the schoolmaster was complete.

My copy of the *Tour* has this inscription: "Mr. Combe presents this volume to Mr. Chester" — I do not know who he was — "with his affectionate regards, May 20, 1812." In the Advertisement, or, as we would now call it, the Introduction, Combe recites the conditions under which the work first appeared.

The designs to which this volume is so greatly indebted ... were sent to me every month and I composed a certain proportion of pages in verse, in which of course the subject of the design was included; the rest depended upon what my imagination could furnish. When the first print was sent to me I did not know what would be the subject of the second, and in this manner ... the artist continued designing and I continued writing ... having no personal communication with or knowledge of each other. I feel no parental fondness for the work, though it was written at a very advanced period of life.

Combe, when he composed *The Tour*, was over seventy years of age, and he continued writing until his death twelve years later.

In recent years only the partnership of Gilbert and Sullivan has in any degree resembled the enormous success of Rowlandson and Combe; the plates, of course, have kept the text alive, for, to quote Dr.

Johnson again, the verse without the plates "had hardly vitality enough to preserve it from putrefaction." But we have the plates, and many pleasant hours may be spent in looking at them, dipping here and there into the accompanying text. There is, of course, a great "likeness" about Rowlandson's work, but this only means that Rowlandson suggests himself rather than anyone else. He is, indeed, strongly individual, and if his men are all big-bellied and his women overflow their stays, they were but slight exaggerations of the people he saw about him. Nothing is lovelier than a young English girl; she seems as fragile as a rose; but with the passing years she not infrequently takes on the habit of a cabbage; indeed Hawthorne goes so far as to suggest that every Englishman should marry his wife a second time, after a lapse of twenty years, because at least half of her was not present at the time the ceremony was first performed.

The success of *Dr. Syntax* was no temporary affair. Edition followed edition; it was translated, I know not how, into the French with French lithographed illustrations, and into the German with German lithographs. Nor is this all: imitations of it appeared in London with cleverly worded title-pages, suggesting to the unwary that Dr. Syntax had broken out in a new place. The illustrations also were imitated: there is a *Tour of Dr. Syntax Through London*, published by J. Johnson, Cheapside, with plates which are obviously imitations of Rowlandson. There are also the *Tour of Doctor Prosody* and the *Adventures of Doctor Comicus* and *Dr. Syntax in Paris,* all probably fakes, but possessing a certain interest, being as they are colored-plate books, and reflecting the taste and manners of the times. Omitting, for the moment, reference to the *Dance of Death,* — in my judgment, the finest of the Rowlandson-Combe books, — we come to the *Second Tour of Dr. Syntax;* for, that good gentleman's wife having died early in the story, he sets out *in Search of Consolation.* Although lacking, perhaps, the spontaneity of the first, it is an amusing volume, dated 1820, and in the introduction Combe says: —

I have been called upon to separate the works written by me, as the Biographer of Dr. Syntax, from those which have been palmed upon the public by others who have pilfered that title . . . *The Tour of Dr. Syntax in Search of the Picturesque, The Dance of Death, The Dance of Life,* and the volumes containing the second and third *Tour,* are the only works in this style of composition which have been written by me.

This would seem to be conclusive, but Combe was, according to some, an unabashed liar. One could believe about half of what he said, but the difficulty was to know which half, and it is quite possible that, although professing his unswerving allegiance to his regular publisher, Ackermann, he at the same time may have done a bit of work for another in t'other end of the town. Be this as it may, on May 1st, 1821 — you see how contagious Combe's style is — the poet set his hand to the Preface of the third and last *Tour of Dr. Syntax*, now *in Search of a Wife*. In this the author — in his eightieth year — with natural pride refers to the pleasure he feels at still being able to amuse the public.

In this way "Dr. Syntax" was an endurance test for the illustrator, the author, and the public. One would not pretend that his interest does not flag here and there in the thirty thousand lines — fifteen thousand couplets — so mechanically supplied, and in which, when a triple rhyme occurred, the printer, as was usual at the time, placed a bracket in the margin to celebrate the event, much as a hen cackles when she lays an egg. The pictures, too, are of unequal merit; but to write and draw acceptably year after year in the same style on the same subject is a task which few but Combe and Rowlandson could have accomplished.

It has seemed best to refer to the three volumes of the *Tour* as though they were one publication, whereas, in point of fact, the first volume appeared in 1812 and the last in 1821. Between these years appeared what many regard as their best joint work. I refer, of course, to *The English Dance of Death* (1816). The *Dance of Life*, published a year later, is obviously an effort to trade on the very great success of the earlier work. Some time ago Mr. Charles Sessler, the bookseller of Philadelphia, had the finest copy of the work in existence. It was formerly in the celebrated Rowlandson collection of Henry Wil-

liam Bruton of London, which was dispersed at auction several years ago. It is made up of parts as
issued, with uncolored plates of all the engravings
and the artist's original drawings, besides a number
of other drawings which for one reason or another
were rejected. He has disposed of it, and whoever
now owns the volume may say in all truth that he
has the finest colored-plate book in the world.

Originally the *Dance of Death* was published in
twenty-four monthly parts; it was then brought out
in two volumes and sold at three guineas. The title-
page bears a translation from Horace: —

> With equal Pace, impartial Fate
> Knocks at the Palace, as the Cottage Gate.

At the risk of hearing someone mutter "sour
grapes," I wish again to say how much I dislike
books in parts, especially if they contain pictures
which one wants to look at. I buy books to read and
to enjoy; it gives me pleasure to show them to an
appreciative friend; if a book is in parts, there is
great danger of a substantial fraction of its value
disappearing each time it is examined. So I content
myself with a volume in its original cloth if I can
get it that way, and if it is very much "shaken,"
as it may be, keep it in a pull-off case or have it
substantially bound in crushed levant morocco — in
which condition it can defy both time and friend.

The personification of Death in the form of a skel-
eton, playing some musical instrument, forcing men
to dance to his music or to follow his steps in the

dance, developed out of Germanic mythology, much as the Faust legend has done. Then it became a mediæval religious drama, and most countries in Europe worked it over according to their peculiar bent. Holbein's "Dance of Death" is certainly the most famous; but in what might be called modern treatment of the subject Rowlandson is supreme. Whether he suggested the subject to the publisher or the publisher to him, is not known, but certain it is that it is his greatest work. In the preparation of this paper I wrote most of the leading booksellers in this country and England, asking what was, in their opinion, the most important color-plate book and — with a reservation, which I shall mention later — the vote for Rowlandson's *Dance of Death* was practically unanimous. I cannot do better than quote Martin Hardie on the subject: —

It is obvious at a glance that the artist bestowed exceptional care on the illustrations for this book. The union of the gruesome and the grotesque appealed strongly to his imagination, and in completeness of detail and carefulness of grouping the illustrations excel nearly all his other work. The hand-coloring also has been delicately and judiciously applied. Combe's versification is full of wit, and shows a force and vigor surprising in a man who had passed his allotted threescore years and ten — a fact that adds a certain grimness to the humor of the work.

Rhyming as an amusement has gone out of fashion, but a hundred years ago it was the usual accomplishment of a gentleman. Perhaps the last American to practise it was James Russell Lowell: asked once to give a lecture, he consented, provided he might give it in rhyme, and leave being granted, he began like this: —

> Ladies and gentlemen! I claim to-night
> With your fair leaves, to use a poet's right:
> Asked for a lecture, 't will be no high crime
> If, for a change, I give you one in rhyme.
> For me 't is easier far, for rhyming grows
> Natural at last, like ropes to dancers' toes,
> And as these oft are clumsy when they walk,
> Poets turn prosers when in prose they talk.

And so on for an hour or more. Combe was a "proser" turned poet in his extreme old age; verse became a medium more natural to him than prose, and he wrote it with greater facility. And here it may not be amiss to say that, for very exalted thought or for comic situations, verse is better adapted than prose, and once one gets into the swing of it, is more easily read. In proof of this statement, read a few pages of the *Dance of Death* and then take up Gilbert à Becket's *Comic History of England* or the *Comic History of Rome*. Both books fairly bristle with puns, jokes, and witticisms, that in verse might have a sort of "punch," but, expressed in prose, give one after a short time a feeling of fatigue. It would be difficult to praise the illustrations of these books too highly: I have indeed never been able to decide which gave me the most pleasure, the *Rome* or the *England*. The illustrations are excellent in drawing, charming in color, and are full of humor — in short, John Leech at his very best. Let the reader throw aside this volume and turn to these "Histories." He has an hour of sheer joy before him.

And then, perhaps, he will welcome a breathing-spell; indeed it might be just as well to get out into the open after the atmosphere of this stuffy library for so many hours. Let us change, and get on the back of a horse or, better still, let us join Mr. Frank Raby, a great friend of mine, and with him go up to London.

XI

WE could have waited for the coach, but with Mr. Raby it's "damn the expense," so we traveled in his post chaise very comfortably up to London at the rate of about ten miles per hour, including stops. Upon our arrival in the metropolis we descended at Stevens's Hotel in Bond Street, and after the removal of the stains of travel from our persons, and dressing with the care which life in town demands, we sauntered forth, and in the course of our wanderings were surprised to stumble upon "Ackermann's Eclipse Sporting Gallery" in Regent Street; upon our last visit to town that gentleman's enterprise was known as the "Repository" and it was located in the Strand. Upon inquiry we were informed that the elder Ackermann was dead; he had suffered a stroke of paralysis, after which time the control of his affairs had passed largely into the hands of his son of the same name. Almost immediately the Repository became the Eclipse Sporting Gallery, and abandoning its old location in the Strand, it moved to a more fashionable situation in the west end of town.

The change in the name suggests the change in character of the business; henceforth "sport" rather than "art" was to reign. Italy for ruins, Germany for music, France for art, but in all that pertains to sport, to games, to life in the open, England is the land! We hear, or used to hear, of the pleasure-loving French, but the Frenchmen's idea of recreation is to grow hair curiously in little tufts upon their faces, and then to sit at little round tables outside the cafés and make eyes at the women as they pass; this is the one outdoor sport in which they excel. They race horses, no doubt, and are adept at cards, but it is pathetic to see them with a bat or ball or gun. Of the manly art of self-defense they know nothing; they can, however, give you a kick that will take the joy out of life for an indefinite period. On the other hand, the English, men and women, old and young, love games, especially such games as take them out of doors. To be supremely happy the man should be mounted upon a good horse, but if he cannot afford this, he can make shift with a stout stick and a dog to keep him company.

The Englishmen are the sportsmen *par excellence* of the world, and for their sports they dress themselves with care: tight-fitting garments for one occasion, loose ones for another; "pink" for one sport, plaid for another; the style is the man, and for style the whole world looks to the one place where it can be found. I feel quite sure that a New York tailor will turn you out infinitely better than an English tailor, but the New York tailor gets his styles and his cloths from London. Where else should he get them? From Berlin? The Germans are the worst-dressed people in the world. Tell a German that he

looks like an Englishman, and he may affect to be
insulted but secretly he is enormously pleased. From
Paris? For madame Paris will do very well, but
Frenchmen dress like freaks unless they copy the
Englishman. I once so far forgot myself as to buy
an expensive hat on the Rue de la Paix, and I was a
marked man until I got rid of it.

The English are very complacent about all this:
indeed nothing less than a world war can shake them
out of their complacency. Even that German lunatic,
George III, before whom they bent the knee, who by
his pig-headedness lost them America, did not greatly
suffer in their esteem. Our loss was greater than theirs,
they said, for we had lost them, whereas they had only
lost us. And "Farmer George" was all right. Had
he not overthrown Napoleon? And what of India?

Never again will England be so completely cock
of the world's walk as in the fifty years after the
Battle of Waterloo. England then was indeed the
right little, tight little island to which all the world
had paid and would continue to pay tribute. The rich
were very rich, and the poor were very poor, but was
that not as God had ordained? The "governors,
teachers, spiritual pastors and masters" were satisfied, and that was all that was necessary. Oh! what
a comfortable thing it was to hear the children promise to order themselves "lowly and reverently" to
all their "betters," and to hear them sing: —

> "God bless the squire and his relations,
> And keep us in our proper stations."

The poor were expected by Church and State to work for pay just sufficient to keep body and soul together, just as the squire was expected to ride and drive and hunt and shoot from one year's end to another. And they gave parties, they did, in those days when George the Fourth was King. Ladies upon these occasions do not seem to have been much in evidence; their place was in the "bower." The parties were, in fact, drinking-bouts, and we read of one at which a butler was so indefatigable with his corkscrew, and it grew so hot under the friction to which it was subjected, that it actually set fire to the cork, the bottle of spirits exploded, and the whole establishment went up in flames.

And this life, so picturesque and so completely a thing of the past, is nowhere so perfectly described as in the "sporting-books" which we are now to consider. We shall only skim the cream of this subject, for it is a study by itself.

Alphabetically and otherwise it is convenient to begin with Alken. One comes so frequently upon the phrase "with plates by Alken" in catalogues and in conversation about sporting-books and prints, that it is somewhat disconcerting to discover that there were several Alkens. Very little is really known about Henry Alken, whose work is in such demand to-day. George H. Sargent, in that excellent Boston paper, the *Transcript*, some years ago published a check list of the works of this great master, and pointed out that the statement of the Dictionary of National

Biography that Alken was born in 1816 and died in 1831 is an obvious error. The family were Danish; for political reasons they left Denmark and, coming to England, abandoned their own name — which was Seffrien — and took the name of Alken. Henry, the most distinguished member of the family, was born in London in 1784. He studied drawing with his uncle Samuel Alken, whose name is not unknown to collectors, and later taught it. There appears to be no truth in the commonly accepted story that he was a stableman or huntsman to the Duke of Beaufort; on the contrary, he is said to have been a gentleman. He died in 1851, being survived by two sons, Henry Gordon and George, both of whom were engravers and lived to a great age; the elder was a conscious imitator of his father's work, and much that is attributed to the father is probably the work of the son.

And now, as though to endorse my statement as to the difficulty of this subject, comes another catalogue, this time from Quaritch, in which I read: —

Alken (Henry). NATIONAL SPORTS OF GREAT BRITAIN. Impl. 8vo., 50 Fine Coloured Plates with descriptive text; half morocco extra, emblematically tooled, by Riviere, gilt edges; Very scarce. Thomas M'Lean, 1825. 48–0–0 This is a quite distinct work from the folio book bearing the same title published 1821, not one design being common to both books. The only resemblance is in the title, a fact which is misleading to many collectors.

So here are two different books with the same title,

published only four years apart. Although he did some landscape work, most of Alken's plates are "horsy." One of his earliest is a set of colored plates entitled, "Qualified Horses and Unqualified Riders"; this is dated 1815, but I shall now take a fence in the most approved style and land in the year 1835, in which he drew and etched the plates for a very famous book, the *Life of Mytton* by "Nimrod." It is a biography of a real man that reads like a work of fiction, while the *Life of a Sportsman*, for which Alken also made the illustrations, is a fiction which reads like a biography. Originally the "Life" of Mytton appeared in the *Sporting Magazine*, where it attracted so much attention that it was reprinted in an edition which all collectors want, and which, on account of its rarity, few can possess. It is an unimportant-looking little volume of one hundred and ten printed pages, with twelve colored plates, bound in brown cloth, and has the imprint, "London, Rudolph Ackermann, Eclipse Sporting Gallery and New Sporting Magazine Office, 191 Regent Street, 1835." The text of this famous sporting-classic by "Nimrod" introduces a new name. "Nimrod" was the pen name of Charles James Apperley, gentleman, scholar, sportsman, and intimate friend of the man whose life he wrote. Financial difficulties led him to exchange the whip for the pen, and he became famous for his sporting-letters in the *Sporting Magazine*.

John Mytton traced his family back for five hundred years; so much for that. His father died when

JOHN MYTTON

From a rare colored print, engraved by Giller after a portrait by Webb

he was a lad, and his mother's efforts to keep him at
school were unavailing; he was expelled from Westminster and from Harrow, and when at the age of
fourteen, a ward in Chancery, he appealed to Lord
Eldon to increase his allowance of eight hundred
pounds per annum, saying he was going to get married,
that gentleman replied wisely and briefly: "Sir, if
you cannot live on your allowance, you may starve;
and if you marry I will commit you to prison." It
would have spoiled a very pretty biography had
Mytton not exercised every Englishman's right to go
to hell his own way. With an iron constitution,
Mytton entered upon a career of dissipation which
ended only with his death from delirium tremens in
the King's Bench Prison in his thirty-seventh year.
He had by that time succeeded in dissipating a fortune of £10,000 a year and £60,000 in ready money
which had accumulated during his minority.

Now I don't mean to say that the *Life of Mytton*
is a work of art, or that it is my favorite biography;
but I do say that if one wants to know in how many
different ways a man can play the fool, it is essential
to read this "Life" and, while doing so, to remember
that it is not fiction: that a hundred years ago Jack
Mytton, Esq., M. P. for Shrewsbury and Major in
the North Shropshire Yeomanry Cavalry, actually
lived such a life as is presented by his biographer.
The "strenuous life" preached by Theodore Roosevelt was the life of a valetudinarian compared with it.

What did he do, you ask? We may suppose that

the high spots in the life of this young barbarian, born
without a nervous system, but with muscles of steel,
are those chosen for illustration by Alken; and opening it at random, we come upon a man in a nightshirt,
with a gun in his hand, squatting on the ice, waiting
for a covey of ducks to appear. This was not done on
a bet; but it appears that Mytton never felt either
heat or cold, and that, far from getting himself up
in proper sporting-togs, as men usually do when they
go out, he, whenever the humor took him, went out
in whatever he happened to have on. Now he happened to have on a nightshirt when he felt a desire
to shoot birds.

Another picture, showing two men being thrown
out of a cart into the road, illustrates this story:
Mytton was driving a friend home when he chanced
to ask his friend whether he had ever been hurt by
being thrown out of a gig. "No, thank God," was his
friend's reply, "for I never was upset in one."
"What!" exclaimed Mytton, "Never upset in a gig?
What a damned slow fellow you must have been all
your life!" And immediately running the near wheel
up a bank, out they went. But the classical story,
without which no reference to this book would be
complete, is the one illustrated by the plate bearing
the title, "Damn this hiccup." The story may be
briefly told: Mytton was in the act of getting into
bed when, annoyed by the hiccups, he exclaimed,
"Damn this hiccup, I'll frighten it away," and taking
a lighted candle, applied it to his shirt tail and was

"WHAT! NEVER UPSET IN A GIG? WHAT A DAMNED SLOW FELLOW YOU MUST HAVE BEEN ALL YOUR LIFE!"

instantly enveloped in flames. When he was finally got to bed he stayed there for a considerable time.

How much he ate and drank — from four to six bottles of port was his daily allowance; the treatment of his wives — he had two; and many other details of this remarkable man, were set down not in sorrow, certainly not in anger, but in wonder by his biographer, and we are quite prepared — as he was not — for his end. Ruined in estate, body, and mind, he fled to France where, port being unobtainable, he lived on brandy. After a time he returned to England, where he was at once arrested for debt, the amount of which no one seemed to know. In a few weeks he was dead, and his remains deposited in all honor in the family vault under the communion table of Halston Chapel. "After life's fitful fever he sleeps well." Let us hope so.

Two years later (1837), a second and enlarged edition appeared, with nine plates from the first edition and nine new ones, eighteen in all. The third edition, published in 1851, is practically identical with the second. Thereafter various editions appeared from time to time: a very fine one, with colored photographic reproductions of the original illustrations, only a few years ago.

Alken's plates require a word; they are no longer the delicately tinted wash-drawings of the earlier colored-plate books, but highly colored opaque watercolor pictures, from which practically all sign of the etched line has disappeared; especially is this true of the first edition. The catalogues call them "spirited," which they certainly are. They have retained all the brilliancy they had when they were made almost a century ago; either water colors were better then than they now are, or the use of them was better understood; certainly, except in stained-glass windows there have never been such brilliant colors, especially the reds and blues; undoubtedly the superior quality of the paper upon which they were painted accounts for much of their permanency.

I would be the last to contend that Mytton was the type of an English country gentleman; but with all his devil-may-caredom, he was a gentleman, not a scoundrel, one of those of whom it may be truly said that he was his own worst enemy. The class to which he belonged has practically disappeared. Addison, in that charming little sketch, *The Tory Fox-hunter*, has painted him to the life; one may make his acquaintance in the pages of Trollope, and to a lesser degree in those of Archibald Marshall, but to see him at his best — and worst — we must consult the pages of the sporting-books we are now considering. A friend, endeavoring to dissuade Mytton from selling a part of an estate, told him that it had been in his family for five hundred years. "The devil it has!" he replied, "Then it is high time it should go." Such seems to have been the feeling of Lloyd George at the beginning of his political career. Then the war came, and the country gentleman, of whom even the radicals were proud, was practically extinguished, but like a true sportsman he made no complaint. Alone and in herds, in Flanders and in Northern France, the sons of the great county families paid the debt they owed their country. The wealth they had is gone, and the life they led is over; they will soon become a tradition; but they will never be forgotten. Such reflections as these must occur to anyone who reads *The Life of a Sportsman.*

If we, who incessantly write and talk about books, were to stop and consider how small a proportion of all that pour from the press survive, for a year say, after publication, we would be more apt to stand at attention when a book is mentioned that has reached its eightieth birthday and is still going strong. *The Life of a Sportsman* is such a book and will, I take it, by succeeding generations be regarded as a sort of "Complete English Country Gentleman." It might have been advertised as "A book for a gentleman — by one."

In reading it as I have done, I have acquired a fund of information which, from all I can now see, will be of no use to me whatever. In these days of motors one need not be told that the horse is going out — he has gone. It used to be said that there was a horse in the zoölogical garden of Venice, which children were occasionally taken to see; and so it may be with us. In our great cities certainly there is no place for a horse, but some of us, who know that life in the country is the only life, will, I take it, continue to get our health and recreation on the back of a horse. What is the old saying? "The outside of a horse is a good thing for the inside of a man." When I began my study of sporting-books, my knowledge of the horse was rudimentary: I could tell the east end from the west, and that was about all; now I am willing to discuss, at greater length than you would wish me to, the care of hunters and the wisdom of feeding "green meat," that is to say, grass, in the summer time, and a hundred similar questions. I shall not permit myself to say anything about hounds, for the reason that a man whose house is not far from mine has a kennel. He is breeding for sound and has secured, I hear, unexpected results.

Men, old and young, with horses and hounds, occupy every page of a *Life of a Sportsman*. It is a novel; that is to say, the hero, Frank Raby, is a fictitious character, but he is placed not in an imaginary but in a real setting and among real people. When it was published eighty years ago it must have produced somewhat the same sensation we experienced a few years ago, when we read Sir Harry Johnston's *The Gay Dombeys*, in which the children of Dickens's imaginary characters were mingled with real people of to-day. The story is briefly told. Frank Raby is the second son of an English squire. His father is not very rich, as great fortunes go in his day, but the substantial sum of ten thousand pounds per annum enables him to live with distinction, provided he is careful of his expenditures. What he does must be done faultlessly; his social position demands it. He

has a pack of "harriers," that is to say, dogs for hare-
hunting, six able coach-horses in one stable, ten
hunters in another, besides a hack or two to carry
messages about the country. And he is very particular about his footmen: they must not differ in height
by the thickness of a hair, and they must be London-
bred. "He never saw a country-bred footman who
could properly enter a room." (I wonder what Mr.
Raby would think of our ideas of service in this
country?) Yet he could not afford his own foxhounds;
therefore he does not "hunt," in the proper acceptance
of that word. From hares, rather than foxes, he gets
his recreation; and it is explained in some detail that
this is a very inferior form of sport.

He has two sons, the elder a delicate lad, fond of
his studies; the younger a fine manly boy, whose one
idea in life is sport. The younger is the favorite of a
rich uncle whose fortune he inherits, and when the
elder brother conveniently dies, and subsequently
the father, the young Squire, having settled a substantial sum upon his mother whom he adores, is
able to devote himself exclusively to the amusement
of his class. He declines a seat in Parliament lest it
might interfere with his hunting, which occupies him
so completely that he never marries. Of night-life
in London there is just a trace — a mere *soupçon*.
From early morn to dewy eve he is riding, driving,
shooting, fishing, and hunting, and when he is not
doing these things he is talking or writing about them.
The *Life of a Sportsman* contains raw material which

Trollope worked over and illuminated with humor, of which this book contains not a trace. A number of rules for the guidance of a sportsman are laid down very seriously, as where Raby is advised not to keep a drinking man-servant nor a very pretty maid-servant on his estate, and never to take the word of any man about a horse he wishes to sell, not even a bishop's. This last, Trollope translated into: "Not even a bishop can sell a horse without forgetting that he's a bishop."

The colored plates in *The Life of a Sportsman* are beautiful; it is the general opinion of the booksellers that the frontispiece, "The Meet at Amsted Abbey," is the finest plate in any colored-plate book. In a chapter on colored-plate books, I said that my friends, the booksellers, had made certain reservations in regard to the *Dance of Death;* they divided colored-plate books into two classes, humorous and sporting. They gave the palm in the one case to the *Dance of Death*, and in the other to *The Life of a Sportsman*. Mr. Sessler, the Philadelphia bookseller who specializes in sporting books, makes the point that the frontispiece in the *Sportsman* is photographic, while the title-page of *The Analysis of the Hunting Field*, another wonderful Alken item, is imaginative. It is a point well taken.

It is remarkable with what skill Alken, in little drawings no larger than a post card, can unfold to you exquisite panoramas of country life such as exist nowhere but in England. Groups of red-coated men

on horses, surrounded by hounds impatient for the
huntsman's signal, are shown in one drawing; in the
next they are going "hell-for-leather" after a little
brown streak that we know to be a fox. Hedges,
fences, and a stream provide the hazards which usually
result in a man being thrown, which seems to be one
of the delights of a hunt, especially if the victim of a
miscalculated brook be a parson, as he usually is. I
remember one plate in which his reverence is shown
struggling in the water. "Shall we fish him out?"
cries someone. "No," says another, "we won't want
him till Sunday; this is only Friday," and on they go.

Fox-hunting is a sport not without its dangers:
Many a man has gone out on a hunt as lively as a
cricket, been thrown, and brought home dead, upon
a shutter; and a hunt need not necessarily be the
best preparation for entrance into life eternal. "God
help me!" exclaimed a dissolute wretch in the fraction of a second before he landed upon his head,
crushing it like an eggshell. "He made a fine end,"
said one of his companions, as they were talking over
the sad event in the gun room after dinner — with
wine. They made it into a hymn: —

> "Betwixt the saddle and the ground,
> He mercy sought and mercy found."

There are many anecdotes of horses and hunting,
but the best story I ever heard has never yet found
its way into a book, and I wish to preserve it. I was
sitting one day with several friends, one of whom was

and still is a lawyer in Philadelphia, a distinguished horseman, a member of the Radnor Hunt. He was telling us of the delight of a fox hunt in which he had taken part the day before. From hunting, riding became the subject of conversation; my own rôle was that of a patient listener. Finally one friend said to the other, "Joe, I think I should like to buy a horse. If you ever hear of a good horse that I can buy cheap, I wish you'd let me know." To which Joe replied, "Sam, I never yet heard of a man who was willing to pay a fair price for a horse. What's your idea of price and what kind of a horse do you want?" "Well," said Sam, who was a distinguished member of the Society of Friends, "I have not ridden much lately, but I used to ride a great deal; I am accustomed to horses. I need a pretty good horse to carry my weight, but I want a horse that my mother can drive; she's an old lady and very nervous. Of course I shall not be able to ride every day, so I'd like a horse that could do odd jobs about the place, there's always a trunk to be hauled to or from the station, or a lawn to be cut, and — " But Joe could wait no longer. "Sam," said he, "while you are look-ing for that kind of a horse, why don't you get one that you can milk, too?"

Is it any wonder that men in town and country, "sporty," and bookworms, like myself, find solace, recreation, and delight in collecting colored-plate books? I eschewed them for years and have lived to regret that I did not "hunt" earlier, before the pace

became so swift, for these books are constantly ad-
vancing in price. At present the market for them is
largely in the East, around Boston, New York, and
Philadelphia. When Pittsburgh, Chicago, and points
West awaken to their charm, as they will, we may
expect to see prices go skyrocketing.

"The proper study of mankind is man," says the
poet. When? we may inquire. When we are making
a living, or when we are amusing ourselves? In our
work we closely resemble one another; we differ in
our amusements. A Frenchman, as has been said,
weather permitting, sits at a little table for hours at a
time, drinking something he calls coffee, talking and
gesticulating madly. A German goes to a beer garden
and, drinking beer, plays dominoes or a game with a
pack of greasy cards. The Englishman's idea is to
get out in the open and follow some sort of sport: he
is said to be happiest when he is killing something,
big game in the proper place; and can there be any
doubt that the fox exists for but one purpose, namely,
to be hunted?

In reading these sporting-books we must remember
that we are for the time being enjoying the best
society in England. Many of the country gentlemen
we meet in *The Chase, the Turf, and the Road*, for
example, men little known out of their own county
would hardly have exchanged their position for any
dukedom going. I once chanced to meet an English
squire, a lord of the manor, to whom in conversation
I happened to mention the name of Marlborough as

great in English history. "Marlborough!" he said disparagingly, "Merely a creation of Anne: my ancestors are in *Doomsday Book;* we have been living on the same estate for eight hundred years."

A century ago, at Melton Mowbray in Leicestershire, the centre of the best hunting-country in England, there used to assemble during the season a group of sportsmen such as the world has never seen before or since. They came with their horses and their servants, and they did nothing but hunt. Six days a week they spent in their saddles, dashing madly from one place to another, following a pack of hounds. On the seventh day they rested, that is to say, they visited one another's stables and kennels, and talked "hunting" — meaning thereby fox-hunting; for to hunt anything else, hares for instance, was in their opinion contemptible. They were enormously rich; one wonders where the money to support such magnificence came from. It was necessary to have, if a man wanted to be properly mounted, from ten to twenty horses. Sir Harry Goodricke, a noted sportsman, had forty-four hunters and eighty couples of hounds, and while this was regarded as liberal, it was not considered excessive: several gentlemen had more. And fox-hunting, be it remembered, was a winter amusement; with the coming of spring, racing took the place of the chase, and this necessitated another string of horses. A man lived for and with horses. When a noted painter was asked why he had given over painting portraits and taken to painting horses, he replied that many a man, loath to spend a ten-pound note on his wife's portrait, made no bones about giving fifty pounds for a good picture of his favorite hunter.

Of the endurance and skill of the riders, we hear much. Not only did they ride from morning till night, but they rode "straight," that is to say, they were prepared to take any fence or hedge or brook that came in their way, and they were able to distinguish the voice of any particular dog above the music of the pack. The price of a good hunter was from one to two hundred guineas, and for a particularly fine couple of hounds two hundred guineas were frequently offered and frequently refused. Verily, as Mr. Jorrocks — of whom more anon — says, "Fox-hunting is the sport of kings." It was the ambition of every man to spend a season in the fox-hunting metropolis, Melton Mowbray, where sometimes as many as two hundred men joined in the chase. And this sporting-life was going on — to a lesser extent, certainly, but going on — all over England. If one criticised it, one was told that it was the foundation of England's greatness. An economist would say that England's greatness depended upon cheap coal, cheap iron, and cheap labor; but who would be an economist that could be a sportsman?

Of the studbook, the only book that Jack Mytton would consent to open, and of the turf I shall not speak; to do so would open up, not a book, but a library. But I cannot deny myself the pleasure of referring to *The Chase, the Turf, and the Road,* as one of Nimrod's most popular books is called. It is, to be sure, not a colored-plate book, but it has plates by Alken, and the portion devoted to coaching-days and coaching-ways is delightful. Let us go back just one hundred years; there were no railways, but listen to Nimrod chanting the glories of England: "The princes of the Arabian Nights' Entertainments were scarcely transported from place to place with more facility or despatch than we are at the present moment." He was not thinking of a wealthy gentleman's traveling chariot and four, with relays of horses all along the road; he had in mind only the regular daily departure of coaches from London for points all over England; but speed alone is not his boast. "Traveling," he says, "is no longer the disgusting and tedious affair our ancestors thought it, but has been converted into something like a luxury. Go back only ninety-four years, when it used to take six days to go from London to York, a distance of two hundred miles; now it can be done in twenty-four hours. What other country under the sun can boast of such an accomplishment?"

We, who live in days when distance can fairly be said to be annihilated, may smile at our author's ideas of speed and luxury, of his "Comets" and "Meteors," his "Quicksilvers" and "Regulators," which at the lightning speed of twelve or fourteen miles an hour made Brighton to all intents and purposes a suburb of London, highways and highwaymen permitting. But no one, not even Nimrod himself, has painted more brilliantly than Amy Lowell, in what she calls "polyphonic prose," life on the post roads of England in the early days of the nineteenth century. In "Hedge Island," that charming little essay of ten pages in *Can Grande's Castle*, we see in imagination the old highways dotted with multi-colored mail-coaches, their highly varnished surfaces flashing in the sun, as they roll along; men set their watches by them — hence the "Regulator." We hear the echoing horn of the guard and the rhythmic beat of the horses' hoofs as they hammer the highway. And the channels marked off by hedges of fragrant hawthorne from the billowy fields lead invariably to an inn, whereat a man receives his warmest welcome — an inn such as Mr. Pickwick loved, with a cozy bar, and a comfortable bed hung with flowered chintz, with sheets smelling of lavender. But at the end Miss Lowell allows a shadow to fall upon the picture: "In the distance there is a puff of steam, just a puff, but it will do. Coaches and coachmen, guards and post boys melt before it like meadow rime before the sun."

I suppose, short of actual war, there has never been anything more tragic to a certain class than the coming of the railways. "Hang up my old whip over the fireplace," said a famous coachman, when the London and Southampton Railway was opened in 1833, "I shan't need it never no more"; and he fell ill, turned his face to the wall, and died of a broken heart.

It is time, and a little more than time, that I introduce another name, great in the history of book illustration, the name of Cruikshank — a name which strikes terror to the heart of every collector, for George alone, of that ilk, is identified with the illustration of some six or seven hundred books or pamphlets. To some he contributed as many as forty full-page engraved plates with countless little vignettes and woodcuts; to others, only the frontispiece.

Men who have been bitten with the Cruikshank craze have spent their lives, and a hundred thousand dollars say, and died unsatisfied; for their collections, while creditable, were not complete. Probably the greatest Cruikshank collection ever formed was given by Richard W. Meirs to Princeton University. I have a suspicion that Princeton does not appreciate it.

Luckily for us, George Cruikshank was not specially identified with colored-plate books. He was, however, a genius who never learned to draw, and he had great originality and imagination. His early drawings were coarse and frequently vulgar. *The Humorist*, perhaps one of his most important, certainly one of his rarest books, was issued in parts in 1819, and was followed by the famous *Life in London* by Pierce Egan. It has thirty-six aquatint plates and numerous wood-cuts, and was enormously popular. From it one gets a fine idea of the amusements of the young bucks of the time, of which getting drunk and beating up the night watch were the most elegant. From the point of view of to-day it would seem to be a curious work to carry, by permission, a dedication to the King, which begins: —

I am encouraged humbly to intreat permission to dedicate this work to your Majesty by that love and patronage which your Majesty has at all times evinced for the protection of Literature.

It then goes on to say that

an accurate knowledge of the manners, habits, and feelings of a free people is not to be acquired in a closet . . . but only by means of a free and unrestrained intercourse with society.

"Free and unrestrained" completely describes many, indeed most of the works of the period.

Cruikshank, who was well over eighty when he died, is a connecting link between the time of Rowlandson and the illustrators of our own day. In his old age he did much to advance the cause of temperance in England, but he had, unluckily, a peculiar aptitude for quarreling with his friends, and he sometimes fancied that he, like Rowlandson, was the creator as well as the delineator of certain famous characters in fiction.

We now come to another well-known name, Robert Smith Surtees, a gentleman, a humorist, and a lawyer. He, while waiting for clients, had written a treatise on the *Warranty of Horses*, the only book to which he ever put his name; he owes his fame to his novels. I have said that "Nimrod" Apperley, in his portrayal of the country gentleman, had treated him not as a man among men, but rather as a god, towering above his fellows. Surtees saw the absurdity of this, and in a series of articles contributed to *The Sporting Magazine* created a sportsman of another type, Jorrocks, who has been the delight of several generations of male readers, and who is still going strong.

John Jorrocks is a city man who, having acquired a substantial fortune in the grocery line, from time to time "sinks the shop" and gives himself a day's outing in the country. All the world has heard of him and of his adventures while hunting, shooting, driving, sailing, and eating — has heard, laughed, and laughed heartily. He is the quintessence of good humor, absurdity, vulgarity, and cunning, and Jorrocks loves an outing with 'orse and 'ounds not less

ROBERT SMITH SURTEES
from a beautiful portrait published by Ernest R. Gee of New York

dearly than Mr. Frank Raby. It will readily be seen
how much fun could be had with such a character.
When the series of articles terminated in the magazine
they were published in book form, illustrated with
etchings by "Phiz," otherwise Hablot K. Brown.
Our interest, however, is with the second edition of
the book, published five years after the first, the
greatly sought edition with colored plates by Alken.
The plates are quite as amusing as the text, and the
title-page — well, Mr. Sessler has given his vote for
the title-page of *The Analysis of the Hunting Field*.
I give mine for "The Jaunts and Jollities of that
Renowned Sporting Citizen, Mr. John Jorrocks, of
St. Botolph Lane and Great Coram St.," combining
in one comprehensive tableau the hero of the yarns
at his favorite amusements.

"That man Surtees could write a novel if he had
a mind to," someone remarked as he put down a
copy of *Jorrocks*, and Surtees "had a mind to," and
he did — a whole series of 'em, of which *Handley
Cross* is by far the best, although much might be
said for *Mr. Sponge's Sporting Tour*. We owe to
the creator of Jorrocks a debt, a debt greater than we
shall ever be able to pay; for the success of the
articles in a magazine led Mr. Chapman of Chapman
and Hall, publishers, to send for a novelist, a young
and practically unknown man, and suggest to him
that he do a somewhat similar series of sketches in
another field, and the immortal *Pickwick Papers* was
the result. Here we see side by side the operations of

talent and of genius: the one produces Jorrocks, the other, Pickwick. If the *Pickwick Papers* had only been issued with colored plates!

> Of all sad words of tongue or pen,
> The saddest are these, it might have been.

But it was not; and so we must return to Jorrocks of *Handley Cross*, who is, I suppose, the most famous character in fox-hunting fiction. The old chap is so inveterate a sportsman that a commission finally sits upon him to determine whether he be mad or no. It is good fooling, all of it. We have "Binjimin," his servant, and "Pigg," his huntsman, and his 'orses, — good at everything, riding, driving, 'unting, and carrying a woman. A grand nag is Xerxes, his master's favorite; when he drove tandem he was the leader, and Arter-Xerxes comes "arter" him, you understand. Once a sporting gentleman, thinking to sell Jorrocks a troublesome horse, wrote to him and received a reply stating that he would have a look at the beast, and as his owner's estate was some distance away, he would stay to dinner and bring his night cap, for, says Jorrocks, "Where I dines, I sleeps, and where I sleeps I eats my breakfast." There is much homely wisdom in the fat old man, who finally becomes Master of the Foxhounds, as when he says, "Arter all's said and done, there are but two sorts of folks in the world, Peerage folks and Post Hoffice Directory folks and it is the Post Hoffice Directory folks wot pays their bills." "'Unting is the sport of kings, the h'image of war without its guilt, and only five-and-twenty per cent of its danger." So Mr. Jorrocks exclaims when called upon to give in public his private opinion of hunting. And perhaps you remember the punning lines of Kipling:

> Certes it is a noble sport
> And men have quitted selle and swum for't,
> But I am of a meeker sort
> And I prefer Surtees in comfort.
>
> Reach down my "Handley Cross" again;
> My run, where never danger lurks, is
> With Jorrocks and his deathless train,
> Pigg, Binjimin, and Arterxerxes!

Leech it was who was joined with Surtees in the success of *Handley Cross*. He is, I think, my favorite of all of England's great illustrators. Austin Dobson has said, "As Cruikshank refines upon Rowlandson, so Leech refines upon Cruikshank, but to a much greater extent." His humor is as keen, his sense of fun as marked, but it is less grotesque, less boisterous, less exaggerated, nearer to truth. Thackeray, whose friend he was through life, once said, "Where would *Punch* be without him?" I might add, where would a whole host of books be without him, and especially the novels of Surtees, and the *Comic History of England*, in two volumes, and the *Comic History of Rome*, in one, which contains, to my mind, some of his very best work.

None of Trollope's novels were issued with colored

plates, hence my mention of them in this paper is out of order; but he has written so many excellent descriptions of hunts and huntsmen that a word may be permitted. A fox-hunting man of my acquaintance who — with his wife, who rides faultlessly — never permits the Radnor hounds to go out without accompanying them, once told me that the best fox-hunting story he knew was the story of "Nappie's gray horse" in *The Eustace Diamonds*. I was inclined to challenge this statement, there are so many excellent hunting-stories in Trollope; and are there not those books by those two wonderful women, Somerville and Ross? I turned to this book and that, picking out delicious morsels here and there, when a letter was received from a college professor with an international reputation, in which I read this: "I have just reread *The Eustace Diamonds*. I don't say that it is a better story than *Vanity Fair*, but I get more pleasure out of it. Do you remember Frank Greystock's hunting on another man's horse? It's what you would call a 'corking story.'" Whereupon I called my friend on the telephone and said, "Arthur, you were right about that hunting-scene in *The Eustace Diamonds*."

To return to Leech, with whom colored-plate books come practically to an end. Beginning with delicate tinting in the early publications of Ackermann, reaching its height perhaps in *The Schools*, we found, at what might be described as its middle period, all trace of the engraved line disappeared in opaque color, in the *Life of Mytton*. In its brilliant close with

Leech, the colored plate became a work of the greatest delicacy and refinement. Leech used a very fine needle, no single line of which was lost in the faint wash of color which was flowed over the entire plate. So we are back where we began in the matter of color, having rounded out a full half-century. In most of his work, Leech employed etching, pure, simple, and black, finishing his plates as though he had no idea that a small army of tinters was waiting upon him. He died in 1864, just as photography as a means of book illustration was beginning to be understood. From it the wood-engraver received a blow from which he never recovered: his art has practically ceased to exist.

The photo, half-tone plate, and other mechanical processes have taken the place of hand work as completely as steam and later inventions have taken the place of the horse. Nowadays we move rapidly, and our happiness seems to express itself in terms of plumbing. Life is more comfortable but it is less picturesque. Having been born to democracy, having achieved votes for women, and had prohibition thrust upon us, we should see smiling faces and contentment everywhere. But do we? The question answers itself. Our labor-and-time-saving devices leave us no leisure in which to enjoy life; as the world grows older it grows sadder, not wiser. We have, in Disraeli's phrase, "established a society which has mistaken comfort for civilization." Our politicians — the scoundrels — are reforming all the joy out of life. If we would live for a time in a world in which everything was wrong but everyone seemingly was happy, we cannot do better than spend an hour or two in turning the pages of the beautiful colored-plate books of the last century.

XII

SKINNER STREET NEWS

WHEN William Godwin, an Englishman who thought himself a philosopher, decided to abandon literature for commerce, — if the vaporings of his mind may be called literature and the publication and sale of children's books may be called commerce, — he looked about him for some location suitable for his purpose and finally pitched upon a little house in Hanway Street, a narrow L-shaped lane leading from Oxford Street into the Tottenham Court Road, the rent of which was only forty pounds a year, of which the greater part was raised by letting rooms to lodgers. He then entered upon a career which was to continue for twenty years: years crowded with such misfortunes as, thank Heaven, seldom interrupt the course of a man who elects to live by the relatively simple method of buying cheap and selling dear — which, reduced to its simplest terms, successful commerce consists in.

Godwin was fifty years of age when he began to do business, his training for which had been peculiar. Almost thirty years before this story opens, five "'Ministers of the Gospel of Christ' certified that he had gone through a course of studies preparatory for the Christian Ministry with great diligence in Mr. Coward's Academy at Hoxton and having exhibited a Theological Thesis in Latin and delivered a sermon in English, and being in communion with a Christian Church, and having maintained a good report as to his religious temper and moral conduct during the whole course of his Academical Education:" therefore these five ministers judged him "to be well qualified for entering on the sacred work of the Ministry" and most heartily recommended him "to the Blessing of God and to the service and acceptance of the Church of Christ." I am able to be explicit in this matter, as the documents in the case are before me, as is also the record of a quarrel which he had, promptly, with one of his earliest congregations — the upshot of which was that Godwin soon gave up the ministry in favor of literature, as he was later to give up literature for commerce.

His business venture he started not under his own name, nor did he yet carry on under that of his wife, — as subsequently he did, — but under that of Thomas Hodgkins, his manager, at what was called "The Juvenile Library." Owing to the revolutionary political and religious opinions which he had developed, he thought it unwise to link his name with such an innocent enterprise as the one he was launching. He was in many respects a shrewd old customer, industrious but self-indulgent, and accustomed, as most of us are, to preach one thing and practise another. The venture was not immediately unsuccessful, for within two years it was removed to more commodious premises at 41 Skinner Street, Snow Hill.

WILLIAM GODWIN
after a painting by James Northcote, now in the National Portrait Gallery

Snow Hill! Does it convey anything to your mind? I seem to have heard of it. Listen: —

Snow Hill! The name is such a good one . . . picturing to us . . . something stern and rugged. A bleak, desolate tract of country, open to piercing blasts and fierce wintry storms . . . lonely by day and scarcely to be thought of . . . by night — a place which solitary wayfarers shun and where desperate robbers congregate. This, or something like this, should be the prevalent notion of Snow Hill. The reality is rather different. . . . There at the very core of London, in the heart of its business and animation, near to Newgate, the jail, and by consequence near to Smithfield, and just on that particular part of Snow Hill where omnibus horses going eastward seriously think of falling down on purpose and where horses in hackney cabriolets going westward not infrequently fall down by accident, stands the Saracen's Head Inn.

Ah, now it comes back to us — the place where Mr. Squeers met Ralph Nickleby and his nephew Nicholas! Exactly; but Skinner Street? Well, Skinner Street had just been built, through the exertions of the man whose name it bore, to connect Newgate Street with Holborn, so that the tortuous, steep, and dangerous Snow Hill would no longer form the chief connecting link between Oxford Street and the City. The street served its purpose for a time, but with the growth of London it was cleared away, and the Holborn Viaduct has now taken its place. To 41 Skinner Street then, on the north side, at the corner of Snow Hill and nearly opposite Turnagain Lane, Godwin removed himself, his family, and his business enterprises and, soon dropping the name of Hodgkins, began to do business as M. J. Godwin & Co., the "M. J." being, of course, "Mary Jane," his wife, "she being a managing woman," while he supplied the inexperience; neither had any capital.

It was from this address that *The King and Queen of Hearts*, that excessively rare Lamb item, was issued. It was one of the first books published by Godwin, and but three copies are at present known; one of them in its dull blue wrappers lies before me as I write. It was my friend E. V. Lucas, Lamb's most scholarly biographer, — who delightfully interrupted the progress of this paper by his unexpected visit to the writer, — who first discovered Lamb's connection with this priceless little trifle. In a letter dated February 1, 1806, only a part of which had previously been printed, Lamb, writing to Wordsworth, says he is sending him a parcel of books, among them "A Paraphrase on the 'King and Queen of Hearts,'

TALES

FROM

SHAKESPEAR.

DESIGNED

FOR THE USE OF YOUNG PERSONS.

By CHARLES LAMB.

EMBELLISHED WITH COPPER-PLATES.

IN TWO VOLUMES.

VOL. I.

LONDON:

PRINTED FOR THOMAS HODGKINS, AT THE JUVENILE LIBRARY, HANWAY-STREET (OPPOSITE SOHO-SQUARE), OXFORD-STREET; AND TO BE HAD OF ALL BOOKSELLERS.

1807.

of which I, being the Author, beg Mr. Johnny Wordsworth's acceptance and opinion." Could Godwin
but know the prices which his early publications
now fetch in the auction rooms, how amazed he would
be! Many of them are worth their weight in gold,
while some of them
would tip the scales
against bank notes,
since scraps of paper
have taken the place
of coin of the realm.

Godwin was not
without ideas: it was
he who suggested to
Lamb that the plays
of Shakespeare,
adapted to the read-
ing of young persons,
would make a nice
little book, especially
if embellished with
copper plates by Wil-
liam Blake; and he it

THE

KING AND QUEEN

OF

HEARTS:

WITH THE ROGUERIES OF THE

KNAVE

WHO STOLE THE QUEEN'S PIES.

ILLUSTRATED IN

FIFTEEN ELEGANT ENGRAVINGS.

LONDON:

Published at the JUVENILE LIBRARY,
41, Skinner Street, Snow Hill; and to
be had of all Booksellers.

1808.

was who published the *Poetry For Children*, the total
disappearance of which in England and its subsequent
discovery in Australia is one of the romances of modern book-collecting. In 1827 Lamb wrote Bernard
Barton, "One likes to have one copy of everything
one does. I neglected to keep one of 'Poetry For
Children,' the joint production of Mary and me, and

it is now not to be had for love or money." What would he have said at the price it brought at the Daly sale in New York twenty-odd years ago? Twenty-two

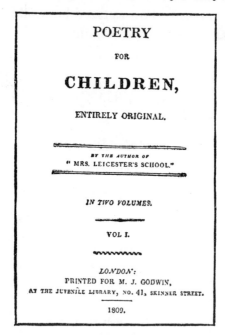

POETRY

FOR

CHILDREN,

ENTIRELY ORIGINAL.

BY THE AUTHOR OF
" MRS. LEICESTER'S SCHOOL."

IN TWO VOLUMES.

VOL I.

LONDON:
PRINTED FOR M. J. GODWIN,
AT THE JUVENILE LIBRARY, NO. 41, SKINNER STREET.

1809.

hundred and fifty dollars! How amazed he would be to see a copy of it in the strong room at "Oak Knoll"!

How sobering is place and responsibility! Take a radical, make him a bishop, and he will roar you as gently as a sucking dove. Godwin, whose name was anathema to the fathers of families, and Lamb, the gentlest of men, fell out over a question as to what was proper for a child to read.

Dear Lamb, [writes Godwin] I address you with all humility . . . hear me, I entreat you with patience: It is strange with what different feelings an author and a bookseller look at the same manuscript. I know this by experience: I was an author, I am a bookseller. The author thinks what will conduce to his honor; the bookseller, what will cause his commodities to sell.

He then went on to state his objections to what

Lamb had written. Lamb made one alteration in the copy he had submitted, and then declined to change another word.

As an author [he wrote] I say to you touch not my work! As to a bookseller, I say take the work such as it is or refuse it. As to a friend I say, don't plague yourself and me —

and Godwin was forced to be content. Doubtless he was getting ready to borrow money from the author, or he would not have yielded so readily.

William Godwin was a cold, contemplative, and selfish man, as innocent of humor as a crutch; he called himself a recluse, which he was not; he spent much time in heated argument with friends and was a regular attendant at the theatre. A few years before he had allowed himself to form a connection with Mary Wollstonecraft, a woman of great talent and beauty, whose life had been one long series of misfortunes, crowned by her marriage — a little tardily — with him. The wedding took place a few months before the birth of a daughter, Mary, who subsequently became the wife of Shelley. She died in giving this daughter birth, and a short memoir, the work of her husband, prompted Roscoe to write of her: —

> Hard was thy fate in all scenes of life,
> As daughter, sister, mother, friend, and wife;
> But harder still thy fate in death we own,
> Thus mourned by Godwin with a heart of stone.

Mary Wollstonecraft, as she is generally called,

for she was legally Mrs. Godwin for but a few months, was only thirty-seven when she died. She was indeed a woman to be pitied. Born in or near London, she suffered much from the neglect of an idle and dissipated father. As a young girl she formed a rather romantic attachment for another girl about her own age, a Fanny Blood, also the daughter of a worthless father, who died in Lisbon; Mary visited her there, arriving just in time to close her eyes in death. Meantime one of her sisters had married a scamp at whose hands she suffered much; indeed it would be amusing, if it were not tragic, to note the misery which invariably followed marriage, as Mary Wollstonecraft saw it exemplified. Small wonder, then, that she wrote "The Wrongs of Woman," a title that would have served admirably for practically all she wrote.

After picking up such education as she could, Mary Wollstonecraft opened a school, which was unsuccessful; subsequently she became a governess in the household of a lady of quality with whom she went to Dublin. While there she wrote a little tale, *Mary*. In it she commemorated the unhappiness of her own life and that of her friend Fanny Blood; it has been called, by courtesy, a novel. I have a copy and I have read it; I venture to say that you, reader, have not. Your loss is small; it is a lugubrious trifle. Poor Mary! All the men she had so far known were brutes, and this fact had distorted her point of view.

Coming to London with the manuscript of *Mary*,

her "Fiction," as she called it, she made the acquaintance of one Johnson, a bookseller in St. Paul's Churchyard, who published the book for her in 1788 and otherwise helped her. The edition must have

been a very small one, for the book is exceedingly difficult to come upon, as is her next publication: *Original Stories from Real Life, with Conversations Calculated to Regulate the Affections and Form the Mind to Truth and Goodness*, as its pious title runs. Of this also I have a copy, which was once Buxton Forman's, and, better still, the original drawings by William Blake, which

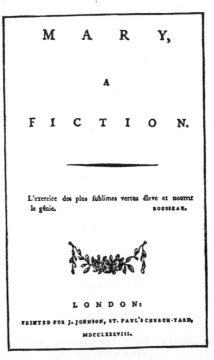

were made for its illustration, — those accepted and those rejected, — which were once the property of Alexander Gilchrist.

It seems curious that we know so little of Joseph Johnson, Mary's publisher, who was at this time a man of considerable importance. Mary Wollstonecraft says he was a man first and a publisher afterward; he is identified with the Edgeworths and also with Cowper, and he was fined and imprisoned for the publication of the writings of the too outspoken Gilbert Wakefield, one of a group of free-thinkers by whom he was surrounded and much influenced. At Johnson's table — for she soon became very intimate with him — she met many of the distinguished radicals of the time: Godwin, Blake, Holcroft, Horne Tooke, Tom Paine, and the rest, who were for rearranging the universe without delay. In this rearrangement she was anxious to do her part, and what more natural than

ORIGINAL STORIES

FROM

REAL LIFE;

WITH

CONVERSATIONS,

CALCULATED TO

REGULATE THE **AFFECTIONS,**

AND

FORM THE **MIND**

TO

TRUTH AND **GOODNESS.**

BY MARY WOLLSTONECRAFT.

LONDON:

PRINTED FOR J. JOHNSON, NO. 72, ST. PAUL'S CHURCH-YARD.

1791.

that her work should take the form of her *Vindication of the Rights of Woman.*

By this time she was known as Mrs. Wollstonecraft, for, as someone has wittily said, in those days the production of a book, like the production of a

child, was regarded as an act of indelicacy if it occurred outside the married state. I have just finished
reading the *Vindication;* how harmless and reasonable
and rather coarse it seems to-day! But it created

almost as much of a
sensation as did God-
win's *Political Jus-
tice,* which appeared
a year later, and for
which, in a manner,
Mary Wollstone-
craft's book blazed
the way. At this
time she would great-
ly have resented Dr.
Johnson's reply when
asked why women
were deprived of
their political rights:
"Why, sir, nature
has given women so
much power that the
law very wisely gives
them very little." As

VINDICATION

OF THE

RIGHTS OF WOMAN:

WITH

STRICTURES

ON

POLITICAL AND MORAL SUBJECTS.

By MARY WOLLSTONECRAFT.

LONDON:

PRINTED FOR J. JOHNSON, N° 72, ST. PAUL'S CHURCH YARD.

1792.

Mrs. Pennell has pointed out in the only Life of
Mary Wollstonecraft that survives, she believed that
coquettish arts triumph only for a day, and that love,
the most transitory of all passions, is inevitably succeeded by friendship, indifference, or neglect.

Though formed for love and friendship, it was

Mary Wollstonecraft's misfortune to be neglected and despised. Within a year after the *Vindication* appeared she had achieved such distinction for herself that conservative people avoided her and her books. Hannah More's attitude was typical. She wrote to a friend: —

I have been much pestered to read the "Rights of Women" but I am resolved not to do it . . . How many ways there are of being ridiculous! I am sure I have as much liberty as I can make good use of now that I am an old maid; and when I was a young one, I had, I dare say, more than was good for me.

A year or two later, when Mary published a poorly digested book on the French Revolution, Walpole, in a letter to Hannah More, concludes with this famous remark: "Adieu, thou excellent woman! Thou reverse of that hyena in pettycoats, Mrs. Wollstonecraft, who discharges her ink and gall on Marie Antoinette, whose unparalleled sufferings," and so forth. This phrase, "hyena in pettycoats," has stuck to her ever since. Poor Mary! In spite of Walpole, I'm fond of you.

About this time there is a story that arose from some gossip as to an affair she had or sought to have with Fuseli, the artist. It is too late in the day to discover the truth or untruth of the story, nor is it necessary, for she soon supplied her critics with a red-ripe scandal, for the truth of which a baby daughter was sufficient evidence. Desirous of seeing a revolution in operation, Mary had gone to Paris, where,

MARY WOLLSTONECRAFT GODWIN

from a portrait now in the National Portrait Gallery (by Opie?)

alone and unprotected in the French capital, she was once more thrown upon her own resources. Under these conditions she met a man — an American, Gilbert Imlay — who assumed the rôle of her protector. Always as strong of will as of emotions, it was not long before she overcame any scruples she may have had, and consented to live with him as his wife. It is probable that, he being an American and she an English woman, a legal marriage in France was out of the question; but her views on the subject of marriage were lax, not to say loose, and she was about to pay the highest price a woman can pay for her laxity. In due time a baby was born, and at nearly the same time she discovered Imlay in amours with other women. His business affairs took him much away from her, and her child, called Fanny after her early friend, was not a blessing as it should have been, but a source of grief, shame, and anxiety. Finally, after her return to London, discovering that Imlay no longer cared for her, she sought to take her own life by jumping into the Thames from Putney Bridge, but was rescued by a passing boat. Her *Letters to Imlay*, written before and during this period, and published shortly after her death by Godwin, make interesting, if pathetic reading. Beginning at first in a glow of passion for the man to whom she had given her heart, the letters by degrees change their tenor, until at last she assures him that she will not again flinch from the duties which tie her to life, and then she solemnly bids him farewell. ·

Assuming now the name of Mrs. Imlay, she once again began to earn her living by her pen, resumed her intimacy with her faithful friend Johnson, the publisher, and gradually regained her old place in literary society. Matured and beautified by suffering, she again met Godwin and interested him; they became friends, and with him, as he says, "tenderness melted into love," and nature took its course. For a time each kept their own lodgings, spending a part of every day together, but the approaching birth of another child led Mary to think of marriage; she had no wish to bring another illegitimate child into the world.

THOUGHTS

ON THE

EDUCATION

OF

DAUGHTERS:

WITH

REFLECTIONS ON FEMALE CONDUCT,

IN

The more important DUTIES of LIFE.

By MARY WOLLSTONECRAFT.

LONDON:

PRINTED FOR J. JOHNSON, N°72, ST, PAUL'S CHURCH-YARD.

M DCC LXXXyII.

While I have no desire to "reflect on female conduct," I may be permitted to observe that the author of this interesting work was the mother of an illegitimate daughter who finally committed suicide. Another daughter, almost illegitimate, eloped with a married man, thus causing his wife to commit suicide! "It is easier to preach than to practise."

One would like to know Godwin's real feelings when he discovered that marriage was expected of him. He had been looking forward to the idyllic time when society would exist without law and when marriage

would be a superior kind of friendship; yet here he
was, confronted not by a theory but by a woman,
and that woman "in an interesting condition." He,
the most methodical of men, made no mention in
his diary that on the twenty-ninth of March 1797,
at old St. Pancras' Church, with only the clerk as
witness, he took vows against which all his life he
had been scoffing. Soon the baby was born who was
to become so famous as Mary Shelley that we almost
forget that she was a daughter of William Godwin.
And with her birth her mother died and was buried
in St. Pancras' churchyard, within the shadow of the
church in which her wedding ceremony had been
performed not many months before.

Mary Wollstonecraft's position in literary history
is unique. Long considered a dangerous radical by
those comfortably placed souls who oppose all change
as revolutionary, she suffered for being consistent,
as the few who are consistent are bound to suffer.
That the world would come to accept her beliefs, she
could only hope: to-day almost the only opinion held
by her which the world has not endorsed is her contempt for the marriage tie; this perhaps chiefly for
the reason that children and property are both affected by its disregard. We may do what we like with
ourselves, and our property may be taken from us
by taxation, but until children become a charge upon
the state — and may that day be far off — we shall
be wise if we conform to the regulations established
by society for its own protection and for ours.

We shall now leave Skinner Street for a time. Indeed, we are not yet there — we are in William Godwin's lodgings in the Polygon in Somers Town. Almost before he realizes that he is a married man, he finds himself a widower and the father of a family. Fanny, his stepdaughter, is three years old; his own daughter, Mary, as many days. Much is in store for him: he has made his bed badly and is about to lie in it. For ourselves, we shall go down into the country.

It is midsummer; and in Sussex, near Horsham, a beautiful and probably naughty little boy is playing. His name is Percy Bysshe Shelley; his parents call him Bysshe; and his home, "Field Place," is a substantial mansion in a park which suggests comfort if not elegance. The boy is tall for his five years, and much inclined to have his own way.

Later on at Eton, and still later at Oxford, this inclination and his wish to challenge any statement put before him, either in a printed book or by word of mouth, led him into many difficulties, culminating in his being expelled from the University. Just before this event took place, a lady — Lady Charlotte Berry, — writing to a friend, said: —

Talking of books, we have lately had a literary Sun shine forth upon us here, before whom our former luminaries must hide their diminished heads — a Mr. Shelley, of University College, who lives upon arsenic, aqua-fortis, half-an-hour's sleep in the night, and is desperately in love with the memory of Margaret Nicholson. He hath

published what he terms her Posthumous Poems, printed
for the benefit of Mr. Peter Finnerty, which, I am grieved
to say, though stuffed full of treason, is extremely dull,
but the Author is a great genius, and if he be not clapped
up in Bedlam or hanged, will certainly prove one of the
sweetest swans on the tuneful margin of the Cherwell.

And it was to be so.

Some controversy about his publication, *The Necessity of Atheism*, was the immediate cause of the lad's
expulsion and, with the doors of his home closed upon
him, we find our young friend in London, frequenting
the hospitals with some idea of becoming a physician.
Shelley, as we shall now call him, is eighteen, a tem-
peramental lad, a reformer, and a dreamer; some day
he expects to be very rich, but he cares nothing for
money except that he may do good with it. He is
tall and of an almost effeminate beauty, which however does not detract from his charm, for his opinions
are as robust as those of a prize-fighter. He has already tasted the joy of seeing himself in print, and
he is determined that his life shall be spent in writing
and fighting for humanity: a noble ambition.

We have been taking Shelley's early life at a bound;
we must now go more slowly. No man's intentions
could have been purer than Shelley's; free, himself,
from every trace of convention, he wished all others
to be free, especially, at the moment, his sisters;
he would not, he said, have their young minds
cramped by orthodox opinions. In the course of his
proselytising he met, at a school which a sister was

attending, a beautiful young girl much beneath him in social position, — her father, indeed, kept a tavern, and kept it well, — Harriet Westbrook by name. She is fire and he is tow — or is it the other way about? No difference: the result is the same; they become attached to each other and part — and absence makes the heart grow fonder. "Harriet" is a beautiful name. Shelley has already had a sweetheart bearing the same cognomen, and so when the second Harriet writes that she is lonely, and suffering for her opinions imbibed from him, and speaks of suicide, what is he to do? He flies to her, takes her in his arms and comforts her; intellectually he is in love with a schoolmistress down in Sussex, but Harriet is at hand. She is well educated for her station, she is good humored, has a lovely voice, a charming figure, and a pretty face. Above all, she is sixteen and he is nineteen, and they are thrown much together by the girl's elder sister Eliza, who, too old for romance herself, has no objection to becoming the sister-in-law of a handsome boy who will in all human probability be very rich and a baronet.

An elopement is arranged; money is borrowed, — I don't think so much money is borrowed to-day as it was a hundred years ago, or perhaps I lack finesse, — and they set off for Edinburgh and are married. Of course both fathers rage, but the girl's father quiets down quickly when Eliza explains matters to him. After all, his daughter is married, that is the great thing; and she has every prospect of some day

PERCY BYSSHE SHELLEY
painted in Rome (not from life) in 1819, after a drawing by E. E. Williams

being called "your ladyship." But the elder Shelley has to be reasoned with, and Shelley the younger is not the one to do it. Friends are called in, differences are glossed over, money matters discussed, and at last terms agreed upon: terms liberal, if not generous, for each father contributes two hundred pounds a year.

It might have been supposed that the young couple could live on this sum quite comfortably, but Shelley was generous to a fault; his mind was on a philosophical poem he was writing; and Harriet, having a pretty face, wanted bonnets and dresses to match it. What more natural than that they should get into financial difficulties? And, as is not unusual under the circumstances, a baby is expected.

Two years passed, and Shelley grew tired of his child-wife who, he found, could not understand philosophy and feel poetry as he did. Shelley, we now know, was a great genius; how was the publican's pretty daughter to hold his love? Or, indeed, the daughter of any man? Yet he had vowed to love, honor, and keep her as long as she should live. He had not, however, sworn to teach her Latin, as he was doing to one girl, nor had he sworn not to read Italian poetry to another girl, as he began to do. Reading poetry in any language to a pretty and sympathetic girl is generally regarded as an extrahazardous occupation; and just as dangerous was a correspondence begun with Godwin about this time. To him he writes: —

Your name excites in me feelings of reverence and admiration. Are you still planning the welfare of humankind?

. . . If I do not have an answer to this letter I shall seek you in London . . . I am convinced I could represent myself to you in such terms as to be thought not unworthy of your friendship.

The correspondence which followed was of such length that we may be sure, had we no other evidence, that Godwin's business was being neglected. One of his letters closes: "All the females of my family, Mrs. G. and three daughters, are much interested in your letters and your history." Whereupon Shelley and Harriet decide to go up to London; there they dine with the Godwins. Once again we are in Skinner Street.

We last saw Godwin almost seventeen years ago, looking at and wondering what to do with a three-days-old baby. After several false starts he had finally joined forces with a widow, also with two children. No one has ever had a good word for Mrs. Clairmont, who became the second Mrs. Godwin. She was no longer young; she was fat, poor, ugly, and disagreeable; she had weak eyes and wore green spectacles. Her views on marriage were not "advanced" and she probably had no illusions about it. She it was who did the courting, and when her deadly work was done she marched her victim off to Shoreditch Church, and there, in the sight of God and the beadle, they took each other for better or for worse.

A story is told of a friend of Godwin's calling shortly after the wedding; he had heard the news and wished to congratulate him, but he was not admitted. Mrs. Godwin met him with a tale that a kettle of boiling water had fallen from the hob and scalded her husband's legs so badly that in drawing off his stockings much of the skin had come with them; the poor man was in terrible agony, quite unable to see anyone. The story goes that the next day the caller met Godwin sauntering down the street with no trace of mishap, the whole incident being a lie from beginning to end. The only sensible woman in the Skinner Street circle, and she was there but seldom, was Godwin's mother. She mildly approved of the marriage; anything was better than such philandering as had been going on. She was a matter-of-fact old woman, holding the old-fashioned belief that husband and wife should live together, although she feared, and did not hesitate to express the fear, that the streets would soon be full of begging Godwins.

A son — named William after his father — having in due time blessed the Shoreditch nuptials, the old lady, in reply to a letter from her son complaining about the trouble his children were giving him, said she did not blame the children but their parents. Godwin's excuse to his mother was that neither his wife nor he had the leisure for reducing their novel theories of education to practice.

As the "Ridiculous Philosopher" sits at the head of his scantily furnished table, let us hastily run over a "Who's Who in Skinner Street": —

EDWARD BALDWIN, Author of a "History of Rome." There was no such person; Mr. Godwin invented him, his own name not being sufficiently respectable for the benign publishing-ventures upon which he was engaged.

MR. GODWIN. An old man of sixty, twice married, although he had written much against marriage, which he regarded as a degrading institution. Originally a preacher, then an author, he is now a publisher, but chiefly occupied in securing loans from friends.

MRS. GODWIN. Second wife of the above. Was the widow Clairmont, — maiden name unrecorded and unimportant, — with two children, a boy and a girl by her first husband, and a boy by her second; no more at present.

FANNY IMLAY. Aged twenty; also called Fanny Wollstonecraft and Fanny Godwin; an illegitimate child of Gilbert Imlay and Mary Wollstonecraft, Godwin's first wife. By no means handsome, but in general prepossessing. Quiet and modest, somewhat given to indolence, and disposed to follow her own judgment.

MARY WOLLSTONECRAFT GODWIN. Aged seventeen. Second daughter of Mary Wollstonecraft. A pretty girl with a strong mind and a high voice, singularly bold and persevering; insufficiently educated, but fond of reading. Of an imperious disposition.

CHARLES CLAIRMONT. Eldest child of Mrs. Godwin by her first husband. Educated at Charterhouse, was for a time employed by the Constables, the publishers. Later, to escape from Skinner Street, he went to Vienna, where he became an English tutor. There he married and died.

MARY JANE CLAIRMONT. Aged sixteen. Second child of Mrs. Godwin by her first husband, who, disliking her name, called herself Claire. A clever, beautiful brunette, with irregular features and a lovely voice; of a romantic and wayward disposition.

WILLIAM GODWIN, JR. A rather colorless lad, inheriting the ample faults of both his father and mother, he became a source of trouble and expense to his half-sister Mary; he will annoy us but little.

Into an establishment thus constituted, Shelley introduced himself and his wife; she was not attracted and came but seldom, but the poet and the philosopher had much in common. Godwin's views upon marriage were especially interesting to Shelley, already tired of his wife and beginning to read life's meaning in Mary Godwin's eyes. There were a few respectable houses in the neighborhood, but Skinner Street was declining almost before it was finished. The great prison, Newgate, was only a stone's throw away, and the periodical hanging-days drew to the locality a crowd of thieves and outcasts. Not long after Shelley's first visit to the Street, in an endeavor to make the punishment fit the crime the authorities hung a sailor only a few paces away from Godwin's door, before a shop which he had been caught plundering. What a place for a poet! for Shelley!

It has always seemed curious to me that fortunes have been made by lending money and fortunes lost by borrowing it; it seems as though it should be the other way about. Godwin contrived to live for many years on borrowed money; he secured funds, how, where, and when he could, from strangers or from friends, in his own name or in names assumed for the occasion. If the sums involved were relatively small, the number and variety of his financial transactions command our admiration. In this sordid atmosphere Mary Godwin had passed, with occasional visits to the country, seventeen years. She hated her step-mother, as did everyone else, and pretty stories are told of her going to her mother's grave under the trees in old St. Pancras' churchyard, to read in her favorite book. There one day she was joined by Shelley, and Mary told him how unhappy she was at home; no one understood her save him, she said. Shelley too was unhappy; his wife did not understand him either, and her sister Eliza had assumed the time-honored rôle of mother-in-law to perfection. An interchange of trouble seems to lessen it; Shelley and Mary left the churchyard together, happier than they had been in a long time. In a voice full of sympathy he had called her "his" Mary and she, in return, had whispered "beloved Shelley" in his ear. In short, they had agreed to elope! With no thought of Harriet, now living at Bath, with no provision for his child, Ianthe, indifferent to the fact that his wife would soon bear him another child, Shelley proceeded with his plan. In Harry B. Smith's "Sentimental Library" there was a letter, now the property of a friend who has sent me a photograph of it, written by Mary to Shelley just before the elopement. It reads: —

MY OWN LOVE:

I do not know by what compulsion I am to answer you, but your porter says I must, so I do. By a miracle I saved your five pounds and I will bring it. I hope, indeed, oh, my loved Shelley, we shall indeed be happy. I meet you at three and bring heaps of "Skinner Street news." Heaven bless my love and take care of him:

HIS OWN MARY.

Elope! Why should they not? Shelley had only taken Harriet out of pity. Should not a marriage tie be broken by either party at will? He loved another; it was no longer binding upon him; and Mary's mother, whose memory she adored, had lived with a man who was not her husband. Godwin's daughter had been taught, if she had been taught anything, that marriage was a silly superstition which wise people disregarded. Marriage vows, if once desirable for the regulation of society, were no longer necessary. Did Mary think of these things, I wonder? Probably not. She thought only of the joy of being forever with Shelley and of escape from Skinner Street.

And what of Godwin? Well, he was in all probability too busy robbing Peter to pay Paul to observe that his daughter was about to set in motion his own pet theories. And so it was that on the twenty-eighth of July 1814 Mary, secretly aided by Claire who accompanied her, left Skinner Street and joined Shelley in an awaiting post-chaise, in which the three runaways started for Dover and the Continent.

But even a philosopher becomes perturbed when a married man runs away with his daughter. We may fancy Mrs. Godwin dashing into the shop and exclaiming, "That man Shelley has run off with your daughter and taken mine with her!" and we may fancy Godwin, who hated to be disturbed when he was meditating, blaming his wife for the disgrace that had overtaken them — for such they considered it. Mrs. Godwin instantly rose to the occasion; no time was to be lost. The fugitives had crossed the Channel in an open boat during a storm and two of them were resting in each other's arms in an inn at Calais, when the landlord disturbed them with the announcement that a fat woman was downstairs, insisting that at least one of the girls should return to London with her. This, of course, was her own daughter Jane, — otherwise Claire, — but Claire would not hear of going back to Skinner Street, neither would Mary; and Mrs. Godwin was forced to depart alone. Sentimental journeys have been made in France before, but surely there was never a more singularly composed party than the one which now set out for Paris on foot, buying a donkey to carry their baggage and one of the girls by turns. One wonders whether Mary felt the need of Jane's moral support at the time of the elopement, or

My own love

    I do not know
by what compulsion
I am to answer you but
your porter says I must
so I do—
    & By a miracle I saved
your £5 & I will bring it—I
hope indeed; oh my loved
Shelley we shall indeed
be happy
    I meet you at three
and bring heaps of Skinner
street news—Heaven bless
my love & take care of him
    his own Mary

THE MARY GODWIN ELOPEMENT LETTER
now in the library of a well-known Boston collector
(*A phrase in the letter supplied the title for this essay*)

whether Jane then for the first — and by no means
for the last — time thrust herself upon the high non-
contracting parties.

Meantime what of the deserted wife? Let us return
to her.

It were bad business to inquire too narrowly into
Harriet's conduct after her desertion by her husband.
They had been living together at Bath, but he had
tired of her — not of her arms but of her soul; soft
arms are more or less alike, but poets seem to require
a variety in souls. It was, if I remember, Wordsworth
who thought that a woman should be a spring and
not a well. Fresh, pure emotions were to be constantly
bubbling up for him; he was not to be put to the
trouble of letting down his bucket, however thirsty
he might be. So it was in Shelley's case; when Harriet
ceased to bubble he sought drink elsewhere.

Nothing can be sadder than a deserted wife, and
when that wife is the mother of one child and is shortly
expecting another her case is pitiful indeed. Shelley's biographers have ranged themselves for and
against Harriet; Professor Dowden, in his *Life of
Shelley*, written at the instance of the "Castle Goring
Shelleys," has by creation, suppression, and innuendo
suggested that the poet believed that his wife was
untrue to him before he left her. I have been unable
to find any basis for this belief, and the fact that
several years after the event Godwin circulated such
a story proves nothing; Godwin, in addition to being

a sturdy beggar, was, when occasion served, a liar also.

And industrious! Godwin was the Complete Letter-Writer of a very letter-writing period. Many of his letters have been published; many remain unpublished in the cabinets of collectors. Through the courtesy of a friend I am able to quote one letter of Godwin's which, though long, — it covers seven quarto pages, — is faultless of its kind. It is addressed to John Taylor, always referred to as "Taylor of Norwich," a money-lender.

SKINNER STREET,
Aug. 27, 1814.

DEAR SIR,

I have a story to tell you of the deepest melancholy. I should not intrude this story at all upon you, if I could help it: first, because it is my temper, as far as with convenience I can, to shut my sorrows in my bosom, and not to disturb all my friends indiscriminately with matters in which they can afford me no aid; and secondly, because I am anxious to confine this story to the deepest secrecy, and not by any indiscretion of mine to allow a breath of it to escape to the world. But it is so unfortunately connected with my affairs, with those affairs in which you have so signally assisted me, that I am under the necessity of requesting that you will have the goodness to be my confidant.

You are already acquainted with the name of Shelley, the gentleman who more than twelve months ago undertook by his assistance to rescue me from my pecuniary difficulties. Not to keep you longer in suspense, he, a married man, has run away with my daughter. I cannot conceive of an event of more accumulated horror.

Mary, my only daughter, was absent in Scotland for her health during Shelley's former visits in London. She returned to me finally on the 30th of March last. Shelley came to London on the 18th of June; and as we expected every day the conclusion of the loan that had been raised, it was necessary he should continue on the spot. He was under apprehension of arrests; and from this consideration I invited him to make my house his principal home, his known haunts being all at the West end of the town. He lodged at an inn in Fleet Street, and took his meals with me. I had the utmost confidence in him; I knew him susceptible of the noblest sentiments; he was a married man, who had lived happily with his wife for three years. Accordingly, the first week of his visit passed in perfect happiness; he was every day impatient to be spared to go into Wales, to secure a retreat he had fixed on, where he might reside with his wife and child, shut out from the rest of the world. When he found that for the moment impracticable, he desired to be absent one night only, that he might visit them at Bracknell, 30 miles from London, where he had left them. On Sunday, June 26, he accompanied Mary and her sister, Jane Clairmont, to the tomb of Mary's mother, one mile distant from London; and there, it seems, the impious idea first occurred to him of seducing her, playing the traitor to me, and deserting his wife. On Wednesday, the 6th of July, the transaction of the loan was completed; and on the evening of that very day he had the madness to disclose his plans to me, and to ask my consent. I expostulated with him with all the energy of which I was master, and with so much effect that for the moment he promised to give up his licentious love, and return to virtue. I applied all my diligence to waken up a sense of honour and natural affection in the mind of Mary, and I seemed to have succeeded. They both deceived me. In the night of the 27th Mary and her sister Jane escaped from my house;

and the next morning when I rose, I found a letter on my dressing-table, informing me what they had done. I had been of opinion from the first that Mary could only be withheld from him by her mind; and in that, by a series of the most consummate dissimulation, she made me believe I had succeeded. I formed the plan of sending her from home, knowing the violence of Shelley's temper, and far from certain what scenes he might be capable of acting; but I was well aware that in sending her from home I should be doing good, if she concurred with me and concealed her retreat from her betrayer, but that if she were capable of an opposite conduct, I should be rather throwing her into his power.

You will imagine our distress. If anything could have added to it, it was this circumstance of Jane's having gone with her sister. Fanny had been for a month or two on a visit to a friend in Wales, and her aunts had come over from Ireland to meet her there; so that Mrs. Godwin and I were left in a moment without a female in the house. We enquired at the neighbouring livery-stable, and found that they had set off post for Dover, on their way to France. Jane, we were and still are, most anxious to recover immediately; and therefore, after much deliberation, it was agreed that Mrs. G. should set off after them by the evening's mail. She overtook them at Calais. I had made it a condition in suffering her to depart, that she should avoid seeing Shelley, who had conceived a particular aversion to her as a dangerous foe to his views, and might be capable of any act of desperation. Mrs. Godwin wrote to Jane the very moment she reached Calais, July 29, who came to her at a separate inn, spent the night with her, and promised to return with her to England the next morning. But when morning arrived, she said she must see the fugitive for a few minutes, and in that interview all her resolutions were subverted. Not the most earnest entreaties of a mother could turn her from her purpose; and on Sunday, July 31, Mrs. Godwin returned once more, alone.

Thus did I find myself left, at once without children and without resources, in a situation calculated to fill the strongest mind with despair. I felt it however still to be my duty not to desert myself, or so much of my family as was left to me, and even to provide, if possible, for the hour of distress (which, I believe, is not far distant), when these unworthy children shall again seek the protection and aid of their father.

I have now, therefore, for two or three weeks past, been looking for the relief to arise from admitting a partner into my concern, and I have made some considerable progress in two quarters, so that it is more likely that I shall be obliged to reject one of two candidates eager for the proposal, than that I shall be rejected by both. This transaction, as far as has yet been calculated, will produce me a sum of at least three thousand pounds, to enable me to discharge any incumbrances that may lie on my share of the concern.

In your last letter you had the goodness to say, that you would still endeavour to do what you could for me as to the discounts, if they should be necessary; but that it was your wish to have your money (referring of course to the £300 for which you have my bond) paid in, as soon as convenient after my receipt of £1500. It is grievous to me to have disappointed you in this. But, alas, my dear sir, you, who I believe have known what it is to be in difficulties, must know how impossible it is with the most earnest desires to fulfill every one's wishes, or with a small and inadequate sum to discharge a whole multitude of demands. And it happens unfortunately in these cases, that the evil-disposed and the illiberal are the persons to whom one is compelled to yield the earliest attention. The sum I was to have received was £3000. But what was sold by auction, and was expected to produce this amount, actually produced no more than £2600. Of this, as you know, I was only to have half; and this half, when all charges were defrayed, yielded me only £1120. Of this I was obliged to give £500 to one person, who had a warrant against my goods, and who could hardly be prevailed upon by any means to refrain from the use of this warrant till the transaction of the loan was completed. I will not trouble you with the detail of the rest. But, I assure you, my dear sir, it was with indescribable difficulty that I could so apply the rest as to produce me any relief; and by the mode of applying which I was reduced to select, I have so far tried the patience of some of my best friends, that my situation is in some respects worse than it was before this relief arrived.

Encouraged by the friendly hint in your last letter, and driven by the urgency of a situation which allows me no liberty of choice, I have taken the liberty to inclose to you bills of the same description and to exactly the same amount, as those with which I last troubled you, of which it will be necessary for me, if you please, to receive £200 by Wednesday next: the remainder I shall not have occasion for before Monday, the 11th of September.

At Mrs. Godwin's request, who has just read what I have written, I forward to you a small parcel by this day's mail, containing the copies of two letters I wrote to Shelley, between the time of his disclosing his licentious passion to me and the catastrophe. From them, you will perceive fully, what were my feelings, and how I conducted myself on the subject. You, I believe, are acquainted with my character on these points, and would, I doubt not, without such an explanation do me justice. But I have many enemies; and Mrs. Godwin thinks I may stand in need of vindication. We are divided in this particular, between justification, and (what we infinitely prefer) the entire suppression of all knowledge of the affair. This, for the present at least, we owe to the poor girls, who may be brought back to the path of duty, time enough to prevent a stigma from being fastened on their characters. I had a thousand times rather remain unvindicated, than publish the tale to a single human creature to whom it might remain unknown.

When I use the word stigma, I am sure it is wholly unnecessary to say that I apply it in a very different sense to the two girls. Jane has been guilty of indiscretion only, and has shown a want of filial sentiments, which it would have been most desirable to us to have discovered in her: Mary has been guilty of a crime.

The bills I shall inclose in the coach parcel. Believe me, Dear sir,

with the sincerest regard and esteem,
yours
WILLIAM GODWIN.

Reference, too, must be made to a letter written by Shelley to Harriet two weeks after the elopement. The runaways were still intent upon increasing the distance between themselves and London, when Shelley took pen in hand to indite one of the most remarkable communications which a sane man ever addressed to a wife.

It begins thus: —

DEAREST HARRIET — I write to you . . . to show that I do not forget you . . . to urge you to come to Switzerland, where you will at least find one firm and constant friend, to whom your interests will always be dear, by whom your feelings will never wilfully be injured. From none can you expect this but me.

One can hardly blame the wife for being not quite

sure that she had forever lost her husband, or the mistress for some incertainty as to whether she was sure of her lover. But however silly Harriet may have been, she was not a fool; she ignored the letter. Had she done otherwise, she would have had her journey for her pains, for by the time she could have reached Switzerland, the fugitives, their funds having given out, were on their way back to London.

In judging Harriet it is to be remembered that Shelley had for several years been her teacher; only a schoolgirl when he first met her, he taught her that chastity was a monkish superstition. What wonder is it, therefore, that forsaken by the man who had sworn to honor and protect her, she took to evil living? Nor did she do that at once; deserted by her husband, she returned to her father's house, and there it was that her second child was born. Shelley had several interviews with Harriet after his return to England, and an arrangement was effected continuing her pension; meantime she had run into debt and had, it is said, taken to drink. Shelley and Mary were now living together, first in the country, then in London, dodging their creditors and Harriet's. An entry in Mary's diary records this: "Harriet sends her creditors here. *Nasty woman!* Now we shall have to change our lodgings again." And move they did; finally they settled down in the country, and just as they were getting established there, Claire Godwin began urging them to go to Switzerland and to take her with them.

A few months before this time Claire had introduced herself to Lord Byron, then at the height of
his fame; he was married, had separated from his
wife, and was — aside from the politicians — the
most talked-of man in England. (Why is it that the
crowd finds the noisy, self-seeking politician so interesting? Why are we so intent upon watching them
play their crooked games that we forget to live the
while, as though it really matters which group carries
off the spoils of office?) But to return to Byron: he
had become a member of the management of Drury
Lane Theatre and was leading a life of "hiccups and
happiness" when Claire determined upon his conquest. Her step-sister Mary had been for some time
the mistress of a poet, Shelley; why should not she,
whose physical charms were infinitely greater than
Mary's, make an even greater conquest? Nothing
venture, nothing have; Claire decided to offer herself
to Byron; she thereupon presented herself at the
theatre, asked for a position, and so deported herself
that, while Byron saw that she would never make an
actress, he noted that she had youth, beauty, and
intelligence — in short, all the requirements of a mistress. "I never seduced any woman," Byron once
declared: perhaps he had Claire in mind at the time.
Be this as it may, Claire certainly laid siege to the
poet, and he surrendered without a moment's hesitation. Then, just as they were getting happily acquainted, Byron announced that he was going to
Switzerland, saying nothing of taking Claire with

him; it was Claire's move, and she moved promptly. Urging Shelley and Mary to leave their newly established home, which had just been blessed by another baby, she prevailed upon them to take her halfway across Europe to Switzerland. Why?

I think it unlikely that Shelley and Mary did not know what they were doing. Excuses have been found for them, but why are excuses necessary? Shelley and Mary were free-lovers, did not believe in marriage — at least Shelley did not. Shelley had a wife in England with whom he could not live; so had Byron, but Byron reveled in vice for its own sake and was not satisfied until he had the reputation of being the most dissolute man in Europe. Shelley, on the other hand, hated vice; had there been no woman in the world he would have been fine. Byron was a devil and delighted in the part; Shelley was an angel playing with fire, and with the usual result.

There is a thumb-nail sketch of the two men drawn by Shelley himself in the Introduction to "Julian and Maddalo": —

Count Maddalo [Byron] is of ancient family and great fortune . . . a person of the most consummate genius . . . but it is his weakness to be proud . . . his passions and his powers are incomparably greater than those of other men . . . Julian [Shelley] is passionately attached to those philosophical notions which assert the power of man over his mind . . . He is forever speculating how good may be made superior . . . he is a complete infidel and a scoffer at all things reputed holy. Maddalo takes a wicked pleasure in drawing out his taunts against religion. What Maddalo thinks on these matters is not exactly known.

A LITTLE-KNOWN PORTRAIT OF LORD BYRON
from an original painting in the possession of Dr. Charles William MacFarlane of Philadelphia

This sketch was written at a somewhat later date than the one I am describing, but it remains true for all time. So it was not altogether by accident that Byron, having issued his famous "Fare Thee Well," upon his arrival at Secheron in Switzerland found Shelley and Mary and Claire awaiting him.

This party of four — five if Byron's friend and physician, Polodori, be included — so lived as to cause a scandal even in a place and at a time when morality was at a very low ebb. The one literary result of this mad meeting was Mary Godwin's *Frankenstein*. All the world knows how the party, amusing themselves one evening during a storm telling ghost stories, finally decided that each should write one; and how Mary, still a girl of less than twenty years, produced a story which for gruesomeness has never been excelled in the hundred years since it was published — for the story still lives, and its name has passed into the language. A few years ago we were telling one another that William Hohenzollern, in creating the German army, had created "a Frankenstein," and that it had gotten away from him and was wreaking vengeance on the world. This seemed to have such sinister meaning that few of us stopped to remember that Frankenstein was the creator of the dæmon and not the name of the monster.

It was Shelley's belief that any woman who lived with him was peculiarly sanctified; Byron had no such delusion: as a nobleman, it was his privilege to have mistresses. Claire pleased him for a time, then he threw her over without remorse; *la commedia e finita*. With his departure there was no longer any reason for Shelley and Mary and Claire to stay, and they returned to England. As for Claire —

> When she found that he was fickle,
>   Was her great oak tree,
> She was in a pretty pickle,
>   As she well might be —
> For his gallantries were mickle
> And Death followed with his sickle,
> And her tears began to trickle

as tears will, when a girl without a husband finds that a baby is coming.

On their return to England Shelley, accompanied by Mary and Claire, settled at Bath. Here in due course Claire's baby was born. This infant, Allegra, — named after a mountain, Mount Alegre, — was a source of much embarrassment. Byron, who was at the moment trying to effect a reconciliation with Lady Byron, had scandals enough on his hands and did not wish another; nor could Shelley very well announce to the world that Lord Byron was the child's father; and as he had taken pains to let people know that love sanctified all things, it was generally suspected that he was its father. Altogether it was an unpleasant and difficult situation.

Listen to a letter which Harriet Shelley, poor woman, wrote her friend Mrs. Nugent: —

Your fears are verified. Mr. Shelley has become profligate and sensual owing entirely to Godwin's *Political Justice;* the great evil that book has done is not to be told! The false doctrine there teached has poisoned many a young and virtuous mind. Mr. S. is living with G's two daughters. I told you sometime back that S. had given G. three thousand pounds!

Poor woman, she actually believed that her Shelley had bought the two girls from their father.

Shelley was indeed in an unpleasant and difficult situation, but it was as nothing compared with the blows which were immediately impending.

We have made little reference to Fanny, Mary Wollstonecraft's daughter by Imlay. She was a plain girl, useful in shop or kitchen, and for this reason was not suspected of having emotions, nevertheless, we have every reason to believe that she too was in love with Shelley. Tyrannized over by an impossible stepmother, she probably compared her lot with that of Mary and Claire, the happy mistresses of poets — handsome, rich, and distinguished; her sisters were butterflies, she was an ugly worm; why wait until she should be crushed under the heel of Fate? Inheriting from her mother a tendency toward melancholy, she decided to put an end to herself, and she accordingly made her preparations. Announcing that she was going on a visit, she journeyed to Swansea, in Wales, where, going to an inn, she engaged a room and, pleading fatigue from the journey, retired. Next morning she was found dead upon her bed. An empty bottle labeled "laudanum" was on the table, and by it a note which read: —

I have long determined that the best thing I could do was to put an end to the existence of a being whose birth was unfortunate and whose life has only been a series of pains to those persons who have hurt their health in endeavoring to promote her welfare. Perhaps to hear of my death will give you pain, but you will soon forget that such a creature ever existed.

A letter from Fanny to Mary, containing a threat of what she was about to do, caused Shelley to set off on a hunt for the fugitive; he went first to Bristol, then to Swansea, where he learned the worst. To one of his emotional nature it was a great shock; but before he recovered from the effects of Fanny's death, a greater one was in store for him: he learned that Harriet, his wife, had also committed suicide.

Very little is known of Harriet's life after Shelley deserted her. That she took to evil living is certain, but the silly statement, made so complacently by Professor Dowden, that "no act of Shelley's during the two years which immediately preceded her death tended to cause the rash act which brought her life to its close," is only one of many absurd statements in a biography which has been sufficiently animadverted upon by Mark Twain in his brilliant essay, — not sufficiently well known, — "In Defense of Harriet Shelley." Perhaps in the scheme of things the death of one woman, or of several, if it contributes to the intellectual development of such a poet as Shelley, is not greatly to be regretted; in nature the higher form of life lives by the destruction of the lower; but Shelley enthusiasts are not content that we should admire him as a poet; they require that we should admire him as a man.

HARRIET SHELLEY SUICIDE LETTER

The last page of a letter written a few hours before the unfortunate woman threw herself into the Serpentine

Harriet's second child was born while she was living in her father's house, which she subsequently left, finally to seek oblivion in the Serpentine. Old Mr. Westbrook, the retired publican, must have cursed the day when the poet first crossed his threshold. On my desk as I write is the last letter — perhaps it should be called the last will and testament — of the poor girl who only a few years before had left school, as she said, "for good." There is that about a letter or a manuscript, which the printed page fails to suggest. Lapse of years tends to increase rather than diminish their interest: they never become cold, but retain forever the vital warmth of the writer. We take them up and seem to feel the pulsations of the heart, agitated, it may be, by sorrow so poignant that death itself seems to afford the only relief. Think of the agony of the poor girl, outcast and broken-hearted, when she penned these lines. They are addressed to her sister Eliza and to her husband Shelley.

SAT. EVE [*December* 1816]

My dearest and much bel'd Sister,

When you read this letter I shall be [no] more an inhabitant of this miserable world. Do not regret the loss of one who could never be anything but a source of vexation and misery to you all belonging to me. Too wretched to exert myself, lowered in the opinion of everyone, why should I drag on a miserable existence embittered by past recollections and not one ray of hope to rest on for the future . . . I have not written to Bysshe. Oh, no, what would it avail, my wishes or my prayers would not be attended to by him, and yet should he see

this perhaps he might grant my last request to let Ianthe
[their daughter] remain with you always, dear lovely
child, with you she will enjoy much happiness, with him
none.

My dear Bysshe, let me conjure you by the remem-
brance of our days of happiness to grant my last will, do
not take your innocent child from Eliza who has been
more than I have, who has watched over her with such
unceasing care. Do not refuse my last request. I never
could refuse you and if you had never left me I might
have lived, but as it is I freely forgive you and may you
enjoy that happiness which you have deprived me of.
There is your beautiful boy. Oh! be careful of him and
his love may prove one day a rich reward . . . God bless
you all is the last prayer of the unfortunate Harriet S.

Poor broken-hearted girl! evidently she could not
bear to write her last name in full.

Her body was not immediately found, but the
Serpentine, called by courtesy a river, — at that time
an evil-smelling pond in the centre of Hyde Park, —
was dragged, and finally the body was recovered.
A newspaper clipping from the *Times* of December 12
completes the gruesome story.

On Tuesday a respectable female far advanced in preg-
nancy was taken out of the Serpentine River and brought
home to her residence in Queen Street, Brompton . . .
She had a valuable ring on her finger. A want of honor
in her own conduct is supposed to have led to this fatal
catastrophe, her husband being abroad.

Mr. Roger Ingpen, the latest student of Shelley,
has discovered that she was buried in Paddington
churchyard under the name of Harriet Smith.

Shelley wrote Mary the details as he understood them: —

It seems that this poor woman — the most innocent of her abhorred and unnatural family — was driven from her father's house and descended the steps of prostitution until she came to live with a groom by the name of Smith; who deserting her, she killed herself. There can be no question that the beastly viper [Eliza], unable to gain profit from her connection with me has secured to herself the whole fortune of her father — who is now dying — by the murder of the old man.

Then Southey took a hand in the mess and wrote Shelley: —

You forsook your wife because you were tired of her, and had found another woman more suited to your taste. You could tell me a history, you say, which would make me open my eyes; perhaps they are already open. It is a matter of public notoriety that your wife destroyed herself. Knowing in what manner she bore your desertion, I never attributed this to her sensibility on that score. I have heard it otherwise explained: I have heard that she followed your example as faithfully as your lessons, and that the catastrophe was produced by shame. Be this as it may, ask your own heart whether you have not been the whole, sole and direct cause of her destruction. You corrupted her opinions; you robbed her of her moral and religious principles; you debauched her mind. But for you and your lessons, she might have gone through the world innocently and happily.

It was not easy for the poet to parry such an attack. The whole tragic affair must have greatly affected such a sensitive nature as Shelley's. Leigh Hunt says he never recovered from the blow. On the other hand, Peacock, with whom Shelley stayed at the time, says: "I never saw him more calm and self-possessed." Invariably, it would seem, authorities differ, but Shelley was not a monster, and Leigh Hunt must be right.

Shelley's first act was to go up to London to secure the possession of his two children. How they were kept from him by Mr. Westbrook, the litigation which ensued, and the decree of the Lord Chancellor that Shelley's conduct made him an unfit person to entrust with the custody of the two infants, is beside the purpose of this paper.

There was now nothing to prevent Shelley's marriage with Mary; he seems to have promised to marry her if ever it was possible; doubtless she wanted to be made an honest woman, and Godwin, who up to this time had borrowed money from Shelley chiefly through the intervention of a third person, doubtless thought, and thought correctly, that he would be able to negotiate loans more expeditiously by dealing directly with a son-in-law. There was no question as to the desirability of a marriage; the only question was — should it be now or later? Mary, wise child, determined that it should be now; consequently, before the year was out, Shelley and Mary, accompanied by Godwin and Mary Jane, his wife, were married by special license in the church of St. Mildred, Bread Street, and Godwin wrote a long letter to his brother. Listen to the old hypocrite!

I do not know whether you recollect the miscellaneous way in which my family is composed, but at least you perhaps remember that I have but two children of my own: a daughter by my late wife and a son by my present. Were it not that you have a family of your own, and can see by them how little shrubs grow up into tall trees, you would hardly imagine that my boy, born the other day, is now fourteen, and that my daughter is between nineteen and twenty. The piece of news I have to tell, however, is that I went to church with this tall girl some little time ago to be married. Her husband is the eldest son of Sir Timothy Shelley, of Field Place, in the county of Sussex, Baronet. So that, according to the vulgar ideas of the world, she is well married, and I have great hopes the young man will make her a good husband. You will wonder, I daresay, how a girl without a penny of fortune should meet with so good a match. But such are the ups and downs of this world. For my part, I care but little, comparatively, about wealth, so that it should be her destiny in life to be respectable, virtuous, and contented.

To "dearest Claire," who was in Bath awaiting the coming of her baby, Shelley, who was devotedly attached to her, wrote a long letter: —

The ceremony so magical in its effects was undergone this morning at St. Mildred's Church in the city. Mrs. Godwin and G. were both present and appeared to feel no little satisfaction. Mrs. G. presents herself to me in all her real attributes of affectation, prejudice, and heartless pride. Towards her I never feel an emotion of anything but antipathy, but her sweet daughter is very dear to me.

Was Shelley falling in love with Claire? Undoubtedly.

By this time, Shelley's grandfather, a rich and

MARY SHELLEY

*painted in 1831 by John Stump when Mary was thirty-four years old.
The large volume is a copy of her mother's "Vindication
of the Rights of Women"*

eccentric old gentleman, was dead, and his father had become Sir Timothy Shelley, a man of fortune. Settlements and agreements were reached, and the poet, having made somewhat niggardly arrangements for the care and education of his children by Harriet, attempted for a time to straighten out the financial entanglements of Godwin, but this was beyond his powers. To escape from the never-ending flood of appeals from the old man, now hopelessly involved, as well as to seek a milder climate after a serious illness, Shelley and Mary finally decided to leave England for Italy, of course taking Claire and her baby with them.

Again they met Byron, now living a life of sordid dissipation; in Venice he had sent for Allegra, but protesting that he would never again see the child's mother; he forced her to give up all claim upon the infant, which she, after many expostulations, finally did.

In Byron, the sensualist, and in Shelley, the idealist, were personified. Matthew Arnold, in his scholarly appreciation of Shelley, calls him "a beautiful and ineffectual angel beating in the void his luminous wings in vain." I cannot agree; Shelley was not an angel, and no great poet ever lived in vain. I have not read, I cannot read, many of Shelley's longer poems, but they form a part of that glorious thing we call English literature, and even I can appreciate the transcendent beauty of "The Cloud." Only in his relations with Harriet was Shelley not a generous and noble-hearted gentleman. To this period belongs "Julian and Maddalo," — Shelley's poem growing out of a conversation with Byron, — the manuscript of which I saw sold several years ago at Mitchell Kennerley's Galleries in New York, and for a moment I was foolish enough to think that I could, perhaps, add it to my collection until its price soared like its author's skylark, "higher still and higher," and the amazing figure of sixteen thousand dollars was reached. Then I discovered, what I might have known, that some person of great wealth would not allow that wealth to dim his appreciation of the beautiful.

Byron's child, Allegra, did not live as Shelley prophesied she would, "to become like one of Shakespeare's women of transcendent worth"; deprived at a tender age of her mother's care, — if indeed Claire could ever have given it such care, — neglected by her father, although he paid handsomely to secure good treatment for her in a convent in which he had placed her, she died when about five years of age. Perhaps Shelley felt the child's death quite as much as Byron, although he did not rave about it as Byron did; she had been born in his house; of her, he said, in "Julian and Maddalo":

> With me
> She was a special favorite: I had nursed
> Her fine and feeble limbs, when she came first
> To this bleak world . . . A lovelier toy
> Sweet Nature never made.

But the total lack of everything included in what
we to-day call hygiene made Italy a poor place in
which to rear English children a hundred years ago.
Shelley lost two of his own children by Mary in Italy,
and Mary only recovered her spirits upon the birth
of her last child, a boy, who grew up to inherit the
title, and who died so recently as 1889.

Shelley left England in 1818 for Italy, that "paradise of exiles," never to return. The few years which
were to elapse before his death were rich, not in
promise, but in fruitage. They produced his greater
lyrics, even to name which were effrontery, and the
finest of his longer poems, his *Adonais*, inspired by
the death of Keats. Of this, in a letter to Claire,
Shelley says: "I have lately been composing a poem
on Keats; it is better than anything I have yet written, and worthy both of him and of me." There was
no great intimacy between the two poets, but Shelley believed, as many did at the time, that Keats'
death was due to the savage attacks made upon him
in the then all powerful Quarterlies. In order that
the poem might escape the errors usual in printing
from more or less illegible manuscript, Shelley decided
to have a small edition of the poem printed near at
hand, "in the cheapest manner," prior to its printing
in England, with the result so well known to collectors.
The edition of *Adonais*, with the curious imprint
"Pisa, with the types of Didot, MDCCCXXI," a
slight quarto, issued in blue wrappers and offered for
sale for 3s. 6d., and for several years unobtainable for

this sum, is now one of the most highly prized of Shelley first-editions. At the Buxton Forman sale, at the Anderson Galleries in New York, several years ago, an immaculate copy brought the then record price of two thousand and fifty dollars: to-day it would probably fetch double that price.

In commemoration of the one hundredth anniversary of the death of Shelley, — July 8, 1822, — which passed almost unobserved in England, my friend Mr. William Andrews Clark, Jr., brought out a fac-simile of the Didot brochure, together with an edition of the poem in perfect format, from the press of that superlative printer, John Henry Nash of San Francisco, with an excellent introduction from the pen of Mr. Clark himself. (And in England they venture to represent American business men as caring for nothing but money!)

In his introduction Mr. Clark says the English edition, the one printed in Cambridge in 1829 at the instance of Lord Houghton and Arthur Hallam, is much rarer than the Pisa edition; I do not know. I have never "collected" Shelley; I have never had the means. Although he was only thirty when he died, he was a most voluminous writer, and all first editions are scarce — some of them priceless. Harry B. Smith, the creator of the "Sentimental Library," — how I envy him that exquisite title! — describes in his library catalogue, which is the only completely read-able catalogue ever compiled, a large number of first editions of Shelley of which he had presentation copies, and says that the poet published or printed privately twenty-nine volumes or pamphlets, two thirds of which are practically unobtainable. I suppose that since Mr. Smith's library was dispersed his distinguished place as a collector has been taken by Mr. Jerome Kern. He is the owner of what I should say is the finest Shelley association-book in the world, namely, the poet's own copy of *Queen Mab*, with the mutilated dedication to Harriet, and full of manuscript notes; he paid six thousand dollars for it: it would fetch several times that sum to-day. Mr. Kern is a very good fellow, but I hate him for the sufficient reason that whenever an item comes up, at auction or otherwise, that I especially want, it almost invariably finds its way into his rapidly growing sentimental collection — for Mr. Smith cannot be permitted forever to have the preëmption of that word.

But to return to Shelley, who had matters other than lyrics and elegies demanding his attention. Try as he would, he could not rid himself of that Old-Man-of-the-Sea, Godwin. Affairs in Skinner Street were going from bad to worse. Discovering in some way that the title of the property which he was occupying was clouded, he declined to pay any rent whatever. The ordinary, simple-minded business man — such, for example, as the writer — desiring to take advantage of his landlord's plight would lay aside the rent as it fell due and await the outcome of legal proceedings with a tranquil mind. Not so the philosopher:

assuming that he was forever to live rent-free, he made no provision against the day of reckoning, with the result that when it came and verdict of the jury called for the immediate payment of a large sum, he let forth such a yell of rage and anguish as seriously to disturb the peace of mind of his daughter and son-in-law in Italy.

Before me are a sheaf of letters from Godwin to Shelley and Mary and their replies, full of recriminations. Godwin protested that he had been lulled into a fool's paradise, that he had rested with "cheerful assurance" upon Shelley's promise to pay his debts. The tune of Godwin's letters makes clear that it was demands, not requests, he was making. "I cannot paint in words my astonishment," he says, "when your letter was put into my hands, to find that it was not accompanied by a shilling!" He had expected a bill for five hundred pounds at twelve months, and that fifty pounds per quarter should be paid regularly — regularly, forsooth! — at his banker's.

In his reply Shelley asks a question which in my amused study of this old horseleech I have often asked. He says, "Put your hand upon your heart and tell me what you do with all this money." Continuing, he says: —

I have given you within a few years the amount of a considerable fortune and have destituted myself, for the purpose of realizing it, of nearly four times the amount. Except for the "good will" which this transaction seems to have conferred on you and me, this money, for any advantage that it ever conferred on you, might as well have been thrown into the sea. Had I kept in my own hands this four or five thousand pounds and administered it in trust for your permanent advantage, I should have been indeed your benefactor. The error, however, was greater in the man of mature years, extensive experience and penetrating intellect than in the crude and impetuous boy. Bankruptcy sometimes surprises the most prosperous concern and is definitely probable in an embarrassed business conducted by a person wholly ignorant of trade. Why, instead of seeking to plunge one already half ruined for your sake into deeper ruin, do you not procure the five thousand pounds from your own active friends? Mary is now giving suck to her infant in whose life, after the frightful events of the last two years, her own seems wholly to be bound up. Your letters from their style and spirit (such is your erroneous notion of taste) never fail to produce so appalling an effect upon her, that on one occasion agitation produced through her a disorder in the child, similar to that which destroyed our little girl two years ago. The disorder was prolonged by the alarm which it occasioned, until by the utmost efforts of medical skill and care it was restored to health. Mary on that occasion gave me the liberty of intercepting such letters as the one to which this is a reply.

It seems to be true that about the time these letters were being exchanged, Claire had made up her mind to become Shelley's mistress, and it seems equally true that Shelley was gradually transferring his affections from Mary to another woman, not Claire. It would seem that for a woman to know Shelley was to love him, and that Shelley had no passion- or fire-retarding material in his composition. The line of his serious love-affairs is a long one. There were

Harriet Grove, and Harriet Westbrook whom he married: there were, too, Elizabeth Hitchener, and Cornelia Turner; and Mary Godwin whom he seduced. There was Claire, whose presence always made Mary nervous, poor dear; and we must not overlook Emilia Viviani and Jane Williams. These attachments in Shelley's case are more difficult to analyze than they would be in any other man, for he was a curious compound of Plato and passion. Poor Mary! she knew, she must have suspected, that troubles were in store for her, but they took a form of all the most unlikely. As for the poet himself, he had become very unhappy. He wrote to Edward Trelawney, "that Corsair," as he called him, with whom he was now intimate:—

Should you meet with any scientific person capable of preparing prussic acid, or essential oil of bitter almonds, I should regard it as a great kindness if you could procure me a small quantity. It requires the greatest caution in preparation, and ought to be highly concentrated; I would give any price for this medicine. You remember we talked of it the other night, and we both expressed a wish to possess it; my wish was serious, and sprung from the desire of avoiding needless suffering. I need not tell you I have no intention of suicide at present, but I confess it would be a comfort to me to hold in my possession that golden key to the chamber of perpetual rest.

There speaks, I think, the real Shelley: Leigh Hunt must have been right. Could one as sensitive and reflective, and introspective, with an honest desire to do good and not evil, be anything but despondent as

he looked back over the havoc he had wrought? How
he was drowned in a sudden squall in the waters of
the Gulf of Spezia, usually so beautifully calm, — I
saw them only a few months ago, — all the world
knows: drowned, we are told, with a volume of
Keats' *Poems* in one pocket and Sophocles in the
other. Some days after his death his body was washed
ashore, and after having been interred in the sand for
a month was subsequently exhumed and cremated
at Viareggio in the presence of Byron, Trelawney,
and Leigh Hunt. But the romance of Shelley's body
was not to end with his death, or burial, or incinera-
tion. His heart, from the manner of his death, would
not burn and was at last snatched from the pyre by
Trelawney, and by him given to Hunt, who gave it to
Mary Shelley. She treasured the relic in a silken bag
together with her copy of *Adonais*. This led her to
be charged with having used the poet's heart as a
"bookmark," and the reproaches caused her to place
it in a silver urn. At her death, in 1851, the heart
was inherited by her son, Sir Percy Florence Shelley,
by whom it was preserved with the utmost reverence,
and on his demise, in accordance with his wishes it
was placed in his coffin.

Therefore the grave of Shelley in Rome, while it
contains his ashes, does not contain his heart, in spite
of the fine epitaph headed COR CORDIUM, with which
it is inscribed. Curiously enough, the epitaph was
written by Leigh Hunt, who was well aware that there
was no heart under the slab, since he himself had

surrendered it to Mary at her request. The famous epitaph at Rome must be regarded as apocryphal, but it is not the less lovely, and the words added by Trelawney certainly could not be bettered: —

> Nothing of him that doth fade
> But doth suffer a sea-change
> Into something rich and strange.

Shelley's death left Mary in a position of peculiar difficulty: she was not, at the moment, on good terms with her father, even had he been in a position to advise and befriend her, and the Shelley family would have nothing to do with her. The heir to the Shelley fortune and the title was not her son, Percy Florence, born a year or so before his father's death, but Charles, his eldest son by Harriet Westbrook; this, of course, was a great grief to her. Poverty stared her in the face, and her husband's executors, Byron and Peacock, were not the best possible advisers. Byron was the last man to go to for advice, and Peacock she did not like. As Dowden, the official biographer of her husband, says, with his usual circumlocution, "Mary was not unlearned in the lore of pain."

In her distress she turned to Trelawney, who agreed with her that she had best return to England, and out of his own fortune supplied the means. So within the year she was found gradually working her way north, stopping for a time in Paris to see a drama based upon her novel, *Frankenstein* — performed for a time with great success. Perhaps she was not the most accomplished woman of her time, but she was

THE GRAVE OF SHELLEY
in the Protestant Cemetery at Rome

one of the most interesting. Under Shelley's direction she had read enormously: she had a working knowledge of Greek and Latin, while French and Italian she spoke fluently. With this equipment, she decided to live by her pen. She was indefatigably industrious. In addition to her own original work, — of no great literary value, — for the thirty years which followed the poet's death, a period in which the neglect and contempt of his poetry gradually waned, Mary Shelley was the custodian of his manuscripts and the chief fosterer of his growing reputation. In 1824 she put forth a volume entitled *Posthumous Poems of Percy Bysshe Shelley*, a collection of lyrics of consummate splendor, to which she added a brief preface, marked by an appreciation of Shelley's genius at once judicious and enthusiastic. Fourteen years later she published an edition of his collected works, enriched with notes of the first importance to critics of her husband's poems. Thus it was her happy privilege to express for many years after Shelley's death that devotion to his genius which she had displayed so clearly during the few short years of his life.

Sir Timothy Shelley finally offered to provide for her son, if Mary would renounce all claim to him, but this she indignantly declined, and ultimately a small allowance was provided for her out of the Shelley fortune. Then, suddenly, a change for the better came: Shelley's eldest son, Charles, died; Mary's son became the heir, and she, as his mother, could no longer be ignored. With the change in her fortunes, her spirits returned. Although she had lived and suffered much, she was still a young woman and very beautiful. What more natural than that she should be sought in marriage? Trelawney seems to have proposed; at least we have a letter from her: "Do you think that I shall every marry? Never! neither you nor anybody else. Mary Shelley shall be written on my tomb — and why? I cannot tell, except that it is so pretty a name that . . . I should never have the heart to get rid of it." To which Trelawney replies, rather enigmatically, "I was more delighted with your resolve not to change your name than any other portion of your letter. Trelawney, too, is a good name and sounds as well as Shelley." To which Mary replies, half playfully, "I must have the entire affection, devotion, and protection of one who would win me. You belong to women-kind in general, and Mary Shelley will never be yours."

Subsequently she may have thought that "Mary Irving" was also a beautiful name; there are good reasons to believe that she had more than a flirtation with our own Washington Irving, but nothing came of it, and she decided to devote her whole life to her growing son. By her literary exertions the young lad was put through Harrow and sent to Cambridge, finally coming into the title and the fortune when about twenty-four years of age. At his mother's request, his first act was to settle an annuity of one hundred and twenty pounds upon their poor and always improvident friend, Leigh Hunt. At last, emo-

MARY SHELLEY
from a portrait in the National Portrait Gallery

tionally exhausted with the struggle of life, she died in London, only a little more than fifty years of age.

Meantime, what of Claire? That Byron's treatment of her was brutal, will be admitted; that she finally came to hate him, is entirely natural. Without resources after the death of her child, she had either to live on Shelley's bounty or get some sort of position. That she loved Shelley and was willing to become his mistress, is certain, and he was undoubtedly attached to her; but Mary, if she drove her husband with a light rein, never permitted him to get out of hand. She knew her husband's failings; she had ministered to them; and, moreover, she knew Claire, who was at last obliged to take a position as a governess. On the death of Sir Timothy Shelley, Claire came into a substantial legacy under Shelley's will, which made her independent. She died in Florence in 1879.

Return we now to Rome. Few visitors interested in English literature and biography will leave the Eternal City without paying at least one visit to the graves of Keats and Shelley. Keats had passed away in the arms of his friend Severn, and had been buried in the old Protestant burial ground, which, before the tombstone with its famous inscription: HERE LIES ONE WHOSE NAME WAS WRIT IN WATER, was erected, was permanently closed. When Shelley visited the grave of Keats, he visited also the new cemetery, separated from the old by a moat and a stone wall. The old cemetery, overshadowed by the pyramid of Caius Cestius, has the appearance of a neglected field, in one corner of which is the grave of Keats; the new cemetery, one of the most beautiful places in the world, caused Shelley to write: "It almost makes one in love with death to think that one should be buried in so sweet a place."

After Shelley's ashes were conveyed to Rome, they were first interred in another part of the ground than that to which, for a century, men and women have been doing reverence to his memory. Trelawney, who visited Rome soon after Shelley's interment, was dissatisfied with the original location of the grave, and chose and purchased another and a better place, in a small bay formed by two abutments supporting a bit of the old Roman wall. Here he secured ground for the grave of his friend and for himself when his time should come, and planted the famous cypress trees. Shelley's ashes were thereupon disinterred and deposited under the flat marble slab with its well-known inscription, and alongside it a similar slab was laid with no name or inscription thereon. More than half a century passed: it was supposed, if anyone gave the matter a thought, that Trelawney was long since dead and buried elsewhere, when quite unexpectedly a lady applied to the director of the cemetery and, handing him a small walnut box, told him that it contained the ashes of Trelawney, and asked that it be buried in the grave next to Shelley's.

There was no doubt as to the proprietorship of the

THE GRAVE OF JOHN KEATS

in the Protestant Cemetery at Rome

*On the Italian photograph from which this print was made, the inscrip-
tion reads: "Grave of the English Poet Young"!*

grave; the difficulty was of another kind. The introduction into Rome of the remains of a dead person
can be legally accomplished only by securing proper
permission and the payment of a considerable sum;
the director expressed his fear that the lady, who
appears to have been Trelawney's adopted niece, had
laid herself open to a considerable fine, ten times the
regular tax; in any event, the matter had to be laid
before the Minister of the Interior. After the usual
delay necessary to securing the documents from London where Trelawney died, and others from Gotha
where he had been cremated, the authorities, having
pondered the circumstances, remitted the tax and
were satisfied with the usual fee of three hundred lire.
A rather verbose inscription, prepared by Trelawney
himself shortly before he died, in his ninetieth year,
was carved upon the slab, and the ashes of "the
Corsair" rest beside those of his immortal friend.

In the Tate Gallery in London is a fine large can-
vas by Sir John Millais; it is just such a picture as
the English love: it tells a story. A young woman,
seated at the knee of an old seaman, is reading to
him of the possibility of a Northwest Passage. The
old man has a far-away look, and is supposed to
be saying, "It can be done, and England should
do it." Fifty years ago it was the sensation of an
Academy season; now it is almost forgotten that
Trelawney, in his old age, sat for his portrait as
the seaman.

Ten years after the burial of Trelawney, a contro-

versy arose between Lady Shelley, the daughter-in-
law of the poet, and Mrs. Call, the daughter of Trelawney, over the proprietorship of Shelley's grave.
Lady Shelley, in place of the flat stone on which for
almost a century pilgrims had been placing wreaths
and flowers, wished to erect an elaborate allegorical
composition, which had been cut in marble by Onslow Ford. Mrs. Call insisted that both graves should
remain as her father had originally planned. For once
we have caught our venerable friend, Herr Baedeker,
napping, for in my edition of his guidebook, I read:
"The present new tomb by Onslow Ford was erected
in 1891," whereas the fact is that it was never more
than threatened. For a time it seemed that a lawsuit
would result, but wise friends intervened, and Lady
Shelley was at last persuaded to erect her work of art,
if such it be, in University College, Oxford, that college from which a century before Shelley had been
ignominiously expelled. There it may be seen, rather
to the bewilderment of those who do not know the
story.

Fortunately, the graves of Shelley and his friend
have been kept inviolate.

One day, several years ago in England, I was listening wearily to a guide earning his shilling by interfering with my reflections as I walked about in the fine
old Priory Church in the ancient city of Christ
Church, which antedates its neighbor Bournemouth
by many centuries. At last the guide drew my attention to a monument I had never heard of, erected to

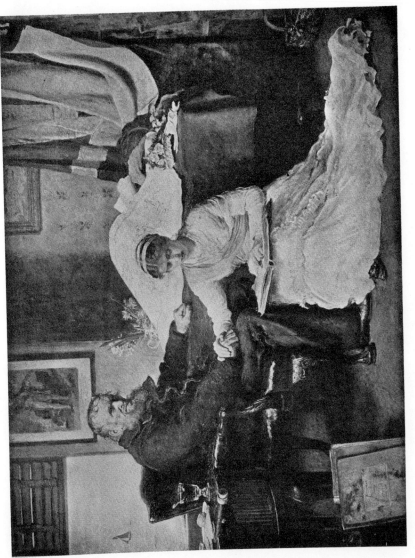

THE NORTHWEST PASSAGE — By Sir John Millais
from the original picture in the Tate Gallery

the memory of Shelley and Mary. To test the old man's information, I asked if Shelley was buried in the church, and this was his reply: —

"No, sir, this is just a monument herected by the Shelley family; there's hanother monument, one somethin' like this at Hoxford but Hi've 'eard that this is considered a better likeness because Mary's in it. No, sir, Shelley's hashes lies in the churchyard of St. Peter's in Bournemouth 'long with several members of 'is wife's family, hall but 'is 'eart; that, sir, as maybe you might 'ave 'eard, was plucked out of the flames by John Keats, the poet, as they was a-burnin' 'is body hin Rome, and buried privatelike, I forget just where."

Staggering under this load of misinformation, to St. Peter's in Bournemouth I bent my steps, if one can be said to bend one's steps in a taxi, and there

---

ESSAY

ON

SEPULCHRES:

OR,

A PROPOSAL FOR ERECTING SOME MEMORIAL OF THE ILLUSTRIOUS DEAD IN ALL AGES ON THE SPOT WHERE THEIR REMAINS HAVE BEEN INTERRED.

BY WILLIAM GODWIN.

Not one of these should perish.
THE BIBLE.

LONDON:
PRINTED FOR W. MILLER, ALBEMARLE STREET.

1809.

high up on a hill, on the fashionable side of a fashionable church, was a tomb which was soon identified as the final resting-place of William Godwin and Mary Wollstonecraft, and their daughter Mary, and Mary's and Shelley's son, Sir Peter Florence Shelley, and his wife Jane. And standing before it, I thought of the "Ridiculous Philosopher" whose last will and testament, never probated apparently, I had at home. I thought of how he had bequeathed all the property of which he died possessed — meaning thereby his debts, no doubt — to his wife Mary Jane, and how he had left to his son and daughter "his most affectionate remembrances." I remembered that his portrait by Northcote, which he had described as "the principal memorandum of his corporal existence," was ultimately to go to Mary, as was the portrait of her mother by Opie. I recalled that he asked that his remains should be interred as near as might be to those of Mary Wollstonecraft Godwin, in St. Pancras's churchyard. Doubtless he loved her: she is, indeed, one of the most interesting figures in English literature — and so little known! I remembered, too, my copy, that was once Claire's, of Godwin's little book, *On Sepulchres*. How pleased, I thought, he would have been with his tomb, and how little he deserved it! Its splendor, which would seem to ensure admission into Heaven, came to him as a result of his daughter being seduced by one of the "Castle Goring Shelleys" — to use a phrase that means much in England.

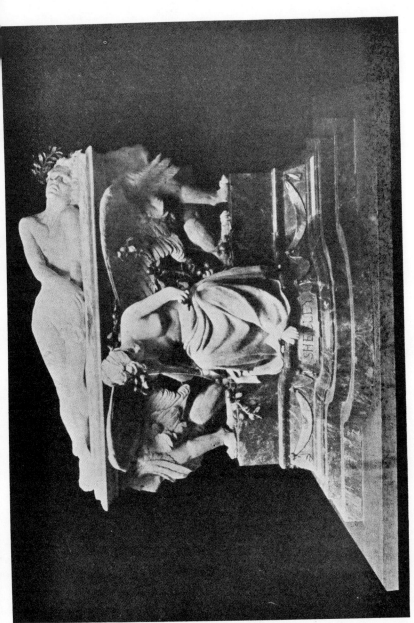

SHELLEY MEMORIAL BY ONSLOW FORD

Erected in a small temple in University College, Oxford. The base suggests a gigantic ink-well on which rests a huge platter, with the rather unpleasant figure of the dead poet thereon. Dreadful as the memorial is in its present location, it would have been still more incongruous had it been erected in the cemetery for which it was designed.

To sum up the Skinner Street News: Here lies the contemptible, middle-class old sinner who, having all his life railed against the laws of God and man, was finally taken from a neglected grave, along with his first wife, and with her interred in the very odor of sanctity, practically in the arms of a wealthy British baronet. If they had not been deficient in humor, this family, all of them, they would turn in their graves and laugh to find themselves in such elegant and exclusive surroundings. In a marble sepulchre, in a fashionable parklike churchyard, exquisitely kept, in an elegant seaside city, lie these once notorious characters. I thought of the squalor of Hanway Street, and of Skinner Street, of Snow Hill, and of the second Mrs. Godwin — she of the green spectacles. What has become of her hashes, I wonder?

XIII

FOUR ardent Dickensians were seated about a long table; all were talking at once; there were no listeners. Listeners are not important — it is the talkers who make themselves heard. All four were collectors. Why should I not name them?

There was the host, Mr. William M. Elkins of Philadelphia, the owner of the most interesting *Pickwick* in the world, the immortal book "in parts as issued, with all the points," as the old-book catalogues have it, given — part by part, as they appeared, with sundry inscriptions — to Mary Hogarth, Dickens's sister-in-law, until her untimely death caused the suspension of its publication, while its author recovered from the effects of the shock, and — but it would be fatiguing to refer to the items in Mr. Elkins's collection; let me say, in a word, that he has what is generally regarded as the finest Dickens collection in the world. There was, too, Judge John M. Patterson, President of the Dickens Fellowship, whose knowledge of first editions is exceeded only by that of another of the group, Mr. John C. Eckel, the author of a *Bibliography of Dickens*, as readable as it is accurate. There was also the writer of this paper, resembling in appearance, it is said, Mr. Pickwick himself, badly distanced in the race as a collector by

THE GHOST OF CHRISTMAS PRESENT

Facsimile of original drawing by John Leech, used in the early editions
of " The Christmas Carol"

these other men either longer of purse or fleeter of foot than he.

The large room in which we were sitting served as a living-room and library. Pause for a moment and think! What is living without a library? What is a library unless one lives in it? The walls were lined with open cases filled with rare books, and it needed only a glance to show that they had been assembled with great discrimination. Easy-chairs, placed with due regard to tables with carefully screened lamps, seemed to invite one to read and rest; but, instead, a violent discussion was going on. It was on that old, old subject — Which is the best of Dickens's novels? *Pickwick* someone urged; then it was admitted that *Pickwick* is not a novel. What is it? Certainly it is n't a romance, or travels! Finally it was agreed that it is in a class by itself, that there never has been a book like it; and just as it seemed as if all four were agreed that *David Copperfield* was Dickens's best novel, someone mentioned *A Tale of Two Cities*, which met with the objection that that was n't in Dickens's manner at all.

Then, above a voice urging *Bleak House*, someone was heard to say that *A Christmas Carol* was the greatest little book in the world. "And if," said the speaker, "you think that a 'rather large order,' name a greater!"

There was silence for a moment, and then a chorus of praise. It was the writer of this paper who made the all-embracing statement. He has the advantage of knowing only one — his mother — tongue; he was talking of books of to-day, not of great little books of ages past; and he was talking with companions who were much too great Dickensians to challenge any statement in praise of the master.

Let there be no misunderstanding. I know all that can be said in dispraise of Dickens: that his characters are not real people, but personifications of virtue and vice and the whole range in between; that he wallows in sentimentality; that all is exaggeration; that eccentric characters pepper his pages; that his women are "impossible," and that his heroes wear side whiskers; that he himself had long curly hair, perfumed, and greasy with macassar oil. I admit all this, and yet I am disposed to say that in the resplendent firmament of English literature there is only one name I would rank above his for sheer genius: Shakespeare. And I make this statement with the less hesitation for the reason that it passed unchallenged — was applauded, almost — when I made it first several years ago, in London. But that story must begin a new paragraph.

That learned and kindly "Wanderer in London," E. V. Lucas, to avenge a fancied obligation, was giving me a dinner, and I was asked to say not only when, but where — and who. I chose the Garrick Club and the guests, and on the appointed evening I found myself next to an old gentleman, one of the handsomest men in London, — he himself admits it, — Sir Squire Bancroft.

Well, after the cloth was removed and the nuts and

wine appeared (how much more friendly than our custom of putting another lump of ice in the tumbler), we fell into our anecdotage, as men will, and Sir Squire challenged attention by saying, "It was at a little dinner in this very room, more years ago than I like to remember, that I first met Charles Dickens." To be sitting next to a man who had known Charles Dickens, to hear anecdotes of him at first hand, was, for me, an unusual experience. Several other men then spoke of the great man, and when it came my turn to say something, or when I thought I could make myself heard, I boldly spoke of him as, next to Shakespeare, the greatest light in our literary heaven, expecting to precipitate a violent argument or at least a discussion. But nothing of the sort followed; on the contrary Augustine Birrell, that wise old book-man, seemed to acquiesce — and he is not always acquiescent; and the late Sir Walter Raleigh, the Oxford scholar, looked at me across the table as if the idea was not new to him.

But it is not my wish to start anything now. I just want to say a few considered words about *A Christmas Carol*.

Dickens had made his first trip to America and was engaged upon that study of selfishness, *Martin Chuzzlewit*, when it occurred to him to write a short story which was to make the world better and happier at Christmas time. The result was the "little Carol," as he affectionately called it. Its composition affected him in a most extraordinary manner: he roamed about London, as was his habit, thinking and talking to himself about it — and no one knew and loved London better than he; and none could describe it better, especially the streets on a winter's day, when the poor suffer; for while Dickens was a boisterous person, overflowing with animal spirits, the poor were always on his mind.

Bear with me while I sing the London streets in winter. Is there, can there be anything colder? The thermometer is not to be depended upon; with true British pluck the mercury keeps up appearances and declines to record the all-pervading dampness which freezes one to the marrowbones. I know; for I have played at hide-and-seek in the fog with well-known landmarks for my playmates, — to keep myself from freezing, — and I am not especially fitted for the game; solitaire I could play better but for the exertion it entails.

But no one has written of a winter's day as has Dickens: listen a moment.

It was cold, bleak, biting weather: foggy withal. . . . The city clocks had only just gone three, but it was quite dark already; it had not been light all day; and candles were flaring in the windows of the neighboring offices, like ruddy smears upon the palpable brown air. The fog came pouring in at every chink and keyhole, and was so dense without, that although the court was of the narrowest, the houses opposite were mere phantoms. . . . It was piercing, searching, biting cold.

Such was the weather in London on that day before Christmas many years ago when Dickens elected to sing a carol which all the world has heard and which all English-speaking people join in singing. Dickens was a man of simple emotions: what did not move him to laughter moved him to tears; some things moved him to both at once. Of nature, in the ordinary acceptance of that word, he knew nothing, cared nothing. London was to him a vast field in which wild flowers grew, the children of the poor, and he gathered them by armfuls. He was a man without what we call taste and, like Shakespeare, he took little interest in either religion or politics, but he had an intense love for humanity. He did not write for the stage, but he wrote dramatically: in tragedy he was apt to be maudlin; in humor he was with the gods. The *Carol* is Dickens in essence, for in it his love for humanity and his love of fun are all-embracing.

May I hum the first stanza of the Carol?

Marley was dead: to begin with . . . as dead as a doornail. Mind! I don't mean to say that I know, of my own knowledge, what there is particularly dead about a doornail. I might have been inclined, myself, to regard a coffin-nail as the deadest piece of ironmongery in the trade. But the wisdom of our ancestors is in the simile; and my unhallowed hands shall not disturb it, or the Country's done for. You will therefore permit me to repeat, emphatically, that Marley was as dead as a door-nail.

But I take it for granted that you can sing the Carol as well as I can, and go on with my story.

It was published a few days before Christmas 1843; six thousand copies were sold the first day, and fifteen thousand more before there was the least sign of the demand slackening. Dickens was in high spirits and wrote to a friend, "The *Carol* is the greatest success, I am told, that this ruffian and rascal has ever achieved." But a minor note was struck when the financial reckoning came in. Its author had been led to expect a clear thousand pounds, whereas considerably less resulted. No care seems to have been taken to ascertain the cost of the publication, when the selling-price was fixed. It is Dickens's prettiest book, tastefully printed and well bound in cloth and gilt; but the illustrations were the chief cause of the trouble. In addition to four woodcut vignettes, engraved by the master hand of W. J. Linton, there were four full-page etchings from drawings by Leech, colored by hand. Such a book costs money to produce, and the retail price was fixed at only five shillings. Dickens was disgusted: it was his first and last experience with colored plates.

It is permissible to refer to the original manuscript of the *Carol*. Dickens gave most of the manuscripts of his novels to his friend and biographer, John Forster, at whose death they passed to the British nation, and can be seen in the Victoria and Albert Museum; the manuscript of the *Carol*, however, he kept himself, endorsing it, "My own and only MS. of the Book," followed by his well-known signature.

But a more impulsive, generous man than Dickens never lived: it was not long before the precious copy was bound and given to an old friend, Thomas Mitton, who, not fully appreciating his possession,

sold it for fifty pounds! Subsequently it passed into
the hands of a Mr. Churchill, who had every one of
its sixty-six quarto pages photographed and reproduced in facsimile. Then, in the hands of a bookseller,
it went to Birmingham; but it soon returned to London, and the price by now having advanced to three
hundred pounds, it passed into the collection of Mr.
Stuart M. Samuel, who ultimately disposed of it to
Pierpont Morgan, and it now rests in the shrine,
frequently called a library, erected by that great
man a few years before his death.

What is more fascinating than the manuscript of
a book? In looking at a picture, we see a work of
art, finished and complete, as its creator intended us
to see it, but in looking at the holograph of a book,
we see the mind of the master at work. We see how
he obtained the effects which so thrill us, and can
study the lights and shades as he applied them.
Dickens was a rapid and clear penman, but in the
excitement of composition he made so many correc-
tions that most of his manuscripts are almost illegible
except to one expert in reading his writing. The
Carol is far from being the chief literary treasure of
Mr. Morgan's library, but it is an ornament to any
collection, and when I held it in my hands, not long
ago, I was told it was one of the items that all visitors
wish to see.

I have referred to the four full-page etchings from
John Leech. I have the original drawings of two of
these, the "Ghost of Christmas Present" and the

"Last of the Spirits"; but where are the remaining two? Who is the happy possessor of the best, "Mr. Fezziwig's Ball"? The gayest little picture in all the world, it fairly exudes Christmas cheer. Who would not love to dance a Sir Roger de Coverly with Mrs. Fezziwig, "one vast substantial smile"? I defy anyone to read the description of that Christmas party and not be a better man for the experience. It is a ripping piece of prose, seemingly written in jig time to the music of fiddles. It should be read — all of the *Carol* should be read — aloud every year before Christmas, when it is cold without and warm within; and there should be children about, girls and boys, especially boys, wide-eyed boys like Pip in *Great Expectations*. The boy who is permitted to grow up without being "read Dickens to" should bring a suit in equity against his parents, preferably before Lord Jeffrey, who has given it as his opinion that *A Christmas Carol* has done more good than all the pulpits in Christendom; and this judgment has been confirmed by the high court of public opinion. I like to think that Lord Jeffrey had in mind the best part of the *Carol*, — if one part can be better than another, — the description of the Christmas dinner at Bob Cratchit's; throw aside this book and read it. Read it now. Was there ever such a goose or such a plum pudding? "Everybody had something to say about it, but nobody said or thought it was at all a small pudding for a large family."

It is just eighty years since the *Carol* was given

to the world, and it still remains a "best seller." It has been translated into almost every language under heaven, though I am at a loss to understand its popularity in Chinese. In London, when it first appeared, people stopped one another in the street with the question, "Have you read it?" and the answer was, "Yes, God bless him, I have." No one spoke more highly of it than Thackeray, except Tom Hood, who maintained that Dickens was inspired when he wrote it. Not long ago, at a sale of autographs, a letter of Stevenson turned up which read something like this: "I don't know that I would recommend you to read the *Carol*, because it is too much, perhaps. But oh, dear God, it is good — and I feel so good after it, and would do anything, yes, and shall do everything to make the world a little better. . . . I shall never listen to the nonsense people tell me about not giving money — I shall give money; not that I have n't done so always, but I shall give now with a high hand."

That is the greatness of the *Carol*: it makes everyone want "to make the world a little better" — that's the idea; and when everyone wants to do a thing, they usually do it.

Dickens gave Christmas a new meaning: from being merely a festival of the Church, kept to some extent by Church people, he made it a universal holiday, and he did this without in any way derogating from its sacred character. What an achievement!

We hear rather too much to-day that art has nothing to do with morals, and it is admitted that an obvious moral may spoil an artistic effect — but not in the *Carol*. We, who know it by heart, hurry to get to the moral we know so well. When the Phantom shrinks, collapses, and dwindles into a bedpost, and Scrooge awakes and "laughs a splendid laugh," we laugh with him. He rushes to a window, throws it open and calls to a boy outside: —

"What's to-day, my fine fellow?"
"To-day!" replied the boy. "Why, Christmas Day."
"It's Christmas Day!" said Scrooge to himself. "I have n't missed it."

How happy he is! How happy we are, too! It is not too late to make amends!

Dickens puts the moral plainly when he makes the ghost of Marley say in reply to Scrooge's "You were always a good man of business, Jacob": —

"Business! — Mankind was my business. The common welfare was my business; charity, mercy, forbearance, and benevolence, were, all, my business. The dealings of my trade were but a drop of water in the comprehensive ocean of my business!"

It is such passages — and they abound in this, the loveliest of fairy tales — which justify the judgment which the world has passed upon this great little book.

The greatness of Dickens is only now beginning to be properly understood. Thousands of books have been written about him, most of them bad, very bad. Indeed, in the "comprehensive ocean" of Dickensiana I know only two books which are thoroughly admirable. I refer to Chesterton's *Appreciations and Criticisms of the Works of Charles Dickens* and Gissing's *Charles Dickens: A Critical Study*. These men are, it seems to me, the forerunners of a new school of Dickens-appreciators.

The bibliography of the *Carol*, John C. Eckel says, has just enough twists about it to make it interesting; but just as we collectors get one twist straightened out, somebody introduces a new one. We are agreed, I take it, that a few, a very few copies were issued with the title-page printed in *red and green*, with the date 1843, with yellow end-papers. These copies all have the chapter heading "Stave I," the numeral "I" not spelled out, "one," as in the second issue. Such copies now fetch from three to five hundred dollars; but speaking by and large a man may be said to have a first edition of the *Carol*, if the title page is printed in *red and blue*, if, in addition to the numeral "I," his copy has the date 1843, with green, not yellow, end-papers — at an investment of, say, from seventy-five to one hundred and fifty dollars. The book should be in good condition and by all means in the original cloth. There recently came upon the market, to the astonishment of all collectors, a single copy of the *Carol* with a Gothic, not a Roman numeral, I. This was evidently a trial copy, and it was the subject of several papers in the bibliographical journals. Charles Sawyer, the London bookseller, secured it for his personal collection, and subsequently a second copy turned up, which is now in the Pierpont Morgan library in New York.

But tell me, ye bibliographers, how it is that all the copies which Dickens himself gave away that Christmas have yellow end-papers? I have one, and I have examined a large number, and I have searched in vain for a presentation copy with green end-papers.

"and so, as Tiny Tim observed, God Bless us every one."

Charles Dickens

London.

Fifteenth march 1844.

Dickens presumably gave the books away on the day of publication; many of them are dated "Nineteenth December, 1843." It is admitted that Carols with green end-papers are rarer than those with yellow end-papers, but I cannot see that that makes them earlier. Maybe we collectors have been fooling ourselves; but after all, what difference does it make?

The important thing is that the book was written, and we have it.

It is said that twenty-four editions were published in its original form. Now, the copyright having long since expired, scarcely a year goes by without a new edition being announced. There are superbly illustrated, printed, and bound books made for the rich, and cheap editions made to sell for a penny to the poor, and both classes buy: its sale has run into the millions. But I have my own idea of the form in which the book should be read. It is admitted that a first edition, be the end-papers of what color they may, is too rare and costly to be read with comfort by the fireside, especially if, when one lays it down for a moment, it may be picked up and carried off by some member of the family, unaware of its value. And equally I do not wish a sumptuous reprint. I have always resented the book being got up in modern fashion, however beautiful; nor should it be read in a large volume out of a set, or expensively bound in leather. The first issues were all bound in red-brown cloth, with a gold stamp on the side, with gilt edges; and subsequent issues were bound in red, as more in the spirit of the season. So I should want my *Carol* bound either in red-brown or holly-red cloth with gilt edges, and I would ask that it be in format as like as possible the little masterpiece which woke the world to its music just eighty years ago. Fortunately they are not difficult to find; several years ago the Atlantic Monthly Press made just such a book as I have in mind. It was an exact facsimile of the first edition; I was honored by being asked to write a brief introduction to it, and gladly did so. And last year, in England, another facsimile was made, the profits arising from the sale of which went to some benevolent book-trade society.

Such editions are and should forever be in demand, for the more *A Christmas Carol* is read, the more it becomes soiled and torn and dog-eared from reading, the better will be the world.

"Are you running a corner in *Christmas Carols?*" a friend once asked me, as he stood in my library facing a little cluster of books in red and red-brown cloth. "No, not exactly," I replied, "but that is the greatest little book in the world. As a Dickens-collector, I am obliged to have all the early issues, and I always keep a few 'spares' on hand for emergencies." "What would you call an emergency?" he inquired. "Well," I answered, "if I were to meet a man at Christmas time who had not read the book, I should consider that an emergency requiring immediate action."

"Would you go so far as to give him a copy?"

"No; but I'd lend him one and not expect to get it back; it comes to the same thing."

Of the reprint of the first edition I usually buy two copies at one time: one to read, the other to lend, when the time comes to read it — and it comes once a year. I frequently find I have lent both copies, and I have to go out and buy another pair.

The *Carol* is a tribute to the race and a glory to the man who wrote it. Its author turned more or less empty phrases into realities. "Good will toward men," for example, he took out of the clouds, brought it down to earth, and set it to work. What an achievement! When we say, "Merry Christmas," we are unconsciously quoting Charles Dickens, who attached to Christmas its modern habit of giving and forgiving. Had he written only the *Carol*, on the basis of good accomplished he would have deserved his place in the Abbey Church of Westminster, where England lays her immortal sons.

XIV

THE LAST OF HIS RACE

Not long ago there died a gentleman, scholar, and book-collector, whose place in the game we are playing it will be difficult and perhaps impossible to fill. Need I say that I refer to Beverly Chew? There have been and there now are greater collectors than he, but I feel quite sure that no other amateur has ever exerted in this country the widespread influence that he did, or had an equal amount of bibliographical learning.

Mr. Chew was born in the beautiful little college town of Geneva, New York, on March 5, 1850, in a fine old mansion situated on a bluff overlooking the lake, and he died in another old-fashioned house not far from the spot where he was born. He was a graduate of Hobart College, a small college in Geneva, and throughout his life he remained closely identified with the institution in which he was educated. After his graduation he went to New York and in due course he became a successful banker. For many years he was Vice President of the Metropolitan Trust Company, until, a few years ago, he retired from active business. At the time of his death he was Geneva's most distinguished citizen, but he was so modest and unassuming that perhaps not all of his neighbors knew this fact. The great passion of his

BEVERLY CHEW

examining a copy of one of his favorite books, Herrick's "Hesperides" (1648)
After a photograph by Arnold Genthe, New York

life was books, and his knowledge of them inexhaustible and impeccable.

I am able to place with some certainty the time when I first met Mr. Chew: it was almost thirty-five years ago, just before I was married, at a reception at the Grolier Club in New York, of which he was one of the earliest members, serving the Club with honor and filling every office from librarian to president. My ignorance in those days was abysmal compared with his knowledge, and somehow in the course of conversation he asked me what I collected and, replying, I said, with some confidence, "The older poets," meaning thereby not Longfellow or Tennyson or Browning, but rather Keats and Shelley. I shall never forget his look of reproach as he said: "You don't call Keats and Shelley 'the older poets,' I hope"; and subsequently, when I came to know him better, I learned that his definition of "older poets" would be those who had died before 1640 — men of whose very names I, at that time, had never heard. But with the passing of years we became warm friends, and those who knew him well will agree with me that no man was more kindly, generous, and courteous than he.

Mr. Chew came of an excellent family, remotely connected with the distinguished Chew family of Germantown, Philadelphia. His grandfather was Collector of the Port of New Orleans and officially entertained La Fayette upon his last visit to this country. It so happened that his father, then an infant, was to be christened at the time of the visit, and the great man held the boy, who was named Alexander La Fayette, the name being handed down in the family.

Shortly after his graduation he married Clarissa Pierson, with whom he lived in the most perfect happiness until her death in May 1889. He had been heard to express the wish that he too might die in May, and this melancholy wish was granted him: after a long period of unconsciousness, he passed away, peacefully on May 21, 1924. He was a high churchman and in New York was a regular and devout attendant of the Church of St. Mary the Virgin. To visit the fatherless and widows in their affliction was a part of his creed; the number and extent of his kindly charities will never be known, for he almost never spoke of these things even to his most intimate friends. His funeral service was held in Trinity Church, Geneva, which he had loved as the church of his boyhood, and his body was carried up the aisle by college boys, members of his fraternity, the Sigma Phi, to which his father and his three brothers belonged. It was a gray day, but the light streamed in through the windows of yellow glass — of which he was so proud; glass made in Geneva a century ago, the manufacture of which is a lost art — and made a golden haze, a proper atmosphere for the beautiful and impressive service of the Church of England Prayer Book. Prior to the service at the church he lay at rest in his library, surrounded by his books, his closest friends, that he knew and loved so ardently.

Next to books Mr. Chew loved prints; portraits, which are a form of biography; especially old examples of famous engravers like Marshall, who engraved the portrait of Shakespeare for the *Poems* (1640), the beautiful Sucklin (*sic*) for *Fragmenta Aurea* (1646), and the Herrick for the *Hesperides* (1648); or Faithorne, who engraved the superb portrait of Killigrew in the 1664 edition of *Comedies and Tragedies*, which Mr. Chew once told me he thought was the finest portrait in any book. And I do not forget the lovely little plates in another favorite book of his, Lovelace's *Lucasta*. Lovelace! what a name for a poet! And Faithorne! "whose charm can save from dull oblivion or a gaping grave," as his friend Mr. Thomas Flatman has it. Mr. Chew's collection of portraits of Milton was, I suppose, the finest ever gotten together. But why call the roll? Whoever did fine work with pen or pencil or brush or type had in Beverly Chew his keenest appreciator.

I have not yet mentioned Mr. Chew's most remarkable characteristic — his marvelous memory. Certain great men are curiously endowed: I have been told that the late Pierpont Morgan could, merely by thinking of figures, make them dance about in his brain, and finally add, multiply, and divide themselves while his confreres were looking for a lead pencil; Mr. Chew's memory was of this same disconcerting order. He never seemed to forget anything relating to a book. And there is so much to be remembered! Think how many books there are; think, too, that every great book has some special characteristic which must be present or lacking, as the case may be, if that book is to pass the scrutiny of a collector such as Mr. Chew was, and find a place upon his shelves. And these points, so important in what they indicate, are seemingly so trifling and insignificant in themselves: a date, a misplaced word — or letter even. Many years ago, I bought at auction a first edition of Hawthorne's *Scarlet Letter*. When I got it home and examined it I found therein a long letter written by Mr. Chew to its former owner, in which he says, "When I returned home and examined page by page the first and second editions of the 'Scarlet Letter,' I find that I was correct in my statement, namely — " then followed a minute description, ending with: "and the book should have the word 'reduplicate' on page 21 instead of the word 'repudiate.'"

Of my personal friends, the only man that I would mention as in the class with Beverly Chew is Mr. Thomas James Wise of London, but Mr. Wise's opportunities have been much greater than Mr. Chew's, for he has sat at the gate, whereas, curiously enough, Mr. Chew never went abroad. No, I can hardly bring myself to think that the present generation of book-collectors is as distinguished as that to which Mr. Chew belonged. I suppose we fall naturally into the way of investing those who have gone with qualities which we may lack, perhaps; and yet, as I think of men like Robert Hoe and Samuel P. Avery, Charles B. Foote and Frederick R. Halsey, Edward Hale Bierstadt, and

William Loring Andrews, it does seem as though there were a falling off in the present generation.

I have referred to Mr. Chew's taking me up so promptly when I spoke of the "older poets"; his own favorites, I came to know, were those of the seventeenth century; I suppose his knowledge of this period was unequaled. Wherever one goes among bookmen, either in this country or in England, the bibliographies published by the Grolier Club are constantly referred to; with the publication of these Mr. Chew had much to do. The librarian of the Club, Miss Granniss, — who succeeded Mr. H. W. Kent, — to whom book-collectors are under so many obligations, has told me of her work on the Club's volumes of *English Bibliography from Wither to Prior.* Most of the collations had been made by Mr. Bierstadt and after his death the work was carried on by a committee. Mr. Chew, it appears, had been appointed to oversee the proofreading, a most tedious and difficult task, one of his countless services to the Club. Questions, of course, arose by the hundred; these Miss Granniss was in the habit of listing during the week for submission to Mr. Chew, and on Saturday afternoons he would punctually appear, and after settling himself in his chair and lighting his cigar, would exclaim, "Fire away!" Whereupon she would begin; and says she, in the letter from which I am quoting: —

I can hardly recall a question which he was not able to answer at once "out of his head," though I remember occasional admonitions to verify this blank leaf, or that variation in spelling by such and such copies or reference books, but I am sure that I never found him mistaken. The information which he had spent a lifetime in acquiring was cheerfully and instantly put at the service of anyone really interested.

Shortly after the war I went to London, and spending, as my custom is, some time in the British Museum, I chanced one day upon that distinguished gentleman, Mr. Alfred W. Pollard, then Keeper of the Printed Books, and in conversation with him I happened to refer to the *Census of Shakespeare's Plays in Quarto* which had recently been published by the Yale University Press, under the joint direction of Miss Henrietta C. Bartlett of New York and Mr. Pollard. The book is a splendid example of scholarly bibliography upon an extremely difficult subject, and Mr. Pollard, referring to the exasperating annoyances and delays incident to sending proof backward and forward across the ocean during the war, said, "I thought the job would never get done, and at last I wrote Henrietta and told her that if she could prevail on Mr. Chew to read the proof I would be satisfied. I was quite willing to put my name to anything that had received his approval." What a tribute from a great scholar to the busy man of affairs! "If you want a thing done, go to a busy man," is an old adage.

Of the many societies and clubs and institutions of which Mr. Chew was a member I shall not speak;

they all, I feel, as we of the Grolier Club do, mourn his loss. An old friend has been taken from us. One may make friends but not old friends — it takes time to make an old friend, as it does to make an old book.

Was Mr. Chew a poet? I do not know, but he wrote at least one poem which has found its way into the anthologies, "Old Books Are Best."

It is a little more than a year ago that, after several days spent in Buffalo with my dear friend and fellow-collector, Mr. R. B. Adam, I decided not to go on to New York without visiting Mr. Chew in Geneva. I am glad that I did. He met me at the station and conducted me — rather ceremoniously, for he was a gentleman of the old school — to his home, pointing out with something like pride the house in which he was born, on the main street of the pretty collegiate town. In the evening after dinner we sat in his library and smoked and talked, and put our hobby horses through their paces until late into the night; and as we retired he told me that my visit to him was a compliment, and I replied that my invitation was an honor. "And so to bed." The next morning, being an early riser, seeing the door of his bedroom closed, I passed very quietly and silently tiptoed downstairs into the library; the old gentleman was there before me. In an easy chair by the window he sat with several newspapers, unopened, by his side. In his hand was a book, which by the help of a magnifying glass he was reading as I entered; he put it by to greet me affectionately, and was I thought, a trifle embarrassed at being seen with this artificial aid to failing eyesight. To change the subject, I spoke of the book he had in his hand; it was a first edition of Herrick's *Hesperides* (1648), and I told him that my copy was a better one. This put him on his mettle at once, and he spoke of the fine copy — bound by Roger Payne, as I remember — that had been in the collection he had sold to Mr. Henry E. Huntington.

It is well known that some ten or twelve years ago Mr. Chew disposed of his library — the greater part of it, that is — to Mr. Huntington. The transaction was a difficult one; Mr. Huntington wanted the books, and Mr. Chew — getting on in years, and never a very rich man — thought that he could not afford to decline a liberal offer. After some delay, due to Mr. Chew's reluctance to part with his books, the proposition was accepted; but when the hour of separation came, it was too much of a wrench. Mr. Chew, with tears in his eyes, went to Mr. Huntington and told him he could not bring himself to part with the volumes, but he said, "If ever I can bring myself to sell, I shall sell only to you." Mr. Huntington was disappointed but understood Mr. Chew's feeling and, fine gentleman that he is, instantly released Mr. Chew from his bargain. Several years passed; the books were becoming increasingly valuable; another offer was made, — and accepted, — and as Mr. Huntington handed Mr. Chew a very large check, he said, "And, Mr. Chew, I would gladly hand you a check for double the amount for your

BEVERLY CHEW'S LIBRARY
in his residence at Geneva, New York

knowledge." Such a compliment is twice blest: "It blesseth him that gives and him that takes." And taking a thought from Omar's *Rubaiyat*, I often wonder what a man does with his money when he has exchanged his library for it. I know what Mr. Chew did: he at once began collecting again, and at the time of his death he had a small but very choice collection, — he would have been the last to call it a library, — for he could not live without books.

A pretty story is told of Mr. Chew's love for a rare book. Hearing that Mr. Huntington had secured two copies of the first edition of Shakespeare's *Sonnets* with the two different imprints, he called upon him and asked for the privilege of holding the two books — they are perhaps two of the most valuable books in the language — in his hands at the same time; one in each hand. I would like to have had a photograph taken of him at this moment, but I have an excellent picture of him, looking at a copy of Herrick, one of his favorite books, the one I saw him examining when I was last with him in Geneva.

Another story. During the last years of Mr. Chew's life in New York it was his habit not to go down town on Saturdays, but to spend the morning quietly among his books in his apartment in the Royalton; knowing this, it became my custom, when in New York on a Saturday, to call upon him. One morning we had spent several hours together when I suddenly remembered that Drake, the bookseller in Fortieth Street, had asked me to call to look at some books just in from London. So cutting my visit short, more especially as Mr. Chew too pleaded an engagement, with professions of mutual regard and regret we parted and I went at once to Drake's. I had not been there more than ten minutes when in walked Mr. Chew; his engagement was the same as mine. We laughed heartily at each other and turned to the books. "Here is something you should buy, if you have n't it," said Mr. Chew, taking up a copy of *Pierce Plowman* in old binding, calling attention to the corrected date, 1550. "But it is out of my line," I replied. "It should n't be," said he. Then my eye chanced to light upon a copy of Blake's *Poetical Sketches*, George Cumberland's copy with his so-called bookplate, one of Blake's last engravings, therein. "And you should have this," I said, knowing that his copy had gone into the Huntington Library. Mr. Drake looked on with amusement. "Go to it, gentlemen; I cannot afford salesmen such as you"; and when a little later we left the shop to lunch together, I was the owner of *Pierce Plowman* and Mr. Chew had a copy of Blake's *Poetical Sketches* in his pocket.

Looking back, one recollects that the year 1918 was a particularly pleasant one for book-buyers, and booksellers too. It saw the end of the war, money was plentiful, and several fine libraries were dispersed at Mitchell Kennerley's Anderson Galleries. I have in mind especially the Hagen collection, sold in May, and the Herschel V. Jones library in December. There was a feeling of good-fellowship abroad, and after these sales a group of us were wont to forgather at the Plaza around a well-spread table, there to fight our battles o'er again. Mr. Chew, who would always be invited to join these parties, was an old friend of Mr. Hagen, and had written an introduction to his sale-catalogue, and was especially interested in the sale of his library. In the introduction he had written: "If I were asked what is the scarcest item in the sale, I should unhesitatingly say that charming little volume containing four of the poems of John Skelton, Poet Laureate to King Henry VII. Two of these little booklets were in the Hoe library, but this lot of four from the Locker library is probably unique." It was not often that Mr. Chew would give a "tip" on a book but this was a sure thing, and the item realized just a trifle short of ten thousand dollars. The high prices pleased but did not surprise him. "They will go higher still," he said. At both of these sales I bought — for me — largely, being guided, as far as my means would allow, by Mr. Chew's judgment. Once again I record that my extravagances were investments, and my economies proved to be a willful waste of money.

> Our friend is gone, if any man can die,
> Who lived so pure a life, whose purpose was so high.

When his will was opened, it was found that Mr. Chew had followed in the steps of the great French collector, Edmond de Goncourt, who left instructions that —

his Drawings, his Prints, his Curiosities, his Books — in a word, all those things which had been the joy of his life — should not be consigned to the cold tomb of a museum, to be subjected to the stupid glance of the careless passer-by; but required that they should be dispersed under the hammer of the Auctioneer, so that the pleasure which the acquiring of them had given him should in turn be given someone of his own taste.

Thus to his friend Mitchell Kennerley, the President of the Anderson Galleries, passed — for sale — Mr. Chew's entire collection, with the exception of four paintings: his portraits of Ben Jonson by Gerard Honthorst, Pope and Dryden by Sir Godfrey Kneller, and a pastel of Dryden by Edward Lutterel; and his fine collection of German, Dutch, and Flemish silver bindings, of which he had some fifty or more specimens; these he bequeathed to the Grolier Club. No doubt he felt, and correctly, that there they would receive the same loving care that they had in his own library, and would serve to link his name with those of other benefactors of the Club, which is the most important, successful, and authoritative book-club in the world. Long may it continue to flourish!

When the announcement was made that Mr. Chew's library would be sold, the book-collecting world was agog. What books had he, and what would they fetch? I knew pretty well what I wanted, and had made up my mind to pay the price. Some day I shall write a paper on the psychology of the auction room: such curious things happen there. Important items are frequently almost given away; occasionally they bring more than they are worth. Who can

tell why? At last the expected evening came; the
sale was well attended.

First let me say that an important book-sale in
New York is very different from a similar event in
London. In London it is hardly apt to be a thrilling
affair, no matter how important the items. At Sotheby's the auctioneer stands or sits in a large pulpit,
while in front of him is a long, narrow table, one end
of which abuts upon the pulpit, while ranged on each
side of the table are the important members of "the
trade," as the booksellers are always called. The
book, if it be an important one, is handed by the auctioneer's assistant to the first man on the right-hand
side, who glances at it and passes it to his next neighbor, who also looks at it and passes it on. At the end
of the table it crosses over to the man on the left and
gradually makes its way back to the auctioneer, who
then knocks it down to the highest bidder with as
much enthusiasm as though he were selling a cabbage. Enthusiasm is never good form in England.
But let us assume that the knock-out is in operation,
as it may well be, and that an outsider, a collector,
seeing an item bringing half what it is worth, ventures
to bid. His bid will be accepted, of course, but instantly there is competition: someone in the trade
will bid quietly but persistently against the outsider
until either he drops out or the book is his at three
times what it is worth. He has made his experience;
if he has secured the treasure he is likely to hate himself and it; if he has lost it, the booksellers are likely

to hate him; in any event he is unlikely to bid again. "The trade" is a ring, and a ring is something which has neither beginning nor end.

A book auction in New York is a very different affair: it may well be a social event, a game in which you may join, if you think you have the skill; but remember that here, too, you are playing against professionals. An amateur swordsman with a broomstick may be able to disconcert a professional with a rapier, but the chances are against it. My own plan, after years of experience, is to give my bids to the particular bookseller most likely to buy, for stock or for a client, the item that I especially covet. For example, if an item like *Robinson Crusoe* is coming up, to free myself from Dr. Rosenbach's competition I will give my bid to him with the highest limit I am willing to pay. He in turn will have to outbid Lathrop Harper and Walter Hill and Gabriel Wells. If, on the other hand, I want a *Songs of Childhood* by Walter Ramal, — De la Mare's first book of poems and now much sought, — or *A Shropshire Lad,* — a slender volume which brought over two hundred dollars at Anderson's not long since, whereas I paid only one hundred and thirty for mine less than a year ago, — I would give my bid to James F. Drake and take my chance with Rosy. If then, having secured the good will of the trade, some little odds and ends come up of no special importance, I do not hesitate to bid myself. But an important item I would never attempt to buy myself; and I have seen thousands of dollars spent uselessly by persons giving important commissions to the wrong agent.

But this is a digression. On the first evening of the Chew sale the room was crowded; all the leading booksellers and many distinguished librarians and collectors were there. I noticed many ladies, particularly Miss Greene and Miss Thurston representing the Pierpont Morgan library, Miss Granniss of the Grolier Club, and Miss Henrietta Bartlett. A few hours before the sale began Mitchell Kennerley received a telegram from the erstwhile collector, Mr. Jones of Minneapolis, reading: "I shall attend the Chew sale not to buy but to pay my respects to a great collector"; the same spirit, I fancy, prompted other collectors to attend. Frank B. Bemis of Boston was there, but I did not see him bidding, and it was not until the sale was over that we exchanged confidences and I learned that several important items would find a resting-place in his lovely home on the North Shore.

Who shall say what a book is worth? I suppose there cannot be a better criterion than the price paid. A *Paradise Lost* in original binding attracted much attention. The volume had a famous pedigree, and had a pencil note dated September 6, 1857, written on the fly leaf by a former owner, Sir M. Digby Wyatt, which read: "This edition is the first and has the first title-page; it is worth nearly £10 and is rapidly rising in value." It certainly is: it brought the record price, fifty-six hundred dollars. Mr. Chew had bought the volume from Quaritch not many years ago for fifteen hundred. I was glad to see a first *Robinson Crusoe*, three volumes, original binding, a fine copy but in no way better than my own, bring fifty-three hundred and fifty dollars, while a Blake *Songs of Innocence and Experience*, for which Mr. Chew paid seventeen hundred and fifty dollars, brought also the record price for that item, fifty-five hundred dollars. The Cumberland copy of Blake's *Poetical Sketches*, which I sold him that day at Drake's for four hundred and fifty dollars, brought nine hundred; while a copy of *Pierce Plowman*, quite as good as the copy he sold me on the same occasion, brought two-thirds less than the price I paid, thus confirming a belief that I have long had: that the tendency in the New York auction rooms is for star items to bring more, and less important items frequently to bring less than they are worth. By a fluke I lost a superb first edition of *Hudibras* in three volumes, in original calf, which I

AMANDA,
A
SACRIFICE
To an Unknown
GODDESSE,
OR,
A Free-will Offering
Of a loving Heart to a
Sweet-Heart.

By *N. H.* of *Trinity*-Colledge in *CAMBRIDGE*

―――― *Unus & alter*
Forſitan hæc ſpernet juvenis――
――*Sed quiſquis eſ accipe chartas,*
Scribe.――

LONDON, Printed by *T. R.* and *E. M.* for *Humphrey Tuckey*, at the ſigne of the black *Spread*-*Eagle*, near St. *Dunſtans* Church. 1653.

had intended to buy, and I discovered later that this desired item went to Jerome Kern; I congratulate him upon its acquisition.

Nevertheless, my "bag" was satisfactory, if not splendid; I especially wanted and secured Hooke's *Amanda*. It is an excessively scarce little volume of poems published "by a gentleman of Trinity College in Cambridge" in 1653, and perhaps owes its vogue among collectors to the lines in Andrew Lang's "Ballade of the Bookman's Paradise":

> There treasures bound for Longpierre
> Keep brilliant their morocco blue,
> There Hooke's *Amanda* is not rare,
> Nor early tracts upon Peru!

I had seen this identical copy sold years ago at the Hoe sale, and since that time only one other copy has come upon this market. I also bought, through "Rosy," a fine Chapman's *Homer* dedicated "To the Imortal Memorie of the Incomparable Heroe, Henrye Prince of Wales," — my "royal book-collector," — the edition which suggested to Keats his famous sonnet; a large paper *Killigrew* with the fine portrait, which Mr. Chew and I have so often admired; and a little Coryat, *Greeting to his Friends in England*, which I have long searched for. These, with a few pick-ups of no great importance, constituted my lot. It seems rather curious to see them in my own library; although I paid for them promptly, I have observed that it usually takes some time for an old book to become accustomed to new surroundings.

When a book-collector dies and his books are disposed of, that ends the matter — except in memory. I have referred to Mr. Chew as "the last of his race"; this is not strictly so. There yet remains one, the last leaf, so to speak, on the noble tree which in its prime was so splendid. I refer to my friend Mr. W. A. White of Brooklyn: he yet remains to us. He is a more distinguished collector than Mr. Chew, and perhaps a better scholar, but his influence has not been so great. He is known the world over for his Blakes, but — with a few other outstanding volumes — chiefly for his Elizabethans. When in 1916, the three-hundredth anniversary of the death of Shakespeare, the Public Library of New York determined to keep the event by an exhibition of books by Shakespeare and his contemporaries, a superb exhibition was made. Miss Bartlett, an undoubted authority on the subject, had the matter in charge, and not everyone then knew that the exhibit was, in effect, a case or two of books from the library of Mr. White. He is so modest, so retiring, so seemingly the scholar, that no one would suspect he is a man of large business interests, yet ever and always ready to place himself, his knowledge, and his library at the disposal of those truly interested in his subject. With his passing, the second and greatest era in American book-collecting will come to an end — an era in which, no doubt, the honored name of Pierpont Morgan ranks highest, as the recent gift by his son of the great library formed by the father so abundantly proves.

Mr. Huntington yet remains to us, but he is not an individual; already he is an institution, and a noble one. Since he began collecting, a few years ago, he has bought twenty million dollar's worth of books and given them away, — to the State of California, — "therefore of him no speech." If nowhere else in the world do we find such fortunes as in America, certain it is that nowhere else are these fortunes so immediately and freely shared with the public.

A new generation of book-collectors is in the making: the names of William Andrew Clark, Jr., R. B. Adam, Frank B. Bemis, Jerome Kern, Carl Pforzheimer, J. A. Spoor, J. L. Clawson, and others, occur to me. I hope, I earnestly hope, that they and others like them will keep alight the torch of learning — bibliographical and other — which, if not originally lit, was for so many years kept aglow by Beverly Chew and kindred spirits of the Grolier Club.

INDEX